The Cross and Creation
in Christian Liturgy and Art

The Cross and Creation
in Christian Liturgy
and Art

Christopher Irvine

A PUEBLO BOOK
Liturgical Press
Collegeville, Minnesota
www.litpress.org

A Pueblo Book published in 2013 for the United States and Canada by
Liturgical Press
Collegeville, Minnesota 56321

Copyright © Christopher Irvine 2013

First published in the United Kingdom in 2013 by the Society for Promoting
Christian Knowledge.

Library of Congress Control Number: 2013939871

ISBN 978–0–8146–6305–9
ISBN 978–0–8146–6330–1 (e-book)

First printed in Great Britain
Subsequently digitally printed in Great Britain

Produced on paper from sustainable forests

For
*GG*CR *and RAW*

Contents

Foreword

What Christians believe about salvation is never expressed completely just in formulae or creeds. Christian faith has always been *enacted*, a matter of physical acts and gestures, ritual dramas of transformation. And Christian art, in its origins, is not about decorative extras or helpful illustrations of stories and doctrines; it is itself a sort of enacting of faith, a means by which we are brought more fully into the mystery being celebrated.

Christopher Irvine, in this original and absorbing book, weaves together what Christians say and what they do, ritually and imaginatively, so as to bring into focus the often hidden core of our beliefs about salvation. We are reminded that what happens in the cross of Christ is the restoration of all things, a renewal of the very stuff of the material world. This event is a new beginning, a re-entry into paradise; and Christian worship affirms precisely this, that we are now brought back into a lost intensity of *presence* to both the world and its maker. The ancient symbolism of the cross as the tree of life in the garden of God's presence is shown to be of cardinal importance to our fuller understanding of what is done once and for all on Calvary.

This study challenges any view of Christ's crucifixion that reduces it either to a human tragedy or to a transaction that 'saves souls': we are taken back into the heart of the biblical and early Christian conviction that this is where the Second Adam breaks the bonds of captivity that have diminished and frustrated humankind and re-clothes men and women in their proper dignity. With an impressively wide range of scholarly reference matched with a lucid and appealing style, Canon Irvine leads us on an exhilarating journey into seeing the central mysteries of faith with new eyes – a true baptizing of the imagination.

ROWAN WILLIAMS
Master of Magdalene College
Cambridge

Acknowledgements

I would like to express my gratitude to a number of friends and colleagues who in recent years have encouraged and supported me. I must thank John Harper for inviting me to be an observer of the Experience of Worship in Late Medieval Cathedral and Parish Church Project, which opened my eyes to aspects of liturgical experience, particularly the visual and the musical in a period that in the past has been generally overlooked by both academic and pastoral liturgists. I must also express gratitude to Gerald Colson and Lance Housley, a former Librarian of the Franciscan International Study Centre here in Canterbury, for locating and assisting in the translation of sources. Gratitude is also owed to those who have read earlier drafts of particular chapters: Paul Bradshaw, Graham Howes, Sarah James, Stephen Bann and Robin Jensen. Their comments have been encouraging and extremely useful in seeing words and arguments that needed to be corrected or sharpened. I must, however, accept full responsibility for any error of fact or infelicity of expression that remain in the book. I must also thank Donald Gray, the Chairman of the Alcuin Club, and Benjamin Gordon-Taylor, its editorial secretary, for their encouragement, and Ruth McCurry of SPCK for her unstinting assistance. In particular, I would like to thank Rowan Williams, former Archbishop of Canterbury, who not only kindly agreed to write the Foreword to this book but whose ministry over a number of years has been a source of inspiration in so many different ways.

This book is the culmination of a good number of years reflecting on the cross. I gained much from discussion with students at the College of the Resurrection, Mirfield, and with those in the Department of Theology and Religious Studies at the University of Leeds who attended my classes on imagination, art and theology. Mirfield was in many ways the crucible of much that has come to fruition in this book; and let me again express here my affection and gratitude to the Brothers of the Community and the College of the Resurrection. I am also grateful to Robert Willis and my colleagues here at Canterbury Cathedral, who have given me the space and much encouragement to continue to reflect on the place of the cross in Christian life, worship and culture. This book has been written not during a period of study leave or a sabbatical but in the margins of a ministry that is set in one of the busiest cathedrals in England. No wonder then that the place, its art and its worship have seeped into what has been written in these pages. Indeed, the sheer wonder of this historic building, its creative community and the rhythm of its shared daily prayer have provided a most congenial setting in which to write this book. Last but by no means least I must thank Rosie, who in kindly reading first drafts of the manuscript realized why so much time was spent during our summer holidays in Italy tracking down crosses in churches, museums and art galleries.

I am also grateful to the following for allowing me to reproduce images as illustrations in this book. To Robin Jensen for her photograph of the Kelibia font in Tunis; to Roger Wagner for his photograph of his *Tree of Life* window at Iffley. I am also grateful to the Chapter of Lichfield Cathedral for allowing me to reproduce their photograph of the Tree of Life nave altar, and to Leonie Seliger and Buffy Tucker for assistance with the Canterbury photographs.

I am grateful to the Community of the Resurrection for permission to cite from the hymn *Immense caeli Conditor* and three psalm antiphons. Other citations are fully acknowledged in the text and fall within what is deemed to be reasonable use. Nevertheless, I here express my gratitude to these authors.

Finally, a work such as this is stimulated and sustained by the regular pattern of daily prayer, and I dedicate this book to two priests who have directed the worship that I have been privileged to share during the long gestation period of this book at Mirfield and at Canterbury Cathedral. These two priests, George Guiver, a member of the Community of the Resurrection, Mirfield, and Robert Willis, the Dean of Canterbury, happily celebrate 40 years of ordained ministry in 2013. This book is affectionately dedicated to them in gratitude for their ministry.

Christopher Irvine
Canterbury Cathedral
O Sapientia, 2012

Introduction

The cross is not only the ubiquitous symbol of Christianity, it is also the very crux of Christian life and worship. A study of Christian origins would reveal how St Paul regarded the very gospel as 'the word of the cross'. He then presented that Word as being ritually enacted in the water ritual of Christian baptism, whereby the candidate entered into the death and resurrection of Christ, and in the Eucharist, which was a ritual showing forth of the death of Christ. Through the ages these rites have been celebrated in specific architectural spaces, which themselves are marked with the sign of the cross. In the design and ground plan of many church buildings the symbols of cosmos and the cross effectively elide, so that on entering the church building the visitor in some sense steps into the cross. Candidates for baptism have been, and in many traditions continue to be, marked with the sign of the cross to indicate their belonging to Christ. In turn, the baptized are sustained in that relationship through the Communion of the eucharistic bread, itself frequently marked with the sign of the cross, and the chalice, which represents the transcendent self-giving of God in Christ on the cross of Calvary. In addition, the president at the celebration of the Eucharist may well make a manual sign of the cross over the gifts of bread and wine during the Eucharistic Prayer.

The cross, in other words, is displayed and enacted in a multitude of ritual acts, and in physical signs inscribed on walls, altars and fonts, each being framed within a designated holy space. From the fourth century the cross was crafted to function as a reliquary, often to contain a fragment of wood from the 'true cross', and then it came to be fashioned as a separate object to be placed on the altar or carried to lead liturgical processions. But what the cross may represent is also shown in what was once known as 'high art', that is, in the plastic arts of

mosaic, sculpture, paintings and glass. The crucifixion became a classic
and central subject in the repertoire of painting, and many crucifixions
are now to be seen in the art galleries of the western world, so much
so that, as Neil MacGregor once noted, Asian visitors to the National
Gallery are somewhat mystified by the prevalence of images of suffering
in the Western pictorial tradition.[1]

The crucifixion of Jesus Christ is the primary reference point of the
cross, and so it is inevitably an object of terrible beauty. Indeed, from
Augustine of Hippo to John de Gruchy[2] in more recent times, Christian theologians have articulated the way the disfigured image of Christ
crucified not only subverts aesthetic sensibilities but, in the mangled
figure of the Crucified, presents the transfiguring beauty of God. In
this reading it is this divine beauty that transforms the Christian into
the likeness of Christ, the image of the invisible God and divine beauty.
But even in this reading the cross is not simply an emblem of universal
human suffering, for as in the New Testament, the cross represents both
the crucifixion and the resurrection of Christ. Later, the cross was seen
to be embedded in a whole related pattern of Christian understandings,
attitudes and outlooks. The doctrine of the cross, in other words, not
only belongs to a doctrine of the atonement but also to our Christology
– our understanding of who Christ is – and our doctrine of creation;
that is, an understanding of how the triune God relates to the natural
environment in which our lives are set. Indeed, Christian doctrines
belong to a whole system of related views and understandings that in
turn shape the very pattern of Christian living.

For this reason, I shall range broadly over a variety of evidence,
textual, ritual and material, in order to recover a sense of the cross that,
in many epochs and types of Christianity, has been subsumed under
the narrower compass of a more personal, not to say individual and
often juridical reading of the divine plan of salvation, and has even been
eclipsed by the understandable twentieth-century emphasis upon a 'suffering God' on the cross. In the aftermath of two world wars, Euro-
pean artists such as Graham Sutherland and Francis Bacon took the
image of the Crucified as an emblem of the human body breached and

1 An observation made in a discussion following the Scott Holland Lecture delivered by
Neil MacGregor at King's College London, November 2008.
2 See John W. de Gruchy, *Christianity, Art and Transformation: Theological Aesthetics in
the Struggle for Justice* (Cambridge: Cambridge University Press 2001).

broken, and theological commentators demanded a historical realism in the portrayal of the cross of Jesus. And yet there were some voices that recalled how the word 'cross' in the writings of Paul and John in the New Testament denoted not only the suffering and death of Christ but also his resurrection. In a considered essay on the symbol of the cross, a pre-eminent Swedish theologian of the atonement, Gustaf Aulén, countered a call to the Church of Sweden to abandon the elegant polychrome medieval art that survived in its old churches and to portray Christ's crucifixion with a brutal realism. Aulén argued that the cross and resurrection belonged together in the witness of the New Testament, and that as a symbol word, the cross held together in tension the suffering, death and resurrection of Christ.[3] The challenge continues to this day as we seek to recover the sense of the symbolic in Christian religious discourse and practice. In part this requires not only a seeing of what is to be seen but a more attentive looking at the design, decoration and art of our places of worship.

And so my first aim in this study is to recover a way of seeing, and for many of us it will be a seeing through our visually cluttered churches to the more focused liturgical art of churches and baptisteries, and to read this in the light of the ritual actions that occur within the architectural framework of our church buildings. Equal attention will be given to what is seen, and what was first commissioned and made for these spaces – to what we may define as the material culture of Christianity. The expression 'material culture' was given particular impetus in the field of history by Eamon Duffy, whose work *The Stripping of the Altars* led to a renewed interest in Christian material culture.[4] It has now become a key issue in the curating of sacred objects in museums and galleries and in the sociology of religion.[5] Concern for the design,

---

3 Gustaf Aulén, *The Drama and the Symbols: A Book on the Images of God and the Problems they Raise* (London: SPCK 1970), p. 167.

4 'A novel feature of this book (*The Stripping of the Altars*) was the sustained use of the material culture of medieval Christianity – the architecture and furnishings of parish churches and shrines, surviving religious imagery in glass and paint, in wood and stone, and printed (and often illustrated) devotional books. This material culture, more often than not the product of lay investment' – Eamon Duffy, *Saints, Sacrilege and Sedition: Religion and Conflict in the Tudor Reformation* (London: Bloomsbury 2012), pp. 4–5.

5 See, for example, the work of Crispin Paine, one of the founders of the journal *Material Religion: The Journal of Objects, Art and Belief,* and David Morgan, particularly his edited collection of essays, *Religion and Material Culture: The Matter of Belief* (London and New York: Routledge 2010).

decoration and furniture of Christian worship is not entirely new in the field of liturgical studies, but I hope that my own work here makes a modest contribution to this fruitful methodology of reading texts, architectural spaces and what occurs within them, and their furnishings and art in relation to each other.

In his work on the English Reformation, Duffy straddled the world of church history and art history, specifically in his study of rood screens. My own liturgical interests have led to an examination of the decoration of the key foci of the performance of the rites of baptism and Eucharist, in particular of altarpieces and baptistery and font decoration, treated respectively in Chapters 2 and 7 of this present study. The identification and the tracing of a specific theme, namely the iconography of the cross and its emerging and repeated linkage with the theme of creation, inevitably narrows the scope of what may be said. But more positively, this thematic approach means that the study is more focused in its attention and in the trajectory of its enquiry. A comprehensive study on the iconography of the cross would require a multi-volume work, but what is presented in these pages, while far from being in any way exhaustive, is a particular mapping of the meaning of the cross. Fundamental to my approach has been a liturgical hermeneutic that has enabled me to both contextualize and read the material and visual evidence in relation to its place and function in Christian worship. This adopted methodology has yielded the sequence of terms in the title: the cross in liturgy and art.

And so although the approach followed in this study ranges broadly over pictorial art, architecture, liturgical rites and text, the focus is on the cross, and particularly on how that image functions in terms of the worship of the Church. The pressing and persistent question throughout the pages of this book is the meaning of what is figured in the imagery of the art of the Church and in the rites that are celebrated in its architectural spaces. Further, in examining the pictorial in relation to the ritual, and the object in relation to its environment, a reading emerges that again and again links the cross with creation. The examination of both textual and material evidence will be selective, as in any thematic study, but what is presented here may well be sufficient proof to show that images of the cross in relation to creation are part of the repertoire of the imagery, both visual and textual, that Christians have used in different epochs and locales to present a public understanding of the two definitive Christian rites of baptism and the Eucharist, and in the liturgies of the cross. To say that something is found within a repertoire of understandings and stock of images is to say no more than that it is one element among many, or that it is a single aspect of the whole.

More can, however, be claimed about the linkage between the cross and creation when we examine the Franciscan tradition of liturgy and art, for here, as I intend to demonstrate, is a paradigm of the cross and creation. It is not that we are constructing a model out of the elements of Franciscan prayer and the art of their churches, but that there is an intrinsic connection between the cross and creation in these sources, a linkage that clearly resonates with our contemporary preoccupation with the environment and its degradation through pollution, the acceleration of climate change through CO_2 emissions and the rapacious exploitation of natural resources. In part, the corollary of the Christian being grafted into Christ in baptism is the task of caring for this fragile planet, and the urgent task of safeguarding its increasingly threatened ecology.

Many years ago, Paul Bradshaw cautioned against a simple application of the Latin tag *lex orandi, lex credendi* (the law of prayer directs the law of belief) and drew attention to the distance between a theoretical understanding of the primacy of worship and the actual experience of worship.[6] More careful enquiry into the historical development of texts for worship has demonstrated that there is a symbiotic relationship between our forms of worship and doctrinal understandings. Nevertheless, although our liturgical texts are shaped by our doctrinal perspectives, it is perfectly valid to argue for a connection between Christian believing and practice, and practice in the widest sense of the term. For, beyond the theoretical, one can observe how faith is in part shaped and grounded in practice,[7] and therefore extend the *lex orandi, lex credendi* axiom to include the *lex vivendi*, giving us *lex orandi, lex credendi, lex vivendi*, which can be rendered 'as we worship, so we believe and live'.

What, we may well ask, does our view of the cross commit us to in terms of the choices we make and actions we undertake? A few years ago, following a presentation I made to a group of Episcopalian clergy in the diocese of Chicago on the figuring of the cross as the tree of

---

6 See Paul Bradshaw, 'Difficulties in Doing Liturgical Theology', *PACIFICA* 11, June 1998, pp. 181–94.
7 Morgan, *Religion and Material Culture*, p. 17.

life, a participant asked me if I could think of a practical outcome that would follow from holding such a view of the cross. I immediately said that one could plant a tree for Jesus. Having seen the vast expanses of corn growing in the Midwest, this was not a flippant comment. If we believe that God's purpose to renew the face of the earth is presaged in the cross, then implications should be drawn regarding agricultural practices, which in turn affect climate change and global food distribution. The framing of these implications and strategies for their effective implementation really belongs to another book, and one written by another author. Suffice it to say here that the ethical outcomes of Christian belief and worship are necessary and, indeed, urgent matters.

Worship, of course, is directed towards the triune God, and elsewhere I have written about its ultimate purpose as being the shaping of the worshipping community to be Christ's Body, and of how the individual worshipper should be both open to and expectant of being changed, specifically of being formed in the likeness of Christ, by being encountered by God's Word and the Holy Spirit.[8] Christians are made and not born, and in Chapter 7 we will examine both material and textual evidence to see how Christians are made through the water and the Holy Spirit in the celebration of baptism. These aspects are already woven together in the imagery of Scripture. In figurative vocabulary that combines language about water, the Spirit and the flourishing of trees, the prophet, for instance, foretells how God would make a people his own: 'For I will pour water on the thirsty land, and streams on the dry ground; I will pour my spirit upon your descendants, and my blessing on your offspring. They shall spring up like a green tamarisk, like willows by flowing streams' (Isaiah 44.3–4).

My intention in this book is to explore and examine further the two-way relationship between worship – both the act of worship and our understanding of what occurs in worship – and art, specifically the iconography of the cross. There are many ways of seeing, but when the cross is seen in a liturgical setting it is regarded as a sign of life. This sign generates the motif of the living cross, a motif that is explored in detail in Chapter 5. The cross as a living cross illustrates the way in which the cross as a sign of God's saving work in Christ is inextricably bound

---

8 Christopher Irvine, *The Art of God: The Making of Christians and the Meaning of Worship* (London: SPCK 2005).

up with creation, a linkage that we will demonstrate is seen repeatedly
in the liturgical art of the cross. This linking of the cross and creation
is wondrously shown in the St Clemente apse mosaic reproduced on
the cover of this book, and yet this lavish artwork, as we shall see, is
closely related to the cross on which Christ died on Calvary. And so
Good Friday, representing the suffering and death of Christ, is a constant point of reference throughout this study. But the cross, that noble
tree commemorated on Good Friday, is the sign of new life, the life
that burgeons in the death, burial and resurrection of Christ. Christ
came to be figured as the tree of life, and from his cross the greening
of creation is prescient. For there on the cross Christ 'handed over' his
spirit, anticipating the promised pouring out of the Spirit when 'the
wilderness becomes a fruitful field, and the fruitful field is deemed a
forest' (Isaiah 32.15).

It could be said that such a reading of the material evidence linking
the cross and creation reflects a cultural preoccupation, if not a neurosis
of our own time. No one would question its topicality, but it should also
be noted that a keen observation and prophetic reading of nature is well
established in Christian sensibility. The theme of the transformation of
nature is often seen in the English visionary art of Samuel Palmer, and
the Jesuit Oxford poet Gerard Manley Hopkins was deeply affected as
a poet and as a person by the landscape and the natural world. In his
poem 'Binsey Poplars' (felled 1879), Hopkins laments how we have
'hacked and hewn': 'O if we but knew what we do / When we delve or
hew / Hack and rack the growing green!' The tradition of the true cross
has a deeper literary and artistic tradition, and its ultimate reference
is to the tree of life, that tree that speaks as much about loss as about
hope, of a curse as much as a promised healing, and of a new life gained
through a sacrificial death and mediated in the rites celebrated by those
whose lives have been configured by the crucified and risen Lord.

This is the message of the Easter gospel, and a recent study of an
Easter sermon by the seventeenth-century bishop, Lancelot Andrewes,
draws attention to how Andrewes saw that the *Triduum Sacrum* – the
three days of Holy Week beginning with the Lord's betrayal in the garden
of Gethsemane on the night of Maundy Thursday to the dawning of a
new day in the garden where Christ had been buried on Easter Day –
holds together the aspects of a single yet temporally extended event.[9]

---

9 Kenneth Stevenson, *Liturgy and Interpretation* (London: SCM Press 2011), pp. 182–4.

For although Christ's betrayal, crucifixion and resurrection are marked and celebrated on separate days, what they signify is inseparable. In a later Easter Day sermon preached before the King at Whitechapel in 1620, Andrewes preached on the Gospel story of Mary Magdalene's encounter with the risen Lord on the first Easter morning, and he playfully teased with the risen Christ's mistaken identity as the gardener. Mary Magdalene supposed Christ to be the gardener, but following the precedent set in a sermon of Gregory the Great, Andrewes affirmed that in a real sense the crucified Lord was indeed a gardener. First, he says, Christ was the gardener of 'the fairest garden that ever was, Paradise'. Now, he says, Christ is the one 'who gives the growth' as Christians mature into the new humanity exhibited by the Lord, and finally, when God's final purpose is fulfilled, Christ will 'turn lands and sea and all into a great garden'.[10]

In the end, it is in the light of the hope of this greening of creation that we come to see the full and final meaning of the cross. This end, as we shall see, is presented in Christian practice as the beginning; that is, the beginning of a Christian life at baptism. But first we must establish how and in what ways the cross is, and has been, seen, presented and received. Here it is the context and the occasion on which the cross is seen that is the key to its fullest meaning. Thus we will speak of ways of seeing and propose a way of seeing the cross and depictions of the crucifixion within and in relation to a liturgical context and its architectural framework.

---

10 Lancelot Andrewes, Sermon XIV, from *Ninety-Six Sermons* (Oxford: John Henry Parker), vol. 3, 1841, pp. 15, 16.

Chapter 1

Seeing liturgically

There are many ways of seeing, and how something is seen depends at least to some extent on where the object is seen and, indeed, on what occasion. The specific aim of this chapter is to establish a way of seeing the cross and images of the crucifixion that takes cognizance of the physical setting in which they are seen, and the building's primary purpose, which in the case of a church is worship. The experience of worship is closely bound up with the ambience in which it takes place and the visual impact of its physical setting. Following the edict of Milan in 313, when Christianity became a legally permissible cult, and the subsequent political annexing of Christianity,[1] Christians in the urban centres of the Roman Empire adopted the basilica – literally, a 'royal hall' – as the most appropriate shape and building plan for their churches. With toleration came a significant increase in the number of Christians, and as their worship became more public, so a public building such as the basilica provided the best model for their worship space. The first secular basilica built in the city of Rome dates back to the time of the Republic (500 BC–AD 31), and served a civic function. The basilica was basically a rectangular shape and typically had clerestory windows and columned aisles on either side supporting a timber roof. In an urban cityscape in which there were temples and shrines on every corner, the basilica did not have a particular religious connotation or significance but provided a gathering space for business transactions and judicial functions and purposes.

---

1 Christianity was privileged in Rome in AD 312 when memories of persecution were still fresh, and then became the sole religion of the Roman Empire by imperial edict in 380. See Bernard Green, *Christianity in Ancient Rome: The First Three Centuries* (London: T. & T. Clark 2010), pp. 225–36.

From the earliest times we know that Christians had adapted domestic architectural spaces for the purpose of worship, but in the second half of the third century, as they grew numerically in cities such as Rome, they acquired larger premises, such as store houses, in which to gather for worship. These were known as the *aula ecclesiae*.[2] Following the conversion of Constantine and throughout the fourth century, there was an ambitious and extensive programme of adapting previous basilicas and of building new ones. Constantine himself was responsible for building a number of new basilicas to mark the significant sites within the Christian world, and by this stage it is evident that important changes were made to the basic ground plan of the basilica in order for them to serve the purpose of Christian worship. Such changes included the orientation of the building,[3] so that on entering it one entered a pathway that drew the eye to its focal point – the concave apse in which the centres of liturgical activity, such as the bishop's chair, the ambo and the altar, were centrally placed.[4] The Christian basilica was an architectural space, specifically designated and adapted for worship, and as such was more than simply a convenient meeting space. Indeed, there is sufficient evidence to suggest that as an architectural space, the development of the Christian basilica deliberately combined notions of the public 'meeting space' with that of the 'sacred space' of the temple in which worshippers invoked and encountered the triune God in worship.[5]

---

2 A detailed account of the adaptation of buildings for the purpose of Christian worship is to be found in Robin Gibbons, *House of God: House of the People of God* (London: SPCK 2006).

3 Thomas F. Mathews, *The Clash of Gods: A Reinterpretation of Early Christian Art* (Princeton, NJ: Princeton University Press 1993), p. 94.

4 On the question of how the architectural design drew the eye to the apse, see Elizabeth C. Parker, 'Architecture as Liturgical Setting' in Thomas J. Heffernan and E. Ann Matter (eds), *The Liturgy of the Medieval Church* (Kalamazoo, MI: Medieval Institute Publications, Western Michigan University 2001). For a summary of how the positioning of these liturgical foci varied from one geographical area to another, see R. Kevin Seasoltz, *A Sense of the Sacred: Theological Foundations of Christian Architecture and Art* (New York and London: Continuum 2005), p. 95. The greatest difference was between the Roman, North African and Syrian basilican plan, where the latter was characterized by a *bema*, or platform, centrally placed in the nave for the readings and the prayers.

5 The basilica emerges as a major and recurring theme in George Guiver, *Vision Upon Vision: Processes of Change and Renewal in Christian Worship* (Norwich: Canterbury Press 2009). Drawing upon recent Italian scholarship on the Christian basilica, Guiver describes the participatory style of its worship. See esp. pp. 19–29.

We know that these buildings, such as the basilica of St John Lateran, built on the edge of the city of Rome and consecrated in 324, were lavishly decorated with glittering mosaics, fabrics and sculpture, and contained certain furniture, such as the altar table, that was assigned symbolic importance and value. The development of the basilica reached its apogee in the fifth century, and a stunning example is the brick-built basilica of Santa Sabina, which was built on the site of a small house-church that allegedly had originally been the titled property of the martyr St Sabina, during the pontificate of Celestine I (422–32), and would have been regarded at the time as monumental in scale. The interior of the building was lavishly decorated, and on one of the surviving cypress-wood doors to the basilica, in relief sculpture, is one of the earliest depictions of the crucifixion, showing an oversized Christ figure with the two thieves on either side.

The deliberate combination of social and sacred space in the Christian basilica led to its name as the *basilica domenicana*, where people were called together by God to be the people of God. The basilica provided an ample and expansive space, a space for all together, and given the scale of ordinary domestic buildings, many worshippers must have been struck by the sheer sense of space that they experienced as they took their place for worship. The very architectural arrangement articulated a dynamic sense of movement as the colonnaded nave drew the worshippers' attention towards the Holy of Holies, inviting them to approach the altar,[6] which came to be covered by a fabric canopy or by an architectural ciborium, and beyond which was the concave apse, the visual climax where the eye eventually came to rest[7] on the place of encounter with the triune God. The basilica provided ample space for worshippers to gather as a corporate body, and as it seems likely, from the material visual evidence of the *orantes* painted by jobbing artists in the Roman catacombs, that Christians prayed with open eyes, the sight lines of the building and their destination must have had a direct and dramatic impact on their experience and understanding of worship.

For Christians worshipping in the basilica, worship was as much a visual as an aural experience. As well as the sight lines there were also clearly defined pathways through the interior space, along aisles

---

6 Jeanne Halgren Kilde, *Sacred Power, Sacred Space: An Introduction to Christian Architecture and Worship* (Oxford: Oxford University Press 2008), p. 48.
7 Mathews, *The Clash of Gods*, p. 94.

that facilitated the flow of the movement of people in and through the building and that were used for a number of liturgical processions and movement, such as the entrance procession, the Gospel reading, Offertory and Communion. And so on entering the great longitudinal architectural space of the basilica, the worshipper may indeed have felt led by the series of columns in that expansive area to step out along a processional pathway into a liminal place of encounter, where sight lines converged in what was the largest unified space for the artist above and behind the altar.[8] The whole architectural design with its deliberate orientation conspired to bring the eye to rest on what functioned as a visual canopy above the particular loci of liturgical activity. Thomas Mathews (1993) has argued that what the apsidal mural or mosaic invariably presented was an aspect of the person or work of Christ. If this view is taken as a correct reading of the evidence, then we can see a correlation between the central visual icon and the one whose presence was understood to be mediated through the proclaiming of the Word, the sacrament of the Eucharist and the assembly itself as Christ's 'body'. In Chapter 5 I will take up the question of what was represented in the visual focal point of the basilica in a discussion of the apsidal mosaics in two ancient basilica churches in Rome, St John Lateran and St Clemente.

Meanwhile, my concern here is not so much to engage in the renewed debate about the ways in which Christian worship was shaped by the ground plan of the basilica but to highlight the visual impact and the kinetic aspects of what it is to enter into a rectangular hall-shaped building, whether that building is an ancient basilica, such as the Roman basilica in Trier, or the lofty Gothic architecture of Rheims Cathedral. In more recent times in London, we have seen a remarkable adaptation of a hall-shaped building for a specifically visual purpose, namely the conversion of Bankside power station into the Tate Modern art gallery. Designed by Sir Giles Gilbert Scott, Bankside was originally an oil-fired power station, and its turbine hall is some 200 metres in length (660 feet).

This building project, designed by the international architects Jacques Herzog and Pierre de Meuron, has been a phenomenal success, converting the inside of a modernist industrial building into a number of light and capacious exhibition spaces. The building work began in

---

8 Mathews, *The Clash of Gods*, p. 97.

1995 and was completed in January 2000, and during its first year the gallery attracted some one million visitors, far exceeding the projected number. On entering the building, visitors find themselves in the cavernous space of the turbine hall, and it would be fascinating to compare the response of visitors on entering that capacious space with those who enter the nave of a cathedral. Comparisons have been made, and the turbine hall was described as being 'cathedral-like' in the official publication describing the building project.[9] Tate Modern occupies a prime site on the south bank of the Thames, directly opposite St Paul's Cathedral, and continues to expand with the addition in 2012 of a new gallery and meeting space in the original industrial oil tanks, for which Tate managed to raise £175 million at a time of severe financial stringency and global economic uncertainty. A second phase of development providing new galleries is expected to be open by 2016. The two iconic buildings of Tate Modern and St Paul's Cathedral are linked by the London Millennium Footbridge, and this linking is not without its ironic dimension. Has the turbine hall at Tate Modern, for which there is currently no charge for entry, become the kind of 'public space' that Christopher Wren intended for his cathedral? St Paul's was built, incidentally, by public subscription to be the sacred space in the City of London for the people of London. It could be said that as both buildings attract a significant high 'footfall' as major visitor attractions in the capital, there is little by way of competition, and some commentators might also add that any comparison between the two buildings is invidious because of the difference in their primary purposes. Nevertheless, in terms of how architectural spaces work, and the visual impact they have on the people who enter them, some comparison seems at least inevitable.

The unquestionable success story of Tate Modern could well be read as irrefutable evidence for the sociologist's theory of secularization. Indeed, an interesting statement is made in the published story of its building that the experience of the visitor to the turbine hall 'is as close to a spiritual experience as one might find in today's secular world'.[10] However, the statement should not be taken on face value as the term 'spiritual' is nebulous and fluid, and the assumption that we live in a

9 Raymund Ryan, *Building Tate Modern: Herzog and De Meuron Transforming Giles Gilbert Scott* (London: Tate Gallery Publishing 2000), p. 24.
10 Ryan, *Building Tate Modern*, p. 24.

'secular world' is one that is increasingly contested. The theory of secularization is constructed from the observation of a combination of social trends, including the mentality that we occupy a closed technologically regulated world that is solely of human making,[11] and the empirical discrepancy between religious belief and actual practice.[12] These social trends underpin the sociologist David Martin's claim that the art gallery and the concert hall are the new foci of high seriousness and contemplation in our plural social world.[13] But this claim, made without any reference to the other factors leading to the prominence of such urban spaces in contemporary society, such as the market-driven art world and culture of celebrity and sensation, merely echoes the confident claim of André Malraux, who in the middle of the twentieth century announced that the gallery or art museum would be the only shrine of the modern age in western democracies.[14]

We may well detect in Malraux's writing a hint of the modern tendency towards opposition; that is, the tendency to oppose categories such as religion and spirituality, the religious and the secular, which in turn can be traced back to the doyen of modernism, the philosopher Friedrich Nietzsche. It was Nietzsche who famously opposed 'Dionysius' to 'the Crucified One'.[15] But there is no necessary a priori reason to posit an opposition between art and religion. They are far from being in competition, and besides, even the theory of secularization, predicated on the empirical basis of the numerical decline of institutional religious allegiance and practice, is now seen to be a more complex phenomenon and is treated in a more nuanced way.[16] The assertion that museums are now our cathedrals and cathedrals now our museums has a definite rhetorical ring, but it is hardly a sufficient statement of the

11 See Bryan Wilson, 'Prediction and Prophecy in the Future of Religion' in Grace Davie, Paul Heelas and Linda Woodhead (eds), *Predicting Religion: Christian, Secular and Alternative Futures* (Aldershot: Ashgate 2003), pp. 64–72.
12 See, for example, Linda Woodhead and Rebecca Catto (eds), *Religion and Change in Modern Britain* (London and New York: Routledge 2012).
13 David Martin, 'On Secularization and its Prediction: A Self-examination' in Davie, Heelas and Woodhead (eds), *Predicting Religion*, p. 38.
14 See Graham Howes, *The Art of the Sacred: An Introduction to the Aesthetics of Art and Belief* (London and New York: I. B. Tauris 2007), esp. ch. 5, 'Holy Places and Hollow Spaces'.
15 Charles Taylor, *A Secular Age* (Cambridge, MA: Harvard University Press 2007), p. 771.
16 Taylor, *A Secular Age*, ch. 14, 'Religion Today'.

intended purpose of both kinds of buildings. It may well be the case that the architectural design of some but by no means all nineteenth-century galleries and museums had architectural similarities to major religious buildings, but it is not simply the case that these buildings, whose primary purpose or function was the display of visual materials and historic artefacts, were superseding the function of cathedrals and other significant religious monuments.

What is indisputable is the notable increase in the popularity of museums and galleries that was noted towards the end of the twentieth century[17] and continues in a particularly huge way with the ongoing developments at Tate Modern. The trend continues, and two impressive new British galleries, the Turner Contemporary Gallery in Margate and the Hepworth in Wakefield, both designed by the architect David Chipperfield, achieved their target for visitors for their first year within seven months of opening. But statistics alone do not in themselves prove that the gallery has become the temple of art in our western mass society. There is in any case a plurality of functions for church buildings as well as for museums and galleries, and both kinds of building continue to attract significant numbers of visitors and pilgrims. According to a pilot survey commissioned by the Association of English Cathedrals, well over 11 million people visited cathedrals during 2006, and among this figure some 45 per cent of respondents to a questionnaire engaged in an explicitly religious act of saying a prayer and lighting a candle.[18] More research is needed here, but this overtly religious behaviour does support the view that cathedrals and churches meet the human need for sacred space. The need, that is, for those places that are described by the poet Philip Larkin in 'Church Going' as a 'serious place', and that, as the sociologist concedes, can provide space for symbolic expressions in times of personal crisis, or of more public anguish and celebration.[19] Further, alongside these occasional uses of sacred space there is the statistical evidence that bucks the overall trend in the decline of affiliation

---

17 See Stephen Bann, 'Art History and Museums' in Mark A. Cheetham, Michael Ann Holly and Keith Moxey (eds), *The Subjects of Art History: Historical Objects in Contemporary Perspective* (Cambridge: Cambridge University Press 1998), p. 230.
18 Visitor research at <www.churchofengland.org/about-us/facts-stats.aspx>, accessed 1 February 2010.
19 Martin, 'On Secularization and its Prediction', p. 70, and Kate Hunt, 'Understanding the Spirituality of People who do not go to Church' in Davie, Heelas and Woodhead (eds), *Predicting Religion*, p. 165.

to religious institutions, and that Grace Davie[20] may count as evidence for a residual or nominal Christian belief and practice, which is the consistent three per cent annual rise in the number of worshippers attending services in English cathedrals during the decade following the turn of the millennium.[21]

It could be the case that what motivates the visitor to a cathedral is the desire to connect in some way to the past or simply to view the art and architecture, but even so, the evidence suggests that in terms of what leads people to visit such a place, one cannot simply equate a cathedral with a museum or gallery. Parallels between the function of galleries and museums and churches and cathedrals have been drawn and analysed. But the mapped similarities have focused on the intended social effect of both kinds of building on their clientele.[22] The fact remains that what is found in the museum may well inform and inspire the visitor, but the artefacts seen in a worshipping context are there as part of the panoply of worship. Both the intention and the function are different. One set of objects is there to educate and even to awaken wonder in the viewer, the other to intentionally evoke and invoke the symbolic exchange in the encounter of the divine and human worlds.

A great number of art galleries were built in the nineteenth century, and they are imposing buildings. The building of some of the earliest galleries in the industrial world may well have contributed to the consolidation of national identity. The intention of the National Gallery, established in London in the 1820s, was to equal the collections of the other great centres in Continental Europe. These institutions with their imposing edifices aspired to be public spaces, and they certainly enhanced a sense of national pride and added an aesthetic value to the perceived achievements of a nation and its people. On a smaller scale, but no less impressive, were the galleries of the major industrial cities of England, such as Leeds, Sheffield and Manchester, which were monuments of civic pride and municipal aspiration. At one level these galleries represent what might be described as the democratization of art. Art was now to be viewed in *public* spaces and not only in the smart drawing

---

20 See Grace Davie, *Religion in Britain since 1945: Believing without Belonging* (Oxford: Blackwell 1994).

21 Headline Mission Statistics, Research and Statistics Department, Archbishops' Council, April 2012.

22 For the classic study of this, see Carol Duncan, *Civilizing Rituals: Inside Public Art Museums* (London and New York: Routledge 1995).

rooms of the rich and fashionable, and it is this desire for *public* space that recalls the motivation of early Christians in adopting the model of the basilica as the ground plan of their cathedrals and churches. Today it is perhaps the experience of space that is the common ground between the visitor to the gallery and the cathedral. There is undoubtedly a similar sense of space in the experience of a person entering the vaulted nave of a Gothic cathedral and the lofty turbine hall of Tate Modern.

In Canterbury Cathedral, for instance, the architectural lines conspire to draw the eye of the visitor entering at the west end of the nave both upward and forward. The space of both the turbine hall and the cathedral nave is an inviting space – it invites the visitor to look beyond the everyday and to step forward into a place of visual encounter. The cathedral, of course, was intentionally built to signal the transcendent, to be a physical sign of the heavenly temple constructed at the very centre of the human city. One can undoubtedly draw similarities between the experience of a visitor entering a cathedral and entering into a large gallery, and although I would resist any opposition between the two kinds of space, there are differences – and significant differences – between the two. Visitors come with an array of expectations, and on entering a space have some sense of what they may see and find there. But the architectural spaces themselves may suggest and evoke inchoate thoughts, memories and associations in the visitor. And so even the most secular visitor entering the space of a cathedral could find that it not only evokes the beliefs of a past religious age but that he or she may feel open on that occasion to the possibility of God and an experience of the transcendent.[23] The tourist can during a visit, perhaps even momentarily, become a pilgrim, a person conscious of the need to journey on in the quest for meaning. There is another debate about what it may be for a space to be a sacred space, a holy place, but suffice it to say here that what differentiates the spaces of a cathedral from the spaces of a major gallery is what actually happens in them, and here, of course, we are brought to the primary purpose of the building, the activity for which it was built, namely worship.

The playwright and novelist Sebastian Barry was commissioned to write a play by Canterbury Cathedral and the Canterbury Festival,

---

23 For an analysis of visitor experience to English cathedrals, see the research report *Spiritual Capital: The Present and Future of English Cathedrals* (London: Theos/The Grubb Institute 2012).

made possible by the support of Arts Council England. The play, *Dallas Sweetman*, was performed in the nave of the cathedral, 'in God's great house', in September 2008. The play is a dense and demanding narrative drama about the difficulties of telling the truth about the past and of the human need for forgiveness. In addition, the technical challenges facing the production team were enormous, and the audibility of the actors for the audience was never satisfactorily resolved. An undulating stage set up at the eastern end of the nave provided a clear visual focus from the gently raked seating, and the lighting effectively drew out the lines and shadows of the unusual architectural setting for the play. After the final performance the cast were unanimous in their view that the space in which they had performed was a rather extraordinary one. In a discussion of what this might mean, one actor said that something else happens in that space. That 'something else', of course, is prayer and worship. This aside could perhaps be read as simply anecdotal or as a piece of qualitative research evidence,[24] but it may give us something of a lead in our consideration of the significance of place and the connections we might draw between what happens in a particular place and what comes to be seen and felt there.[25] In the case of a church or a cathedral, one could argue that the physical building, its design, furnishings and the various worship practices that occur within it, contribute to the effect the place has on the sensibility of both worshippers and visitors alike.[26]

As we begin to tease out the question of the relationship between a church space and a gallery space, we can see that there are both similarities and significant differences, not necessarily in architectural terms but in terms of the feel and spirit of a place. Both spaces are highly visual and yet they are in their own ways quite distinctive, and what may be

24 In this connection, it is also interesting to note with Paul Bayley, who has curated significant exhibitions of contemporary art at St Paul's Cathedral and other London churches, that a number of artists are keen to exhibit their work in a sacred space, presumably because they feel it gives them some cachet and adds a certain gravitas to the artwork that is shown in that context.

25 For a discussion of what makes a space a 'holy place', see Christopher Irvine, 'Liturgical Space' in Juliette Day and Benjamin Gordon-Taylor (eds), *The Study of Liturgy and Worship: An Alcuin Guide* (London: SPCK, 2013).

26 For a range of theoretical considerations, see Gordon Lynch, 'Object Theory: Toward an Intersubjective, Mediated, and Dynamic Theory of Religion' and David Morgan 'Materiality, Social Analysis, and the Study of Religions' in David Morgan (ed.), *Religion and Material Culture: The Matter of Belief* (London and New York: Routledge 2010).

described as the institutional and ideological differences between them are probably quite significant. Simply by being publicly designated and recognized as being a particular kind of space – a church or a gallery – gives them a distinctive function. It is interesting to note, for example, that in discussions about what it is that makes modern art, the very fact that it is placed in a gallery is a sufficient qualification for an artwork or installation to be deemed art.[27] The context in which art is seen is undoubtedly critical for the reception of art as art, and for most of us it is the gallery that provides the appropriate space for the exhibiting and viewing of art. Within the setting of the gallery, a key skill of the curator is the placing of the artwork. In setting up an exhibition, the good curator will be concerned with matters such as appropriate lighting for the viewing of the artworks and appropriate interpretation. But the key factor in showcasing works of art is the placing of exhibits, of what exactly should go where and in what space to show the relationships between the artworks exhibited in the gallery. So from the general consideration of the context in which the art is viewed, there is the more specific question of the placing of artworks, the spatial relationship between them, suggesting how one painting, for instance, may be read and responded to in relationship to the others displayed in the gallery or brought together for a particular show or exhibition.

The question of what we see when we view a piece of art will depend to some extent on where it is seen and on the context of where it is seen, and we shall have to return to this crucial point at a later stage in our discussion of seeing liturgically. At this stage we can turn our attention from the place in which we see art to the question of the placing of art, and tease out in reference to some modern art this question of placing, of where an artwork is displayed and how this is not simply a matter of showcasing but also of interpretation – of how a picture is viewed, received and understood by the viewer. What comes into play here, in what curators are increasingly calling recontextualizing,[28] is not simply the setting in which artwork is sited, or where it is placed, but the other

---

27 The very placing of a work in a gallery brings that work into an institutional and a conceptual space in which the viewer may see and respond to it as a work of art. See Daniel A. Siedell, *God in the Gallery: A Christian Embrace of Modern Art* (Grand Rapids, MI: Baker Academic Press 2008), esp. pp. 24–6.
28 See James Hall's review of the Cy Twombly and Poussin exhibition at the Dulwich Picture Gallery, *Times Literary Supplement*, 12 August 2011, p. 17.

objects that will come into the viewer's fields of vision as he or she looks at a painting or other work of art.

At the 'Turner and the Masters'[29] exhibition at Tate Britain in 2009, a number of canvases painted by J. M. W. Turner were, as the show's title suggests, placed side by side with a range of classical works, including the then fashionable Poussin, Titian and Rembrandt. The intention was to illustrate not simply the art that influenced Turner but to show what he aimed to do in his art, which was, when first shown publicly, greeted in some quarters with derision. He copied the masters whom he admired, and tried, with mixed success, to exceed what they had produced through the vitality of colour and light. The arrangement of the exhibition certainly illustrated the technical innovations made by the artist, but what was even more striking was the way viewers not only saw Turner's work in relation to the style of the fine representational artwork from which he was deliberately wanting to break away, but also, side by side, could see something they probably would not see were the works viewed separately. This illustrates precisely what I want to say, first, about the importance of the *placing* of art. Where a painting or artwork is placed is vital in allowing it to speak to the viewer. In the following chapter, we will explore this in relation to the proximity of altarpieces to the altar, the primary locus of liturgical activity. But a brilliant example of the placing of an artwork in a gallery, and one that understandably elicits a wry smile, is the placing of Francesco Botticini's painting *The Assumption of the Virgin* (c. 1475–7), originally painted as an altarpiece for Matteo Palmieri's family chapel in Florence, on the wall facing the top of the wide staircase in the Sainsbury Wing of the National Gallery that leads to the first floor. As the visitor reaches the top of the 48 stairs, he or she can look up and is then faced by Botticini's painting. In this painting, placed above the staircase in this voluminous rectilinear space, the nine choirs of angels are grouped into three bands, with the figure of Christ blessing the crowned Virgin Mary, painted at the centre of the top band, which extends the sense of ascent.

The placing of an artwork in its spatial architectural setting and in relation to other works of art is critical to how its visible language may be read and its meaning conveyed. The physical placing of a work of

---

29 'Turner and the Masters' at Tate Britain, September 2009–January 2010, an exhibition curated by David Solkin.

art, in other words, is more than just making it visible. It effects how it is perceived and understood by the viewer. The placing of a Craigie Aitchison painting of the crucifixion next to the artist's painting of canaries in a tree, for instance, may well lead the viewer to see the cross as an image of the tree of God's kingdom, in which is to be found colour and form and song.[30] In the physical placing of a work of art, one is actually setting it within a particular visual and conceptual frame of reference, and this changes how the piece actually works.

A liturgical example of the importance of the siting of an artwork in relation to how it is read and responded to can be seen in the recently installed water-stoup at Canterbury Cathedral, crafted by the sculptor Stephen Cox. This capacious water-stoup, whose elliptical bowl standing on an elegantly sculpted pedestal and measuring 150 by 60 centimetres, is made of Fouakir Breccia, an ancient Egyptian hard silt stone compacting brightly coloured pebbles into the green marble. When it is filled with water, it is like seeing the pebbles on the bed of a clean stream, as in Piero della Francesca's painting of the baptism of Christ in the National Gallery in London. The water-stoup is placed against the pillar by the south-west door, the principal entrance for visitors, and is exactly aligned with the Cathedral's seventeenth-century font, which stands between two pillars on the north side of the nave. Because the water-stoup is placed where it is, it resonates with a range of symbolic meanings – as a sign of welcome, of a line of liminality marking the threshold into sacred space, and as a place to remember baptism. Symbols may indeed be found in works of art exhibited in the art gallery, but the kind of symbolic resonance I have alluded to in connection with the siting of Stephen Cox's water-stoup is to a large extent dependent upon its setting. Indeed, I would contend that within a church building that is used for worship, the delineated architectural spaces, artefacts and works of visual art combine to form a matrix of communicative signs and symbols.[31]

When we enter a church building we enter a symbolic world. There we find symbolic objects, and perhaps more importantly, those who participate in worship are caught up in intentionally symbolic actions. For what constitutes a sacred space is what actually happens there, the

---

30 See the image of the eschatological tree in Ezekiel 17.23, 31.6 and Daniel 4.9–17, and the parable of the mustard seed in Mark 4.30–32.
31 Anne Dawtry and Christopher Irvine, *Art and Worship* (London: SPCK 2002), ch. 5.

rituals that are performed there and the marking out of the space as a place of encounter with others and with the mystery of God. The crucial difference between a church and a gallery is that the former is a consecrated building, ritually marked out as 'holy space'. In Christian terms, the designation of sacred space and the marking of objects placed there as holy things is performed by literally making a specific mark or sign. In the earliest centuries the celebration of the Eucharist was sufficient to sacralize a space, but the rites of consecration became more elaborate and by the seventh century included the incorporation of relics in the new church as well as the designation of the building as a holy place by the signs of the cross.[32] Likewise, the key furnishings of the church, such as altars and fonts, were and still are consecrated by being ritually signed with the sign of the cross. And so if you go and see the new font by the sculptor William Pye that has been installed at Salisbury Cathedral, you can still see the mark of the cross that was made with the oil of chrism by the then Archbishop of Canterbury, Dr Rowan Williams, at the consecration ceremony as part of the 750th anniversary service of the Cathedral on 28 September 2008.

As I have written elsewhere,[33] the cross is a condensed symbol. It is in one sense the signature of the God whose story is told in the Gospels. It is the universal sign of Christianity, and those who are made Christians are themselves signed with the cross at baptism to indicate their belonging to Christ. The cross marks a holy site, and even the architectural ground plan of some churches is in the shape of a cross, so that as one enters the building one is spatially entering the cross. At prayer some Christians make the sign of the cross to personally appropriate the blessing and protection that Christ offers and brings.

One second-century Christian writer, Irenaeus, Bishop of Lyons,

---

32 Since earliest times, places of worship were marked out ritually as holy spaces. We know of the dedication of the early Christian basilicas, and a number of Pontificals (liturgical books produced for the use of bishops) tell us that by the eighth century, consecration rites assimilated aspects of the baptismal liturgy, with walls being washed with holy water and pillars and walls being marked in the oil of chrism with the sign of the cross. See John Wickham Legg (ed.), *The English Orders for Consecrating Churches in the Seventeenth Century* (London: Henry Bradshaw Society, vol. 41, 1911); R. W. Muncey, *A History of the Consecration of Churches and Churchyards* (Cambridge: Heffer 1930); G. G. Willis, *Further Essays in Early Roman Liturgy* (London: SPCK 1968), ch. 3.

33 Christopher Irvine, *The Use of Symbols in Worship* (London: SPCK 2007), ch. 1.

saw the cross as being stamped into the physical fabric of the natural world, and regarded the event of Jesus' crucifixion as making visible the ubiquitous sign of God's engagement with the whole of creation.[34] The cross is there for all to see, but ultimately its meaning, how it works as a symbol, depends on its being seen in the wider context of the Christian story and the arena of the Church's worship.

What I am attempting to do in this chapter is to construct a cumulative case in support of the view that the reception and reading of religious art, rather like the perception of a sense of place, is related to the distinctive activity or behaviour with which the space in which it is seen is associated. We have already indicated that the architectural setting in which a cross is placed is vital to the releasing of the power of its symbolic meaning, and we will need to address the wider question of the context, of the occasion in which the cross is placed, seen and responded to by the viewer. The first question, of course, is where the work of art is placed and the setting in which it is seen. Does it matter if a religious work of art is seen in the worshipping space of a church or in an art gallery, with its adjustable track lighting, bare white walls and controlled environmental conditions?

'Devotion by Design', an exhibition at the National Gallery during the summer of 2011, addressed the issue by setting a number of Italian altarpieces in its collection in ways that helped the viewer appreciate the original church setting of these works of art. One of the galleries in this exhibition was a simulacrum of a church interior, fitted out with an altar, candlesticks and a serried row of benches facing the altar. But even with the playing of suitable ambient music, this fabricated church setting was finally unconvincing because the key contextual factor was missing, namely the space in which the liturgy is actually celebrated. Again, context is the key, and the context is wider than the physical setting in which art is viewed and responded to. But there is a dilemma about the placing of art, particularly those works that are considered to be great and that need to be kept in appropriate environmental conditions and, crucially, a place that allows for maximum access by the viewing public. On this basis, it is understandably assumed that an artwork is best seen *as art* in the conditions of a gallery or a museum. But in some cases there is a risk of decontextualizing the work in a

---

34 Irenaeus, *Proof of the Apostolic Preaching*, 1.34.

sanitized white space,[35] and possibly limiting its meaning(s) to the assumptions and expectations brought to it by the viewer.

We can continue to tease out this question of the setting in which a work of art is seen a little further, but at this stage of the exploration we may also consider the idea of the 'viewer as worshipper'. This further dimension, including the dispositions and indeed preconceptions that the worshipper brings to a work of art in a church setting, widens the scope of the discussion beyond that of the physical context in which the artwork is placed and seen. Even so, the context in which religious art is placed and seen remains crucial, and as a test case, I shall look at the much discussed Isenheim altarpiece in Colmar (see Plate 1).[36]

This multi-panelled altarpiece, painted around 1515 by the enigmatic artist we know as Matthias Grünewald for the monastery of St Antony at Isenheim in the Alsace region of France, is now in nearby Colmar in the Unterlinden Museum, itself a converted church building. In a highly influential study of the Grünewald altarpiece, the art historian Andrée Hayum drew attention to the importance of the *context* in which the work is seen. Although the main point Hayum wants to make is that this work of art might not resonate for contemporary viewers from a more secular culture to the extent it did for its original audience, the implication she draws is that seeing a work of art originally commissioned for a church setting in a gallery is rather like seeing animals in a zoo rather than in their natural habitat.[37] The point Hayum articulates here applies to the more general observation that was made earlier, albeit in a different context, by the famous critic

---

35 The convention of painting the modern art gallery white can be traced back to the American-British artist James McNeill Whistler (1834–1903) and his one-man show at the Goupil Gallery in London in 1892.

36 See, for example, the major studies of Jane Dillenberger, *Style and Content in Christian Art* (London: SCM Press 1986); *Images and Relics: Theological Perceptions and Visual Images in Sixteenth-Century Europe* (Oxford: Oxford University Press 1999), pp. 27–32; David Brown, *Tradition and Imagination: Revelation and Change* (Oxford: Oxford University Press 1999); Tina Beattie, 'Insight beyond Sight: Sacramentality, Gender and the Eucharist with Reference to the Isenheim Altarpiece', *New Blackfriars*, vol. 88, no. 1014, March 2007, pp. 170–86, and more recently, David Jasper's erudite study, *The Sacred Body: Asceticism in Religion, Literature, Art and Culture* (Waco, TX: Baylor University Press 2009). Jasper argues (pp. 20, 42–3, 112) that the Grünewald crucifixion panel is an artistic representation of the final *kenosis*, or self-emptying, of the incarnate God, presenting the viewer with a paradoxical image of absent presence.

37 See Andrée Hayum, *The Isenheim Altarpiece: God's Medicine and the Painter's Vision* (Princeton, NJ: Princeton University Press 1989), p. 8.

André Malraux. Malraux was not the first to contest the role of the art museum to remove material visual work from its original setting in order to display it according to some presupposed schema of display and way of seeing. As early as 1807 the German archaeologist C. A. Böttiger had described the placing of antique artefacts in the museum as the final degradation of classical art, on the grounds that the Greeks considered art as being inseparable from its religious and public functions.[38]

Malraux worked with the same logic and implicit critique, and argued that the removal of artworks from church buildings and the placing of them in an art gallery not only isolated an artwork from its original context but, more significantly, 'tended to estrange the works . . . from their original functions'.[39] The implication is that the art works differently in different contexts, and this observation is insightful and needs to be teased out further. In the vocabulary used by both authors we see first, in the case of Hayum, a reference to what may be described as 'the form of life' of which the work is an integral part, and second, in the case of Malraux, a reference to the 'functions', the complex activities engaged in by the community for whom the art was commissioned, made, seen and responded to. What both these commentators have said is that the removal of an artwork from its primary context may well result in highlighting its artistic value but shrink its range of original, intended and received meanings. In short, how an artefact or a work of art functions depends in a variety of ways on the context for which it was made and the occasion in which it was originally intended to be seen and responded to. Every designated public space is associated with a complex of beliefs, assumptions and practices, and these are not immediately transferable from one kind of space to another.

The Isenheim altarpiece shows what has been described as a gruesomely horrific painting of the crucifixion. It can, of course, be read in many ways, but the visual impact is that of the figure of the Crucified, with his head slumped on his right shoulder, sagging under the dead weight of his already decaying body. But this dark crucifixion panel, dense with symbolic references, belongs to a multi-panelled altarpiece,

---

38 Cited by Bann, 'Art History and Museums', p. 237.
39 See André Malraux, *The Voices of Silence*, trans. Stuart Gilbert (London: Secker & Warburg 1956), p. 14.

and so it also needs to be 'read' alongside the other panels, which include a painting of the risen Christ emerging from a fiery ball of light. The interesting question of whether this painting actually works as a painting of the resurrection is a different one, and not really the issue here. What is important in this discussion is that Grünewald's dark image of the dead and decaying figure of Christ on the cross, which influenced such twentieth-century artists as Pablo Picasso in the late 1920s and early 1930s and Graham Sutherland in the 1940s more than any other artistic representation of the crucifixion, is seen as part of a wider visual field in this complex multi-panelled altarpiece.

Andrée Hayum's classic study draws attention to how the painting of the crucifixion in Grünewald's altarpiece (in its closed position) would have originally been seen by those who gathered for the celebration of the Mass at the high altar of the chapel of the monastery of St Antony at Isenheim. Both the artist and the patron may well have been familiar with the graphic descriptions of Christ's physical suffering on the cross in the writings of contemporary Christian mystics such as Birgitta of Sweden or Julian of Norwich; but they were also aware of how the painting would have been seen and received by those suffering from the disfiguring and agonizing symptoms of St Antony's fire, an excruciatingly painful skin disease caused by eating poisoned rye bread that caused boils, rupturing of the skin and gangrene.

What the patients of the Antonine hospital who attended Mass in the monastic church would have seen in this depiction of the decaying and pock-marked flesh of the dead Christ was a mirror image of their own diseased and disfigured bodies. What was seen by the worshippers in this figure of Christ crucified, far larger than the other figures painted in the panel, would have been a startling image of the God who empathized with their condition. Indeed, this figure of the Crucified would have elicited in the worshipper a sense of a God who knew the extremities of suffering and who in Christ had been 'counted among the afflicted'. If this is how the terrifying image of Grünewald's crucifixion was perceived, it must have been of some consolation to the sufferers of St Antony's fire to see that the God they worshipped was a God who knew their suffering. Nevertheless, the range of responses to this panel may not have been restricted to this psychological one of solidarity, compassion and empathy. The panel is a complex composition and contains a variety of symbolic images that would have been read and responded to by the viewer as a worshipper as well as a patient.

There is, for example, the symbolic figure of Mary Magdalene. She is painted kneeling upright, her spine arched back, arms raised and hands together, the fingers loosely interlaced. To her left Mary, the mother of the Lord, swoons from grief into the arms of John the beloved disciple at the sight of her dead son. By way of compositional contrast, on the other side of the cross stands the figure of John the Baptist. His posture is poised and purposeful. His left arm outstretched, his elongated hand and exaggerated index finger point to Christ. Pictorially, the declarative figure of the Baptist corresponds to the performative character of liturgical celebration.[40] His inclusion in this crucifixion scene is anachronistic, but John the Baptist was the one who witnessed to Christ and declared him to be 'the Lamb of God who takes away the sin of the world!' (John 1.29, 36). It is my contention that the way the figure of Mary Magdalene is painted, particularly her posture in this symmetrical composition, presents us with a model of how the viewer as worshipper is intended to respond to the visual declaration of the Baptist. Unlike the larger figure of Mary immediately behind her, Mary Magdalene's eyes are open and fixed on the figure of the Crucified. The gestural language of Mary Magdalene, so eloquent in the monastic culture of silence, is also significant. She is depicted kneeling, which is the posture of penitential and supplicatory prayer.[41] She neither wrings her hands at the sight of the calamity of Christ's death, nor do her fingers tightly grip her hands as though she were in a state of desperate despair. Rather, her hands are together and are raised. The fingers are loosely splayed, so that if she were to drop her arms slightly, her hands would open and form a receptive shape. Moreover, her head is raised, and with open eyes she looks up directly in the face of Christ, whose head has fallen to the side. In terms of the picture's composition, when we look at the direction of Mary Magdalene's gaze we can trace a diagonal line between her face and the face of the Crucified.

---

40 A reproduction of this painting hung above the desk of the reformed theologian Karl Barth, who saw the figure as representing the witness, or testimony to the cross to which the only response is a worshipful 'Amen'. See James E. Davison, 'Karl Barth and Matthias Grünewald: The Continuing Life of a Painting at Pittsburgh Theological Seminary' in *Panorama*, a publication of Pittsburgh Theological Seminary, vol. 45, no. 3, Spring 2006.

41 Simon Tugwell OP, 'The Nine Ways of Prayer of St. Dominic: A Textual Study and Critical Edition', *Medieval Studies*, vol. 47, 1985.

What I am suggesting is that the way the figure of Mary Magdalene is painted is an answering pose to the indicative declaration of the Baptist, and that the gestural language of her raised hands is a gesture of supplication. Specifically, the visual pose strikes the supplicatory cry of *Agnus Dei* at the Eucharist: *Agnus Dei, qui tollis peccata mundi, miserere nobis*, 'Lamb of God, you take away the sins of the world: have mercy upon me.'[42] The painted figure of the kneeling Magdalene, in other words, shows the viewer, whether it is the brother of the Order of St Antony or a hospital patient worshipping in the church, how they are to respond to the declaratory witness of the Baptist as a worshipper at the Mass. The viewer is the worshipper who is here being invited to worship the paschal Lamb who was slain and yet who lives for ever, and who wipes away every tear of suffering (Revelation 5.6–14; 7.17).

It is in this sense that the altarpiece is complete when it is seen and responded to by worshippers during the actual celebration of the Mass. The eucharistic reference becomes explicit in the foreground figure of the lamb at the feet of John the Baptist, whose blood flows from its gashed chest into a chalice, and in the so-called lamentation, or painting of entombment on the predella, the low oblong section below the main panel of the altarpiece. Here the dead Christ is gently being laid on to the pure white winding cloth, adjacent to the tomb, rather as the priest in celebrating the Mass would have lowered the elevated host on to the corporal following the dominical words of consecration: 'This is my body'. The altar, with its *mensa* stone, was held since the time of Charlemagne to signify the tomb of Christ. The predella extended along the whole back edge of the surface of the altar table at which the Mass was celebrated, and so would have set up, immediately for the priest at the altar, a visual correspondence between the physical body of Christ and the sacramental body of the Eucharist which, following the Fourth Lateran Council of 1215, had been dogmatically considered to

---

42 According to the *Liber Pontificalis*, a book recording the deeds of the Bishops of Rome, the *Agnus dei* was introduced into the Mass at Rome by Pope Sergius 1 (687–701). It was probably appropriated from the Greek Liturgy of St James, and in the Roman Rite was placed after the Lord's Prayer. It was sung by 'the clergy and people' as the consecrated host was broken (the 'fraction') in order to be distributed in Communion, and thereby functioned as a prayer of preparation for Communion. See Joseph A. Jungmann, *The Mass of the Roman Rite: Its Origins and Development*, trans. Francis A. Brunner, revised Charles Riepe (London: Burns & Oates 1959), pp. 485–9; Kenneth Stevenson, *Eucharist and Offering* (New York: Pueblo 1986), pp. 276–80.

be of the same substance.[43] As well as the proximity of the altarpiece to the altar, the multiple eucharistic references were also signalled by the compositional arrangement of the crucifixion panel painting. Indeed, as indicated above, we can trace a whole nexus of interrelated signs within the crucifixion panel, and perhaps most explicitly, as Hayum observes, the blood flowing from the chest of the lamb into a eucharistic chalice is on the same vertical axis of the lance wound in Christ's body figured in the lamentation painting.[44] So looking at the artist's placing of his images on this painted panel, we can say that the image of the lamb and the dead body of Christ are brought into a kind of eucharistic alignment, so that the life that is seen to be given on the cross is mediated through the body.

The story of Christ being pierced by the lance (John 19.31–34) is accentuated by the artist in the terrible and pictorially dominant figure of the Crucified in the visual field, as the crimson blood gushing out of the wounded chest contrasts with the dark background of the painting.

The crucifixion panel depicts a painting of the dead Christ, and yet when one reads this figure in relation to the other compositional elements, this death is not the total extinguishing or emptying out of the redeeming power of divinity.[45] For the viewer as worshipper may well have read the witness of John in this composition and seen Christ as the Lamb of God, which as a sacrificial figure is simply 'gift', as was the ram that mysteriously appeared caught in a bush when Abraham was about

---

43 This will be discussed further in the next chapter. See also Richard Kieckhefer, 'Major Currents in Late Medieval Devotion' in Jill Raitt (ed.), *Christian Spirituality: High Middle Ages and Reformation* (London: SCM Press 1988), pp. 96–100.

44 Hayum, *The Isenheim Altarpiece*, p. 75.

45 David Jasper refers to the Russian novelist Dostoevsky's reaction to the painting of Hans Holbein the Younger, *Body of the Dead Christ in the Tomb* (1522), which he takes as typifying the Orthodox aversion to the naturalistic visual presentation of the agony and death of Christ because of its apparent erasure of divinity (Jasper, *The Sacred Body*, pp. 32, 36, 110). David Brown similarly posited a simple dichotomy of views between the Christian East and West (Brown, *Tradition and Imagination*, pp. 333–4, 351), but such a polarity of view between East and West is difficult to sustain. Viladesau, for instance, quotes the modern Catholic theologian Karl Rahner, saying 'it does not help me to escape from the mess and mix-up and despair if God is in the same predicament' – Richard Viladesau, *Theological Aesthetics: God in Imagination, Beauty, and Art* (Oxford: Oxford University Press 1999), p. 197. In other words, if the cross has salvific significance, then the crucifixion cannot be seen as the final *kenosis*, or emptying of divinity (*pace* Jasper), and so our iconography and the liturgical portrayal of the cross must contain some visual symbol of redemption, or intimation of resurrection and new life.

to sacrifice his son Isaac (Genesis 22.1–14). This unsettling incident was read in the earliest Christian centuries as a type of the sacrifice of Christ, and its subject became woven into the thickly textured fabric of sacrificial language in the fixed written Eucharistic Prayers, where we find expressions such as 'unbloody sacrifice', in the Anaphora of St James and the 'unblemished sacrifice' in the canon of the Mass of the Latin West. In the eucharistic pleading and commemoration of Christ's sacrifice on the cross, the gift of communion is the means whereby the worshipper can again be made 'at one' with God.

During a plenary session at a recent conference on cathedrals and the visual arts,[46] one delegate asked in a rather exasperated tone why we could not see cathedrals as places for displaying art in the same ways as galleries. In some respects the answer could be a straightforward yes, we could, if there is a suitable space for exhibiting art in the cathedral and its precincts. But the more interesting question is what happens when we place a work of art within a space that is used for worship, and attend to how it is seen and responded to in that context – rather than in a gallery – as an integral visual feature of the worshipping environment. Returning to Hayum's implication that the removal of the Isenheim altarpiece from its original context to a gallery or museum is like removing an animal from its natural habitat, we could extend the metaphor and say that the celebration of the liturgy is a vital element in the complex ecosystem of the sacred space in which the artwork is placed. As Hayum acknowledges, when we now look at religious art in the museum or gallery, we need to remind ourselves of the original context in which the work was placed and to see it in relation to the cult that was celebrated in that original setting.[47] As with the Isenheim altarpiece, the original viewers were actually participants in an action, respondents to a liturgical rite for which the altarpiece provided a visual focus behind the altar in what was a complex and richly sensual experience of various sights, sounds, physical movements and even smells.

What I have said about the Grünewald crucifixion panel is an example of seeing artwork liturgically; that is, seeing the artwork as part of the total worshipping environment and experience in its

---

46 The conference brought together artists, theologians and people working in cathedrals, and was held at Sarum College, Salisbury, in September 2009.
47 Hayum, *The Isenheim Altarpiece*, p. 118.

originally intended setting where the Mass was celebrated. This may strike the reader as a rather overconfident claim, and one that ignores the fact that every work of art is in one sense open to interpretation each time it is viewed. But there are grounds for thinking that where an artwork is seen, and by whom, does affect how the artwork is perceived. In drawing attention, as I have attempted to do, to the context in which the altarpiece was originally seen, I have underlined its liturgical setting, a setting in which it is viewed as part of the whole ambience of worship rather than in isolation, an 'artwork in itself'. This is not to deny that one may look simply at the architecture, decoration, icons, sculpture, paintings, furniture and fittings as individual works of art, but to recover the fact that these various elements are all of a piece, a whole and interrelated complex worshipping environment, and to register the visual impact this may have on worshipper and visitor alike.

It may be the case that Émile Mâle, in his classic 1910 study *The Gothic Image*, overemphasized the visual impact of medieval churches and what was actually communicated by their art and architecture, but the visuality of medieval worship and devotion can hardly be denied.[48] When this art is taken out of context, the viewer may well admire the making of sacred works of art but be baffled by them, and this is confirmed by eavesdropping on what visitors say to each other as they walk around a gallery exhibition of religious art and artefacts. What is overheard would suggest that many lack the cultural frame of reference that really makes sense of the exhibits. The organizers of the National Gallery's winter 2009–10 'The Sacred Made Real' exhibition of seventeenth-century Spanish religious art, made deliberate attempts to address this by providing some theological commentary and suitable music on the audio guide made available to visitors. But watching the behaviour of visitors, Tina Beattie recorded that many seemed uncertain as to how they should respond to these polychrome religious artefacts, and some were even a little embarrassed by what they saw.[49]

---

48 Émile Mâle, *The Gothic Image: Religious Art in France of the Thirteenth Century*, trans. Dora Nussey (London: J. M. Dent 1913). For a discussion of the educative role of art for laity in medieval churches, see G. W. Bernard, *The Late Medieval English Church: Vitality and Vulnerability before the Break with Rome* (New Haven, CT and London: Yale University Press 2012), pp. 97–101.
49 Review of exhibition in *Art and Christianity 61*, Spring 2010, p. 10.

The problem goes beyond the question of whether viewers comprehend the religious meaning of what is viewed, to that again of context, of the setting in which religious artworks are placed and how they work when they are removed from a setting of prayer and worship to that of the art gallery or museum.

It could be objected that such 'liturgical seeing' requires a degree of liturgical formation and biblical literacy for people to understand what they see. Indeed, we could ask whether previous generations, such as those early Christians who gathered for worship in the basilica or the ordinary people who attended their parish church on the eve of the Reformation, understood what was going on, what it was all about. A post-Reformation perspective, privileging conceptual ways of understanding in a literate culture, may well conclude that the level of understanding among such people was lamentable. But perhaps such a reading of history is an ideologically motivated handling of the evidence. Moreover, we should also recognize how meanings are apprehended differently, and that our formation as worshippers in particular occurs in a variety of ways. In short, our knowing of something, or someone, is not always dependent upon knowing *about* that thing or person. And when it comes to the apprehension of religious meanings, these may well be, and often are, understood through the repeated patterns of behaviour within a particular cultural environment – in our case by the worshipper in a church building.

At this point in the argument we could invoke the liturgical theologian Aidan Kavanagh's fictional character, 'Mrs Murphy'.[50] She is something of a caricature representing a regular churchgoer who, though unable fully to articulate the official meanings of the liturgy, has a sense of its meaning built up by the habitual practice and participation in the Church's worship.[51] Here, in other words, is a person who inhabits

---

50 Aidan Kavanagh, *On Liturgical Theology* (New York: Pueblo 1984), pp. 146–7.
51 The word 'participation' became the watchword in the recent decades of liturgical revision and renewal, and came to mean the active involvement of worshippers in what is said and done in worship. More recently, the formative aspect of worship has come to the fore, with the accent not solely on what the worshipper does but what worship may do for the worshipper. There are many ways in which worshippers may be attentive to the liturgical act and its setting, and in so doing find themselves caught up in something that is transformative and that may question assumptions and change attitudes. For an erudite account of how participation occurs at a number of different and complementary levels, see Mark Searle, *Called to Participate: Theological, Ritual, and Social Perspectives* (Collegeville, MN: Liturgical Press 2006).

the practice of the Church's prayer and for whom what is celebrated in the liturgy resonates with her own life experience, with all her personal joys, losses, terror and wonder. Whatever reservations or criticisms we may level against this caricature and the claims Kavanagh makes about a *theologia prima*, 'primary theology',[52] one can, on the basis of insights derived from the emerging discipline of ritual studies, postulate an understanding, or sense, of God that is mediated through the actual and repeated participation in the liturgy. This is not to claim that the connections that are felt and known can be or are articulated, but that the arena of worship is where the worshipper first gains what may be called 'ritual knowing'; that is, a tacit form of knowing and understanding, which I have summarized elsewhere.[53] It is this form of knowing, accumulated through the actual practice of liturgy, that gives participants a sense of what it is about, even if they are unable to articulate that sense fully or set it out in a way that approximates to the 'official' or even 'public' meaning of the rites that are celebrated in the church.

The notion of 'liturgical seeing' is more than simply the act of seeing religious art in a specific context, of viewing art in a setting designated for worship. In an essay entitled 'Seeing Liturgically', Aidan Kavanagh expounds the development of the root Christian metaphor of the Body of Christ through the celebration of Christian worship in public space.[54] In one section Kavanagh alludes to the mosaics in the late fifth- and sixth-century churches of Rome and Ravenna as a particular cultural test case, and argues that what was seen in these mosaics was what was proclaimed and ritually enacted in the celebration of the liturgy, so that the meaning of what was preached and enacted in ceremony and ritual was shown in the art of that sacred space. The point Kavanagh makes here, that what was seen was done liturgically, is a valid insight, and my purpose is not simply to reiterate it but to extend and apply it more generally, and say that the meanings of what is said and done liturgically can also be apprehended visually. It is solely a question of opening our

---

52 For a study on the relation of liturgy and personal (articulated) belief, see Ian Paton, 'Liturgy and Belief: Conversations with Mrs Murphy and her Pastor', *Anaphora* 2.2, December 2008, pp. 21–32.
53 See Christopher Irvine, *The Art of God: The Making of Christians and the Meaning of Worship* (London: SPCK 2005), esp. pp. 98–101, 133–4.
54 Aidan Kavanagh, 'Seeing Liturgically' in J. Neil Alexander (ed.), *Time and Community* (Washington, DC: Pastoral Press 1990), pp. 255–78.

eyes and seeing what there is to be seen in the triangulation of artefact, place and ritual action.

Such an assertion moves beyond Kavanagh's particular observation regarding the mosaic decorative scheme in the nave of St Apollinare in Classe, near Ravenna, and I should be careful, at least methodologically, about making a universal principle out of a particular observation of how art functioned in a particular place. Sacred art, such as the cross, was presented in various ways in churches of different historical epochs, cultural contexts and geographical locations. Nevertheless, there is some scope for both refining and developing Kavanagh's suggested notion of 'liturgical seeing'. The expression undoubtedly has a rhetorical force, for although it is recognized that religious meanings are communicated and apprehended through a range of media, of which the aural is often taken to be the most important, 'liturgical seeing' also serves to redress the balance and encourage the worshipper to be more *visually* aware of the setting of the liturgy and its art, and more attentive to the ritual performance of worship. At surface value these things undoubtedly need to be said and heard, but there is also the deeper sense that our seeing in a liturgical context also functions in a hermeneutical way in the communication of meaning.

Such a liturgical hermeneutic takes the context in which worship occurs as being primary to both the transmission and reception of meaning, and would regard that context as encompassing all the visual stimuli that would strike the worshipper, both consciously and unconsciously, during an act of worship. To put this in other terms, we could say that liturgical seeing has the power to connect the worshipper to the meaning of what is being played out in word, song, music, silence and ritual action occurring in the worshipping environment. This may read as a bold and possibly overstated claim, so perhaps it should be recognized that this function of liturgical seeing can, as we have indicated above, work both ways. It can extend, but also limit, the focus of the meaning of the sacrifice of the Mass, or of the water of baptism. We shall see how this occurs as the discussion unfolds, and sharpen our focus on the cross in liturgical art and architectural settings in subsequent chapters.

In arguing for such 'liturgical seeing', one also has to reckon that visual meanings can be as many and as varied as any readings or interpretations of a written text. And so it is for this reason that I would suggest that the final arbiter has to be the intended context of what is seen, where, by whom and on what occasion. Over time, meanings are neither fixed nor static, and as David Brown has demonstrated, both patrons and artists themselves have extended and enlarged the meaning of religious events and images.[55] In some instances this attenuation of meaning is achieved through the placing of images in relation to particular texts. An example regarding the image of the cross and a set of prayer texts is a miniature crucifixion scene that is drawn and delicately coloured on the facing page of a series of prayers 'to the holy cross' in an Anglo-Saxon prayer book made around the first quarter of the eleventh century for a monk of New Minster, Winchester.[56] In this example, the figure of the Crucified, with large open eyes, is flanked by the traditional figures of Mary and John. But around these two figures are drawn tall stylized plants with coloured flowers. Although the prayer texts themselves, incorporating the seven traditional penitential psalms, focus on sin and death, the image, by contrast, speaks of life and hints of creation in bloom. This motif of the flowering of creation in relation to the cross is one to which I shall return in more detail in Chapter 3 in relation to the work of Renaissance artists.

From the time of Giotto and the emergence of the artist not as an artisan – literally 'a maker' – but as one skilled in drawing a narrative scene and in depicting individual character in ways that captured the emotional responses of the figures portrayed, we see a definite shift from the iconic to the pictorial. Giotto was acclaimed as the one who originated the stylistic shift from Greek to Latin, when pictorial art became more 'realistic'[57] and less symbolic. Painting now tells a story,[58] and figures, which in Giotto's case are a little statuesque and restrained in their gestures, reveal emotional responses in their expressive faces. Such broad generalizations, of course, mask the various stylistic currents that are evident throughout the time of the Renaissance. Some elements of the Byzantine style persisted, and in some instances were incorporated

---

55 See Brown, *Tradition and Imagination*, pp. 89–92, 341.
56 *Aelfwine's Prayer Book*, ed. Beate Günzel, Henry Bradshaw Society, vol. 108 (Woodbridge: Boydell Press 1993), p. 12.
57 Art came to be conceived as a faithful representation of nature. See Jules Lubbock, *Storytelling in Christian Art from Giotto to Donatello* (New Haven, CT and London: Yale University Press 2006).
58 For a detailed study of Renaissance pictorial narratives, see Lubbock, *Storytelling in Christian Art from Giotto to Donatello*.

into new styles and compositions. We might consider, for example, the cross attributed to the Master of St Francis.

The period of the Italian Renaissance, with its renewed interest in antique statuary, classical learning and mythology, led to a greater naturalism in painting and in sculpture. The classical religion of ancient Greece and Rome had presented its pantheon of gods in a divine human form. And so as the Renaissance artists and sculptors looked back and recovered the aesthetic ideals of classical times; the human form, somewhat idealized, was taken as the measure of things divine. This is supremely seen, of course, in the monumental work of Michelangelo at the beginning of the sixteenth century. Such a movement towards natural realism may be seen to have begun a century earlier in the way in which the figure of the Crucified came to be portrayed in art and sculpture.

The figure of the Crucified carved by the sculptor Donatello for the church of Santa Croce, Florence, around 1408–12, may be taken as an early example of such a muscular and well-proportioned naked figure. The story is told that having sculpted this figure, Donatello sought the opinion of his associate, the architect and sculptor Filippo Brunelleschi, and in what has been construed as a game of artistic one-upmanship,[59] Brunelleschi carved a corpus, now to be seen in the church of Santa Maria Novella, Florence, that he considered to be both more realistic and audaciously more beautiful than that carved earlier by Donatello. There was undoubtedly an element of competition between these two Florentine artists. But what was it exactly that they were trying to achieve in their respective carvings of the figure of the Crucified? Brunelleschi's corpus certainly shows the strain of physical suffering, and yet the composition is serene, as befits the divine Son of God as he hangs dead upon the cross, the instrument of death. In this sculpture the head is slumped forward and the figure hangs down with the dead weight of the body, giving us that 'Y' shape that is often found on the back of a Gothic chasuble worn by a priest to celebrate the Mass. Were the two artists competing to show the most naturalistic representation of the human figure of Christ sacrificed on the cross? A clue to the

---

59 Richard Viladesau, *The Triumph of the Cross: The Passion of Christ in Theology and the Arts, from the Renaissance to the Counter-Reformation* (Oxford: Oxford University Press 2008), pp. 55–6.

question may be found in Brunelleschi's claim to have made a beautiful figure of the Crucified, a claim that would suggest that their aim was more than making the most realistic portrayal of the crucifixion. What this was may be seen when we look at the particular setting and patronage of Donatello's figure of the Crucified.

Donatello's crucifix was commissioned for the principal church of the Conventual Franciscan friars in Florence dedicated to *Santa Croce*, 'the holy cross', and as we shall see in subsequent chapters, this places the crucifix within a wider frame of reference that is both architectural and theological. The crucifix, which was probably suspended originally above the altar in the Bardi chapel in Santa Croce, was worked in such a way as to fit its context, both visually and liturgically. The near-naked figure resonates with the Eucharist in visually showing the body and in giving prominence to the blood that is seen to flow from the wounds of Christ, and the placing of the cross opens into another frame of interpretation that connects the cross with creation. Recent research has demonstrated that Donatello finished the wood of the cross in such a way as to resemble more closely the material from which it was made, thereby turning the cross back, as it were, into wood.[60] It has the grain and texture of wood, and so relates to the story of the discovery of the true wood of the cross by Helena – mother of the Emperor Constantine – illustrated in the fresco decoration in the Cappella Maggiore (chancel) in Santa Croce, executed by Agnolo Gaddi, the son of Taddeo Gaddi, in the early 1390s. As we shall see in Chapter 6, this decorative scheme illustrated a story of the finding of the holy cross recorded in the thirteenth-century work of the Dominican friar and archbishop of Genoa, Jacobus de Voragine, *The Golden Legend*. Voragine's work gathered the disparate stories and legends in circulation about holy people and holy things, and arranged them according to the cycle of the feasts of the liturgical calendar. The story of 'The Finding of the Holy Cross' was provided in this classic literary source for the feast of the Invention of the Holy Cross (3 May), and was particularly favoured by the Franciscans because it related the material wood of the cross with the biblical image of the tree of life. So in making the cross look

60 I am indebted to Dr James Harris of the Courtauld Institute for drawing this point to my attention in a paper, 'The Meaning of Stuff: The Materials of Donatello's Painted Sculpture', delivered to a seminar organized by the Centre for Medieval and Early Modern Studies at the University of Kent, December 2010.

like wood, Donatello was deliberately evoking the story of the true cross and triggering that train of associated scenes that relates the cross to the tree of life. In showing the near-naked figure of the Crucified, the artist publicly portrays Christ as the incarnate, literally the enfleshed Son, who through the instrument of his death, the cross, restored the tree that was first planted in paradise.

In the following chapter I will look a little more closely at the function of the altarpiece, and to see it as one might see the scenery in a theatre as the backdrop to the liturgical action – specifically, the performance of the Eucharist or the Mass, which is the commemoration and celebration of the whole saving mystery of Christ.

Chapter 2

Salvation seen

In the previous chapter consideration was given to the architectural spaces that were adapted and specifically designed for the purpose of worship. In these architectural spaces, sight lines draw the viewer to particular foci, the loci of liturgical celebrations, such as the ambo and the altar. Each of these foci occupies a designated space, and the configuration of these spaces conspires to draw and focus the eye. The intentional visuality of the sacred zones of a church building came to be enhanced by monumental works of art, both the altar itself and, from the thirteenth century, the so-called altarpiece which, given its proximity to the altar, became part of the liturgical ensemble and provided visual clues to the multiple meanings of the Eucharist in close focus. What exactly may have been seen, and by whom, are important questions in examining individual altarpieces, but as a permanently fixed item the altarpiece would have been visible, even if not always entirely legible, for those who came into the church. During the offering of the Mass, the celebrant would have had the most privileged position since he literally stood and faced the altarpiece as he celebrated the Eucharist (see Plate 2). And what his eyes saw was a figural representation of that mystery of the Word made flesh, the flesh of the one whose sacrifice was in some sense represented at each celebration of the Eucharist.

The language of representation belongs to the vocabulary of what is visible, and as a complex term it is inextricably bound up with presence. The word serves to denote an object in our field of vision and further-more connotes a presence. It is both something that is seen as well as a reality that becomes present to the viewer. The Latin term *repraesentatio* was a key one in medieval discourse on the Eucharist and encapsulated the repeated vocabulary of sacrifice in the Canon of the Mass, in which the offering of the eucharistic bread and wine mirrored and was caught up with the sacrifice of Christ on the cross at Calvary. What Christ offered on the cross was his very self, and it is the presence of that divine and human 'self' that was believed to be manifest in the sacramental bread and cup. The presumed coincidence of image and reality was contested and played out through successive episodes of iconoclasm, culminating in the many controversies of the Reformation. In this regard, it is interesting to note that in one detailed theological critique of Reformation iconoclasm, a clear suggestion emerges that a close correlation can be drawn between the prominence of visual art in a church and the degree of sacramental realism in the official teaching of that church.[1] It is as though the greater the visual impact of the art within a worship space, the higher the degree of sacramental realism – and the altarpiece would have provided the most artistically accomplished and most detailed visual representation in the medieval church building. As we shall see, the exquisitely painted and constructed altarpiece rarely depicted an explicit eucharistic subject, such as a Last Supper, but through a combination of symbols and figural painting it provided a complex eucharistic frame of reference. So the way this worked was not in any simple illustrative or functional sense but in providing a visually complex key to a number of eucharistic understandings and liturgical ritual practices.

Altarpieces have attracted considerable attention from art historians in recent years, and in their discourse the term has become a rather fluid category.[2] But although their form and functions varied at different times and from place to place, it can be said that the altarpiece developed to complement the liturgical action at those altars used for an eastward, as distinct from the *versus populum* ('facing the people'), celebration of the Eucharist at a free-standing altar in a church. The classic example of the free-standing altar was seen at St Peter's in Rome and in those churches modelled on the Roman arrangement, such as Fulda Cathedral, where Boniface was buried, and the Ottonian Cathedral in

---

1 I am indebted to Professor Mia Mochizuki for drawing my attention to Sergiusz Michalski's work, *The Reformation and the Visual Image: The Protestant Image Question in Western and Eastern Europe* (London and New York: Routledge 1993).

2 For a comprehensive survey and critical evaluation of discussions of altarpieces by art historians, see Beth Williamson, 'Altarpieces, Liturgy and Devotion', *Speculum*, vol. 79, no. 2, 2004, pp. 341–406.

Cologne.[3] The altarpieces that were constructed and painted between the thirteenth and the sixteenth centuries were intended, though not exclusively, as a visual backdrop to the liturgical action, the celebration of the Mass, which came to be considered and experienced in the high Middle Ages as a highly visual performance.[4] And given their position, directly behind and above the locus of liturgical action, the altarpiece was brought into the closest relationship with the ritual action performed at the altar.[5] Not all churches had retables or altarpieces to physically frame and enhance the altar, but looking at those that did, it is clear that the altarpiece came in a variety of forms.[6] The first were generally composite wooden constructions with multiple images, like the low horizontal panels that became fashionable in the late twelfth-century churches in Umbria and then in neighbouring Tuscany. Some of the Franciscan churches in this region, being modelled on the basilica of St Francis in Assisi, had retro-choirs for the friars located in the apse behind the main altar, and double-sided altarpieces were commissioned for these churches.[7] In these cases, as we shall see in Chapter 6, a large painted cross was suspended above the altar and was integral to the whole ensemble.[8] The construction of altarpieces bearing multiple

3 Kees van der Ploeg, 'How Liturgical is an Altarpiece?' in Victor M. Schmidt (ed.), *Italian Panel Painting of the Duecento and Trecento*, Studies in the History of Art, vol. 61 (Washington, DC: National Gallery of Art 2002), p. 104.

4 The point is conceded by Dyrness, who traces the development of the visuality of medieval religion to the interiorization of images and a closer correlation between word and image, visuality and aurality in religious practice – William A. Dyrness, *Reformed Theology and Visual Culture: The Protestant Imagination from Calvin to Edwards* (Cambridge: Cambridge University Press 2004), ch. 2.

5 An attempt to set out a methodology for examining the interaction between the visual and the ritual in the context of the celebration of the Mass is offered by Staale Sinding-Larsen, *Iconography and Ritual: A Study of Analytical Perspectives* (Oslo: Universitetsforlaget 1984).

6 For a summary of the different forms and their construction, see Scott Nethersole, *Devotion By Design: Italian Altarpieces Before 1500* (London: National Gallery 2011).

7 These Franciscan double-sided altarpieces have recently attracted the attention of art historians, but there is no compelling reason to endorse the emerging consensus, first proposed by Henk van Os, that their primary function was to screen the laity in the nave from the friars in Choir. See Donal Cooper, 'Franciscan Choir Enclosures and the Function of Double-Sided Altarpieces in Pre-Tridentine Umbria', *Journal of the Warburg and Courtauld Institutes*, vol. 64, 2001, pp. 1–54; Dillian Gordon, 'Thirteenth- and Fourteenth-Century Perugian Double-Sided Altarpieces: Form and Function' in Schmidt (ed.), *Italian Panel Painting of the Duecento and Trecento*, pp. 229–49.

8 Gordon, 'Thirteenth- and Fourteenth-Century Perugian Double-Sided Altarpieces', p. 230.

images became more complex in design, and these polyptych panels were tall polygonal shape constructions, with multiple images around a central panel. Duccio's double-sided altarpiece, the *Maesta*, was so massive that it had two polychrome decorated piers or pillars fixed to the floor to support the wooden structure.[9] Duccio's famous altarpiece was made for the high altar in Siena Cathedral, and installed, following a procession through the town, for the feast of Corpus Christi in 1311. In this famous and complex altarpiece, a dominant image of the Virgin Mary and Child occupies the central panel on the front of the altarpiece facing the nave, as appropriate for a city that called itself the *Civitas Virginis*, the city of the Virgin.[10] On the reverse side, placed back to back, was a panel of the crucifixion set within a series of christological scenes, including seven panels depicting the resurrection appearances.[11]

Following the multi-image painted panel came the single panel or painted canvas, known in Italy as the *pala* or *tavola*, and then, finally, the complex Gothic arrangement of the multi-panelled or folding altarpiece, as we saw with the winged Isenheim altarpiece in the previous chapter. The winged folding altarpiece, most closely associated with Germany, which could be opened or closed in order to give a visual focus for the theme of the liturgical season or commemoration, has its antecedents in the kind of altarpieces favoured by fourteenth-century Cistercians, who apparently used them to articulate the particular feast or liturgical season being celebrated.[12] And apart from the painted image of Our Lady, the altarpiece was the most elaborate artefact in their elegantly simple Cistercian abbey churches. Whatever the location, the subject or subjects painted on the altarpiece functioned as an important visual backdrop to the liturgical action of the celebration of the Mass.

---

9 On the structure of this altarpiece, see Christa Gardner von Teuffel, *From Duccio's Maesta to Raphael's Transfiguration: Italian Altarpieces and their Setting* (London: Pindar Press 2005), pp. 128–35.

10 Henk van Os, *Sienese Altarpieces, 1215–1460: Form, Content, Function*, vol. 1 (Groningen: Bouma's Boekhuis 1984), p. 11.

11 The German art historian Peter Seiler has proposed a convincing hypothesis that the Eucharist was reserved on the reverse side of Duccio's altarpiece. See Peter Seiler, 'Duccio's Maesta: The Function of the Scenes from the Life of Christ on the Reverse of the Altarpiece: A New Hypothesis' in Schmidt (ed.), *Italian Panel Painting of the Duecento and Trecento*, pp. 251–77.

12 Van der Ploeg, 'How Liturgical is an Altarpiece?', p. 109.

More often than not the altarpiece of the high altar of a church depicted an aspect of the Passion of Christ, such as the crucifixion, or showed the figure of the infant Christ with Mary his mother. The latter image of the Madonna and Child was not unrelated to Passion imagery and the cross, for the infant Christ was often depicted naked, literally 'in the flesh', the flesh that was formed in the womb of Mary and in which Christ suffered and died upon the cross. The flesh, in other words, pointed forward to the redeeming cross and, further, resonated directly with eucharistic meaning. For in this range of dominant imagery, what was visually presented, namely the body of Jesus, was that which was believed to be made present in the sacrament of the altar. In this sense there was a coincidence of the visual representation in the altarpiece of the incarnate Christ and the sacramental sign of Christ's body and blood, understood to be confected by the priest when he rehearsed the words of Jesus, the high priest, at the altar in the celebration of the Mass.[13]

The thirteenth century saw the emergence of influential lay confraternities, often dedicated to a particular saint or mystery of the faith, and they invariably had their own altars and side chapels for offering particular votive Masses. The proliferation of side altars in a church reached its climax in the fourteenth century, and the retable or altarpiece behind these altars may well have shown the particular saint to whom the chapel was dedicated. In these instances, as well as a cross being placed on the altar, a crucifixion or another motif of Christ's Passion was generally rendered in the central panel of the predella, the low oblong section below the main panel of the altarpiece. The donors of altarpieces were often portrayed in the altarpiece and conventionally rendered as smaller figures in comparison to the subjects of the painting. The negotiations between the patron and the ecclesiastical body responsible for the church, or between, say, a religious community commissioning an altarpiece and the artist, would have been within set parameters or ecclesiastically agreed conventions regarding

---

13 The metaphysical and logical precondition of Christ's sacramental presence, according to Aquinas, was the incarnation of the Word, whereby the Father placed the Son 'in the order of [visible] signs'. Following from this premise, the efficacy of the sacramental sign was the Passion of the incarnate Christ, the high priest and principal actor in the liturgical celebration. See Aidan Nichols OP, *Lost in Wonder: Essays on Liturgy and the Arts* (Farnham: Ashgate 2011), ch. 1, 'St. Thomas and the Sacramental Liturgy'.

the appropriate subject for an altarpiece.[14] But unlike the altar, whose prominence, size and form were regulated by canon law, an altarpiece was subject to less stringent ecclesiastical control.

However, in the broadest terms, and given the preferences both of the particular church community commissioning a work and of patrons covering the financial cost in exchange for prayers and requiem Masses to be offered on their or their family's behalf, a measure of control was set by the official understanding of the Mass celebrated at the altar and the contemporary doctrinal nexus connecting the Incarnation and the Eucharist. This came to be formularized in the preamble to the fourteenth-century statutes of the painters' guild of Siena. The primary purpose of the ecclesiastical artist was to reveal the mysteries of 'the Holy Faith', a goal that we may put in terms of seeking to make visible the mysteries of the invisible God. This was, in the broadest sense of the term, a sacramental aim, and so the figures or the event that were artistically rendered in colour, line and form had to be congruent with the official and conciliar teaching of the Church. Although art historians often discuss religious paintings in terms of either 'liturgical' or 'devotional images', it is probably best not to see them as strictly oppositional terms but to see the later 'devotional images' as effective ways of extending the meanings of the Eucharist and the liturgical year. So-called 'devotional paintings' would have given the viewer the opportunity to see, and to return and possibly see something new, in a complex nexus of symbolic motifs that signalled the mystery of Christ's Incarnation, suffering, death and resurrection. The very mystery, in other words, that was explicitly commemorated at each celebration of the Mass and temporally unfolded in the dramatic celebration of the Christian year in its cycle of feasts and fasts.

The Fourth Lateran Council convened by Pope Innocent III at the Lateran in November 1215 was the first official church council to use the word 'transubstantiation' in connection with the bread and wine being miraculously changed into the very body and blood of Christ at

---

14 For a detailed essay examining and comparing Italian tempera- and oil-painted altarpieces in the Netherlands, see Diana Norman, 'Making Renaissance Altarpieces' in Kim W. Woods (ed.) *Making Renaissance Art* (New Haven, CT and London: Yale University Press 2007). For an account of the didactic altarpieces of later Lutheran churches and their communicative function, see Joseph Leo Koerner, *The Reformation of the Image* (London: Reaktion Books 2004), esp. ch. 5, 'A Reformation Altarpiece'.

the Mass. But the Council itself did not venture to spell out or eluci-
date how this actually occurred. A doctrine did develop, principally, as
we shall see later in the chapter, through the work of Thomas Aquinas
(1225–74), but it did not become an official dogma of the Roman
Church until the thirteenth session of the Council of Trent in 1551.
Suffice it to say at this stage of the discussion that there was a vital sense
of the 'wondrous exchange' of the eucharistic bread and cup and the
body and blood of Christ, and so it is probably the case that this developing doctrine of transubstantiation encouraged the practice of eastward celebration, as the priest with his back to the people would have
added to the dramatic mystery of the ritual action. In this eastward-
facing position, the priest, certainly by the thirteenth century, would
have directly faced the central panel of the altarpiece, and what he saw
there corresponded in some direct way to what was believed to happen
at the altar, namely the changing of the substance of the host into the
body of Christ.

This belief in the changing of the eucharistic bread into the fleshly
body of Christ was graphically shown in the late medieval paintings
and illuminations of the Mass of St Gregory[15] both south and north
of the Alps. This is a key image and one to which we shall return.
The point to be drawn here is that the sacramental focus on the body
invariably had a visual counterpart in what was depicted in the altarpiece. Altarpieces had various subjects, but whether it was a Madonna
and child,[16] the visit of the Magi, a crucifixion, the deposition or the
entombment, each showed the physical body of Jesus as the central
figure, and therefore would have had multiple eucharistic connotations
and associations. For what was pictorially seen, at least by the celebrant
if not so clearly by the worshipper, was the body of the one whose
sacrifice was set forth and re-presented ritually in the Mass, for and on

---

15 This became a popular subject in the fifteenth century in book illustrations and
northern oil-painted altarpieces. See, for example, the mid fifteenth-century Book of
Hours in the British Library; and a Gregory Mass scene is commonly found in missals
and other liturgical books.

16 Regarding altarpieces of the Blessed Virgin Mary, the focus was invariably on the
Christ figure rather than Mary per se. Even in the case of Duccio's multi-panelled *Maesta*
painted for Siena Cathedral, it is the Christ child that is being shown to the viewer. See
Charles Hope, 'Altarpieces and the Requirements of Patrons' in Timothy Verdon and
John Henderson (eds), *Christianity and the Renaissance: Image and Religious Imagination
in the Quattrocento* (New York: Syracuse University Press 1990), p. 546.

behalf of both the worshippers who were present and those for whom the Mass was offered.

To illustrate the point we may consider a Netherlandish oil-painted altarpiece. Rogier van der Weyden (1399/1400–64), the 'painter of Brussels', was much admired for the brilliancy of his colour and the expressive rendering of human emotion. Rogier's altarpiece *The Descent from the Cross*, painted around 1435 and measuring some two by two and a half metres, was regarded as the apogee of Flemish naturalistic oil painting. It became a model altarpiece, and its composition was frequently copied in northern Europe. It was commissioned by the civic archers' guild for their guild church in Leuven. It was subsequently requisitioned by the young King Philip of Spain, and now hangs in the Prado Museum in Madrid. Painted with glittering painterly bravura, it is an exquisite painting of passion and compassion, with the eight life-size figures around the dead Christ looking red-eyed and tearful because of their loss. The under-drawing serves the narrative of how the dead weight of Christ's body was taken down from the cross, but in the actual painting the hold on the body by the figures of Joseph of Arimathea, Nicodemus and a young stranger on the ladder behind the cross, is loosened. This change in the painting reinforces the whole composition of these monumental figures who, occupying the whole of the surface of the painted board, seem to be stepping out of the frame, as though the body of Jesus, showing his wounded side, is being proffered to the viewer.

This painterly illusion of the body presented to the viewer, which also occurs in Rogier's Entombment painting, now in the Uffizi Gallery in Florence, confirms Barbara Lane's contention that the altarpiece requires a liturgical reading, for it is not only a vivid portrayal of the story of Christ's Passion but also dramatizes the eucharistic sacrifice as the showing and giving of the sacramental body to the worshipper.[17] The pictorial illusion, in other words, has its ritual counterpart in the making present of Christ's sacramental body in the Eucharist. Further, the way the viewer is expected to respond to this gift of the body is modelled in the posture and gestural language of the painted figure of Mary Magdalene to the far right of the picture, who with hands

---

17 Although Lane is sometimes criticized for giving a pan-liturgical explanation of altarpieces, her analysis in this case seems sound. See Barbara G. Lane, *The Altar and the Altarpiece: Sacramental Themes in Early Netherlandish Painting* (New York: Harper & Row 1989), pp. 79–90.

together and head bowed seems to be reverencing the physical body of Christ. Here, we could say, is a pictorial representation of the belief that the sacramental body of Christ became present at the consecration,[18] and that when it was seen, it was to be adored.

The understanding of the mode in which Christ was present in the sacrament has a varied history, dating back to the controversy instigated by Paschasius Radbertus, the ninth-century Benedictine monk of Corbie. As Gary Macy has demonstrated, the doctrine was far from uniform in its formulation by the schoolmen, such as Berengar of Tours and Lanfranc of Bec and Canterbury.[19] Although it is not possible to postulate a single and consistent linear development of the doctrine of 'real presence', there was a broader consensus by the thirteenth century, when the doctrine received its fullest articulation by both Franciscan and Dominican scholars, among whom was the Dominican theological colossus Thomas Aquinas. Aquinas articulated his understanding of real presence using the Aristotelian categories of 'substance' and 'accident'; that is, what a thing really is and what it appears to be.[20] Aquinas, building upon the legacy of Augustine of Hippo,[21] argued that God communicated himself in ways that were the most appropriate to the

---

18 The popularity of the subject of the Mass of St Gregory, depicting the appearance of the Christ figure as Gregory celebrated the Mass, visually reinforced the doctrinal articulation of the 'real presence' of Christ in the sacrament.

19 See Gary Macy, *The Theologies of the Eucharist in the Early Scholastic Period* (Oxford: Clarendon Press 1984), pp. 21–31. Lanfranc distinguished between the body of Christ, glorified in heaven, and the flesh of Christ, taken from Mary through the Incarnation, offered in sacrifice on the cross and received in the consecrated bread and wine of the Eucharist. He conceded a figural interpretation to Berengar in so far as it also allowed a realistic view of the flesh and blood of Christ in the sacrament. Berengar's views became heterodox as he was drawn into controversy and had to answer for them under duress at the Council of Rome in 1059. On the basis of a reading of Scripture and the patristic sources, Lanfranc asserted that the inner reality of the sacrament changed through the ministry of the priest in consecration, while admitting that the sacrament continued to look and taste like bread and wine. See G. R. Evans (ed.), *The Medieval Theologians: An Introduction to the Theology of the Medieval Period* (Oxford: Blackwell 2001), pp. 88–9; H. E. J. Cowdrey, *Lanfranc: Scholar, Monk and Archbishop* (Oxford and New York: Oxford University Press 2007), pp. 70ff.

20 Gary Macy argues that it is misleading to read Aquinas' account of 'transubstantiation' in the light of later sixteenth-century Tridentine formulation. See Gary Macy, *Treasures from the Storeroom: Medieval Religion and the Eucharist* (Collegeville, MN: Liturgical Press 1999), pp. 81–105.

21 *On Christian Doctrine*, Bk 1, ii–iv in Philip Schaff (ed.), *A Select Library of the Nicene and Post-Nicene Fathers of the Christian Church*, vol. 2 (Edinburgh: T. & T. Clark 1993).

conditions of our corporeal existence, and cited Dionysius in support of his argument.

Furthermore, in his schematic view of the make-up of the human person, again drawing on the categories of Aristotle, Aquinas proposed a hierarchy of bodily senses and placed the sense of sight as the highest of the five human senses through which the perceiving subject was understood to receive the world.[22] In this life, human beings aided by God's grace could apprehend spiritual realities through the sense of sight, and in the life to come the pious Christian hoped for nothing else than the perfect vision of God.[23] As Augustine's views were received by later medieval theologians and philosophers, so more nuanced accounts of human perception came to be articulated, particularly by thirteenth-century scholars such as Matthew Paris and Roger Bacon. The shared supposition was that our knowledge of things, both material and spiritual, was mediated through the physical sense of sight. As the process of perception was being thus elucidated through Platonic sources,[24] so the sense of sight came to be seen not only as passive reception but as an active reaching out to grasp the objects of the human gaze.[25] Given the privileging of 'looking' in this anthropological understanding, it is not surprising that the sense of sight became, as we shall see, the most prominent and popular way medieval Christians participated in the mystery of the Eucharist, a liturgical rite that provided them with the perfect paradigm and source for the symbolic ordering of the physical, social and moral world in which they lived.[26]

Such a claim may well jar with the modern reader, who would be suspicious and critical of a view that seemed to cast the worshipper in the role of a mere spectator. The modern view that worshippers should be active rather than passive participants in the liturgy may be traced back to one of the tenets of the twentieth-century Liturgical Movement.

---

22 *Summa Theologicae*, Pt 1, Q1, Art 9, vol. 1 (New York: Benziger Bros 1948).

23 See Augustine, *City of God*, Book 22, ch. 29.

24 See, for example, *Timaeus*, 45b–c.

25 Michael Camille, 'The Internal Senses and Late Medieval Practices of Seeing' in Robert S. Nelson (ed.), *Visuality Before and Beyond the Renaissance: Seeing as Others Saw* (Cambridge: Cambridge University Press 2000), p. 205.

26 See Eamon Duffy, *The Stripping of the Altars: Traditional Religion in England 1400–1580* (New Haven, CT: Yale University Press 1992), esp. ch. 4; Catherine Pickstock, *After Writing: On the Liturgical Consummation of Philosophy* (Oxford: Blackwell 1992), esp. pp. 140–54.

Ildefons Herwegen, the abbot of the Rhineland abbey of Maria Laach, and pioneer scholar of that movement, opined that visual piety, what he called *Schaufrommigkeit*, resulted in the corrosion of a corporate liturgical life. His protégé, Anton Mayer, sharpened the critique of visual piety and delivered a most scathing attack on fourteenth-century 'Gothic piety'. With full-blown rhetoric, Mayer argued that Gothic visual piety undermined and distorted the very corporate nature of liturgical celebration by focusing on the individual's subjective experience which, he claimed, led to the disintegration of the liturgy.[27] This view soon came to be shared by a number of twentieth-century liturgical scholars – even Joseph Jungmann cast the laity in the role of passive spectators in his description of medieval worship[28] – and grew to an unquestioned assumption, constantly reiterated by those seeking to promote a more active participation of the faithful in the action of the liturgy. But a more nuanced view of liturgical participation, and more recent historical research, mean that the full-blown rhetoric of a medieval distortion of the liturgy can no longer be sustained.

There were undoubtedly developments and changes of sensibility during the Middle Ages, but the more recent work of church historians such as Eamon Duffy and the art historian Paul Binski present a more complex and nuanced picture of religious practice that cautions against the simple judgement that medieval piety was a distortion and diminution of liturgical life. As we have seen, underlying the practice of visual piety was a developed anthropology that privileged the sense of sight and the variety of ways of religious looking that, even if they were not framed within a liturgical celebration, intentionally extended it. As Thomas Lentes has recently argued, visual piety needs to be examined in a more differentiated way, and apart from the practical question of

---

27 See A. L. Mayer, 'Die heilbringende Schau in Sitte und Kult' in O. Casel (ed.), *Heilige Überlieferung: Ausschnitte aus der Geschichte des Mönchtums und des heiligen Kultes*, Festschrift Ildefons Herwegen (Münster: Aschendorff 1938), and for his trenchant remarks on the liturgical distortions of the high Middle Ages see A. L. Mayer, *Die Liturgie in der europäischen Geistesgeschichte* (Darmstadt: Wissenschaftliche Buchgesellschaft 1971).
28 See Joseph A. Jungmann, *The Mass of the Roman Rite: Its Origins and Development*, trans. Francis A. Brunner (New York: Benziger Bros 1951), p. 117; Theodor Klauser, *A Short History of the Western Liturgy*, 2nd edn (Oxford: Oxford University Press 1979), pp. 98, 101–13. A more considered and welcome view of the Mass in the medieval West is given by Paul Bradshaw and Maxwell Johnson in their recently published *The Eucharistic Liturgies: Their Evolution and Interpretation* (London: SPCK 2012), pp. 210–31.

the visibility of objects in a liturgical setting, one also needs to ask questions about what is seen, when and by whom.[29]

The practice of elevating the host at the consecration, following the recital of the words of Jesus in the institution narrative in the Canon of the Mass, *Hoc est corpus meum*, 'This is my body', was probably introduced in the eleventh century at the very earliest. There is no reference or even allusion to the practice in the hugely influential early ninth-century allegorical interpretation of the Mass by Amalarius of Metz, and it may have begun as a fairly localized custom, and one whose introduction may well have been in response to lay devotion.[30] As previously mentioned, the elevation was far from being a uniform and universal practice in the twelfth century, and we must reckon with the likelihood of considerable regional variation of the ritual practice and its interpretation throughout the Western Church during this time and well into the thirteenth century. It is likely that the elevation of the host became more commonly practised during the time of Pope Innocent III. It is known, for instance, that in some places the host was elevated three times (possibly to indicate the Trinity?), and at Laon the priest celebrating the Mass would turn as he elevated the host to face the congregation. The use of unleavened wafer bread certainly made the elevation a convenient custom, and these thin white discs were often stamped with a particular motif, such as the *Agnus Dei*, and it seems that the motif, imprinted on the dough before it was baked, varied according to the liturgical season.[31]

Certainly by the mid thirteenth century, the ritual gesture was being actively promoted by Franciscan theologians and preachers, whose own tradition would have given some warrant to such a development. For the earliest biographical sources tell how Francis presented the gospel in visually graphic ways,[32] and although the writings attributed to him make no direct reference to the ritual practice, the reflections attributed

29 Thomas Lentes, 'As Far as the Eye can See: Rituals of Gazing in the Late Middle Ages' in Jeffrey F. Hamburger and Anne-Marie Bouche (eds), *The Mind's Eye: Art and Theological Argument in the Middle Ages* (Princeton, NJ: Princeton University Press 2006), pp. 361–2.
30 Lee Palmer Wandel, *The Eucharist in the Reformation: Incarnation and Liturgy* (Cambridge: Cambridge University Press 2006), p. 19.
31 Wandel, *The Eucharist in the Reformation*, p. 23.
32 See Roland Recht, *Believing and Seeing: The Art of Gothic Cathedrals*, trans. Mary Whittall (Chicago and London: University of Chicago Press 2008), pp. 74–5.

to him on physical seeing and spiritual perception in regard to the eucharistic elements could well be taken to endorse and encourage a devotional looking at the host during the elevation.[33] In one passage in *The Testament*, for instance, Francis seems to imply that the only way a person could physically see 'the most high Son of God' was by looking at the sacrament of Christ's 'holy body and blood' on the altar.[34] This was sufficient reason for the Franciscan friars to have adopted and promoted the ritual practice of the elevation. A direction to elevate the host following the words of consecration was included in a Franciscan missal, the *Ordo Missae*, and in the priest's manual for the saying of the Mass, the *Inductus planeta*.[35]

So one could argue that it is more than geographical coincidence that some of the first altarpieces to be painted were for churches under the care and direction of the Friars Minor.

Without any doubt a painted altarpiece would have visually enhanced the altar on which the Eucharist was celebrated, but it would be too much of a logical jump to propose, *pace* the art historian Henk van Os, that the relationship between the developing Italian altarpiece and the increasing practice of the elevation was a causal relationship.[36] What is more likely is that they developed in tandem. Indeed, on the basis of our reflections so far we can confidently say that the altarpiece in most instances would have visually complemented the elevation and, as we have seen, provided a dramatic backdrop to the ritual action of showing Christ, who was believed to be sacramentally present.

The origins of the practice, however, appear to be elsewhere. The earliest documentary evidence witnesses to a decree issued at a synod by the Bishop of Paris, usually identified as Eudes or Odo de Sully, sometime between 1197 and 1210. The decree stated that the host should be elevated after the dominical words. It has been suggested that the

---

33 See Elvio Lunghi, 'Francis of Assisi in Prayer before the Crucifix in the Accounts of the First Biographers' in Schmidt (ed.), *Italian Panel Painting of the Duecento and Trecento*.

34 See 'The Testament' 10 and 'Admonitions' 1 in *Francis of Assisi: Early Documents*, vol. 1 (New York: St Bonaventure University 1999, pp. 125, 128.

35 For details, see Anne Derbes, *Picturing the Passion in Late Medieval Italy: Narrative Painting, Franciscan Ideologies, and the Levant* (Cambridge: Cambridge University Press 1996), p. 187, n. 31.

36 Henk van Os, *Sienese Altarpieces, 1215–1460: Form, Content, Function*, vol. 1, pp. 12–17.

motivation for this specific synodical direction was to deter any gesture
of reverence being made to the eucharistic bread before it was consecrated.[37] Whatever prompted this specific ruling, it does seem to legis-
late for an existing practice in the region around 1200. For at this time,
Peter of Roissy reports what he considers to be the admirable practice
in the region of the faithful bowing their heads and raising their hands
at the elevation of the host. Reviewing the evidence, Paul Binski concludes that the practice was established in England in the early 1200s,
and that the Archbishop of Canterbury, Stephen Langton, insisted at a
provincial synod in 1214 that the elevation should be visible and that
the clergy should instruct their people to genuflect after it.[38] From the
outset, Langton expected the laity to deport themselves reverently from
the elevation until the host was consumed in Communion, for the
elevation was not only a visually climactic moment but also marked
a point of what was considered to be the intensification of being in
the presence of the divine, as is wonderfully illustrated in a *Mass Tract*
believed to have been produced in London or in East Anglia in the
thirteenth century.[39]

As well as synodical decrees and episcopal directions, further evidence for the promotion of the practice of elevation can be gathered
from liturgical books. The celebrant was directed to show the sacrament to the people in the rubrics of mid-thirteenth-century missals.[40]

---

37 See texts cited by V. L. Kennedy, 'The Moment of Consecration and the Elevation of
the Host', *Medieval Studies*, vol. 6, 1944, p. 149, and a useful summary of the scholarly
literature to date by Burkhart Steinberg in 'The Theology of the Elevation in the Eucharist', *Theology*, vol. 113, no. 873, May/June 2010, pp. 183–91. Regarding reverence
paid to the eucharistic bread prior to the consecration, one may compare the practice of
kneeling and crossing oneself as the 'approaching sacrifice' is carried through the people
in the nave during the Great Entrance in the Byzantine Rite. See Hans Joachim Schulz,
The Byzantine Liturgy: Symbolic Structure and Faith Expression (New York: Pueblo 1989),
pp. 33–9, 118–19. Robert Taft records his experience of the devout prostrating themselves in front of the procession in Romania so that the priest had literally to step over
them. See Robert F. Taft, *A History of the Liturgy of St. John Chrysostom*, vol. 2, *The Great
Entrance* (Rome: Pontificio Istituto Orientale 2004), p. 7.
38 See Paul Binski, *Becket's Crown: Art and Imagination in Gothic England 1170–1300*
(New Haven, CT and London: Yale University Press 2004), pp. 153, 154.
39 Aden Kumler, *Translating Truth: Ambitious Images and Religious Knowledge in Late
Medieval France and England* (New Haven, CT and London: Yale University Press
2011), p. 114.
40 Miri Rubin, *Corpus Christi: The Eucharist in Late Medieval Culture* (Cambridge:
Cambridge University Press 1992), p. 56.

Exactly how the gesture was received and interpreted by lay people attending Mass is not known in detail, but it is easy to see that during the elevation at an altar where there was an altarpiece depicting Mary with the infant Christ, or a crucifixion scene, there would have been a visual alignment between the eucharistic host and the figure of Christ's physical body at that moment of gazing at the consecrated host. For the priest and for those worshippers in close proximity to the altar or with clear sight lines, the elevation of the host would have been experienced as a momentary visual coincidence of 'body' and 'body'.

The picture that emerges when we combine the various threads of pictorial and literary evidence is that the host was regarded – literally – by the faithful as a condensed symbol of the divine in their midst, a highly visual 'making present' of Christ. In some respects the elevation was a momentary extension of the Incarnation and an intensification of the experienced somatic dimension of Christian faith and worship focused on the gift of Christ's body.[41] Indeed, it could be said that for both priest and lay people alike, the elevation came to be the ritual high point of the celebration of the Mass, particularly in northern Europe throughout the high Middle Ages. The practice was reinforced in the popular imagination through the seasonal performances of Mystery and Passion plays, where it was not uncommon for the actor playing the part of Christ in the scene of the Last Supper to mimic the ritual gestures of a priest saying Mass, including an elevation of the bread.[42]

The elevation was certainly a common subject in the religious art of this high medieval period. It featured particularly as illustrations in ecclesiastical books, such as the *Decretals* – a codification of canon law – of Pope Gregory IX, and these illustrations provide some clues as to how the ritual was performed and how the priest and the people were configured in the area of the sacred space. A magnificent double folio illustration of the elevation in an early fourteenth-century English translation of the Anglo-Norman *The Lay Folks' Mass Book* shows the congregation kneeling at the moment of consecration to 'welcome [the]

---

41 For a discussion of the trope of 'the body' and the embodied nature of Christian liturgy, see Christopher Irvine, *The Art of God: The Making of Christians and the Meaning of Worship* (London: SPCK 2005).

42 See Wandel, *The Eucharist in the Reformation*, p. 25; and the classic study of O. B. Hardison, *Christian Rite and Christian Drama in the Middle Ages* (Baltimore: Johns Hopkins 1965).

Lord, in form of bread', as the celebrant's assistant raised a large burning torch and the church bell was tolled.[43] Such a pictorial representation is confirmed by the rubrical directions in both the Sarum Missal and later editions of the York Missal. The purpose of the elevation is set out in these rubrics in terms of enabling the people to *see* the consecrated host: *Hostium et elevet eam supra frontem ut posit a populo videri.*[44]

But how were the faithful to respond to this central visual cue to their participation in the Mass? The answers are various: it was an act of reverence, an act of greeting and an occasion for prayer. The ringing of the bell drew the attention of those gathered in the church and signalled a shared, corporate moment in the Mass, said inaudibly in Latin, when attention was drawn to the altar at which the Mass was being celebrated. For some of the worshippers, it may have been the awaited moment when they would silently bring their petitions to Christ, the heavenly mediator, and for others, a moment of intense devotion when they would greet and quietly adore Christ in his sacramental presence. Manuals to assist the unlettered laity in their prayer during the Mass were written in the vernacular and often in verse form in the later fourteenth and through the fifteenth centuries. The *Merita Missae* ('the Virtues of the Mass'), dated around the third quarter of the fifteenth century, is a good example of one of these manuals expressly written to help the laity pray during the offering of the Mass. What is interesting is that the manual was selective in its comments on the Mass and, unsurprisingly, the largest section, in two parts, concerns the intentions and devotional posture of the contemporary worshipper at the elevation of the host:

---

43 See Binski, *Becket's Crown*, plate 129 and pp. 157, 198. The original French text of *The Lay Folks' Mass Book, or the Manner of Hearing Mass*, as it was also called in its English translations, is no longer extant but was probably written towards the close of the twelfth century, and may well have reflected Gallic practices from the Rouen Usage. At the elevation, the text requires the layman to remain kneeling and to hold up both his hands in prayer. See Thomas Frederick Simmons (ed.), *The Lay Folks' Mass Book, or the Manner of Hearing Mass*, Early English Texts Society (Oxford: Oxford University Press 1879, repr. 1968).

44 Although the original York Missal did not contain a rubrical instruction about the elevation, a direction was added later to bring it into conformity with the Sarum Usage. The York rubric is cited in P. S. Barnwell, Claire Cross and Ann Rycraft (eds), *The Mass and Parish in Late Medieval England: The Use of York* (Reading: Spire Books 2005), p. 158. On the Use of York, see J. H. Arnold and E. G. P. Wyatt (eds), *Walter Howard Frere: A Collection of his Papers on Liturgical and Historical Subjects*, Alcuin Club Collections 35 (Oxford: Oxford University Press 1940).

And when he ringeth the cross-bell,
Pray then for another skill,
That thou be worthy to see that sight,
That shall be in his hands light.
And when he resteth him up on height,
Kneel a-down with all thy might,
And if thou ask any thing,
Speak dreadfully as to a king.[45]

This is a comparatively late source, and it is impossible to reconstruct all the specific responses that were elicited or even expected at the elevation from the geographically dispersed beginnings of the ritual act in the thirteenth century to the universal practice of the early sixteenth century. Suffice it to say, the scant rubrical evidence, the comments in manuals written for the laity and the evidence of contemporary artwork all indicate that at the elevation both the priest and people were caught up in a single and singularly *visual* liturgical moment. The raising of the chalice after the dominical words, 'This is my blood', provided an element of ritual symmetry, but the crucial difference was that in the elevation of the host the material sacramental sign was visible whereas the contents of the chalice obviously were not.[46]

The elevation during the Mass is depicted in *The Mass of St Giles*, painted around 1500 and now to be seen in the National Gallery in London. This consummate work is a narrative painting and has as its subject the story of the Emperor Charlemagne attending a Mass celebrated by the hermit St Giles before the sumptuously decorated altar and cross of Abbot Suger at St Denys. The saint is elevating the host, and the Emperor, gazing at the host, is depicted with his hands extended in a gesture of greeting, a posture we may construe in more contemporary terms as an opening of oneself to the sacramental presence of Christ. An angel appears above Charlemagne holding a parchment on which is written the sin that Charlemagne is unable to confess with his lips, and

45 Original text, British Library, Cotton MS Titus, A. xxvi, folios 154–6, and reprinted by John Harper in the unpublished briefing notes for the Experience of Worship in Late Medieval Cathedral and Parish Church Project, 2011.
46 John F. Baldovin sj, '*Accepit Panem*: The Gestures of the Priest at the Institution Narrative of the Eucharist' in Nathan Mitchell and John F. Baldovin (eds), *Rule of Prayer, Rule of Faith: Essays in Honor of Aidan Kavanagh, O.S.B.* (Collegeville, MN: Liturgical Press 1996), p. 126.

the assurance of God's absolution. The scene is framed within a liturgical context, and although, unlike the viewer of the painting, neither Charlemagne nor St Giles can see the angel, the appearance of the angel's message coincides with the elevation, thereby communicating to the viewer the message that what is conferred by Christ's sacramental presence is the gift of forgiveness. It is in this sense, one could argue, that the painting makes present what is invisible.

A similar purpose could be applied to the many fourteenth- and fifteenth-century painted panels and engravings of the popular subject of the Mass of St Gregory, which has received a great deal of interest from scholars.[47] The image usually shows St Gregory the Great at the altar with assistant ministers, and the appearance of Christ, usually portrayed as the living Man of Sorrows. Almost invariably it is the viewer, not Gregory or his assistants and any others who may occupy the painted scene, who sees the vision of Christ. It is possible that what we see in this compositional arrangement is a deliberate caution and official unease about the eucharistic host appearing as flesh. But even more likely, we see a clear visual statement of the view, articulated by a number of writers and teachers, including Thomas Aquinas, that the sacramental presence of Christ in the arena of a liturgical celebration was an invisible and hidden presence. This essentially paradoxical view is one that we shall discuss in more detail below.

What is clear in these examples is that the liturgical context of 'visual piety' is the key, and that the elevation is a prominent ritual act to facilitate such spiritual seeing. But like other ritual actions, the elevation attracted other symbolic meanings in allegorical readings of the Mass, such as the lifting of the body of Christ on to the cross at Golgotha.[48] Nevertheless, the rubrical directions and the desired devotional

---

47 A database containing and commenting on a large number of Gregory Mass images can be viewed at <http://gregorsmesse.uni-muenster.de>.

48 Amalarius, the ninth-century Bishop of Metz, provided an allegorical reading of the Mass, and from the time of William Durandus (1230–96) until the high Middle Ages, the Mass was interpreted allegorically in relation to Christ's Passion. These commentaries rarely commented on the shape of liturgical action, or its intrinsic themes, but indicated points that resonated with the wider story of Christ, particularly the story of his Passion. Some later vernacular commentaries perpetuated typological symbols, such as the incident of Moses raising the serpent in the wilderness as Christ being elevated on the cross. One late fourteenth- or fifteenth-century English example sees the ritual of the elevation as combining both Christ being raised on the cross and his exaltation, as celebrated in Philippians 2. The example, set out against the text of the Canon of the Mass, is in

responses are consistent with the primary and presumably public meaning of the elevation as a ritual that had to do with the visuality of the faith, enabling the faithful to see and read the sign of Christ's presence. Such visuality is not without its antecedents in Christian reflection. Seeing, of course, is a recurring theme in the Johannine literature in the New Testament. The Johannine Christ declares: 'whoever has seen me has seen the Father', and the Greeks are reported as coming to the Apostle Philip with the request that they too 'would like to *see* Jesus'.

A more systematic understanding of sight was set out by Augustine of Hippo in the fifth century. Following classical precedent, Augustine argued that knowledge was conveyed through the senses, particularly through the faculty of sight. Further, as he argued in *De Doctrina Christiana* (On Christian Doctrine),[49] it was through the seeing of signs, a constant key term in the definition of a sacrament, that we are able to see the things of 'the invisible God'.

In a later work, *De Genesi ad litteram* (The Literal Meaning of Genesis), Augustine drew a distinction between what is perceived through the physical sense of sight and what was deemed to be 'spiritual seeing'; that is, between the corporeal, spiritual and intellectual modes of seeing.[50] He acknowledged that seeing was not without its dangers (the most serious being idolatry) and ambiguities (the confusion of sign and reality), re-affirmed the primacy of the sense of sight and provided the language and logic for later medieval thinkers to speculate on how the sentient embodied Christian could participate in the things of God. To summarize this medieval speculation, we could say that what was physically seen was understood to be imprinted upon the mind's eye, and that there was a sense that what one perceived deeply affected the mind, the outlook and the attitude, as we might say today, of the perceiving subject. It would be pushing the logic too far to say that the early medieval thinker

Gordon Jeanes, *Signs of God's Promise: Thomas Cranmer's Sacramental Theology and the Book of Common Prayer* (London and New York: T. & T. Clark 2008), p. 40.

49 See *Teaching Christianity* (*De Doctrina Christiana*) (Bk 1, ii–iv), in *The Works of St Augustine: A Translation for the 21st Century*, ed. and trans. Edmund Hill OP (New York: New City Press 1996), pp. 106–8.

50 The corporeal level of sight is the perceiving of objects through the physical eye, the spiritual level is the recall of images from the memory and the generation of images through the faculty of the imagination, and the intellectual, the highest level, is the perception of divine truths. See Cynthia Hahn, 'Visio Dei: Changes in Medieval Visuality' in Nelson (ed.), *Visuality Before and Beyond the Renaissance*, p. 171.

believed in a Neoplatonic way that a person became what they saw, but there does seem to be a consensus that spiritual realities could indeed be apprehended through the sense of sight, and that material things, such as a decorated cross, could radiate what is truly divine and illuminate the mind.[51] Such an understanding applied not only to objects but also to words fixed and written on parchment; for again, as Augustine said, letters and words are also signs to be read through the eye, and as such resist any simple opposition between words and images.

In concluding this brief excursus on the theoretical understanding of spiritual seeing, we may conclude that throughout the early and high medieval period (say 400 to 1500), words and material images were regarded as belonging together, and that of the five senses, sight was the privileged sense through which the human person perceived and interacted with all that he or she encountered. This view is stunningly illustrated in the so-called Fuller Brooch, a brilliant piece of Anglo-Saxon jewellery now exhibited in the British Museum. The inscribed decoration of this brooch shows the personification of the five senses, the largest, set in what could be a cross at the centre of the brooch, being the sense of sight. So it may be that this beautifully crafted arte-fact could represent for us an icon of 'salvation seen'.

But what was conveyed by this showing and seeing? Thomas Aquinas had drawn a clear distinction between the sacramental grace conveyed through Communion and the blessing gained by gazing upon the con-secrated host, which as we have seen increasingly became the most common way of participating in the Mass. The impetus behind this tendency in lay devotion in the West[52] was not only the physical fencing off of the altar and the definition of priesthood in terms of the power to confect the sacrament, but also the increasing anxiety people had about receiving the sacrament unworthily.[53] St Paul's warning about

51 For references and historical examples, see Hahn, 'Visio Dei', pp. 176–84.

52 The emphasis in Western popular devotion to seeing and adoring the host during the celebration of the Mass was detailed by Gregory Dix in *The Shape of the Liturgy* (London: Dacre Press 1945), pp. 14, 482, 620.

53 Three conditions were conventionally sought in those who received Communion: first, a discerning of the sacramental body of Christ, second, a penitent heart and resolve not to sin again, and third, a mind that meditated on Christ's saving life, Passion and resurrection. See Charles Caspers, 'Augenkommunion or Popular Mysticism?' in Charles Caspers, Gerard Lukken and Gerard Rouwhorst (eds), *Bread of Heaven: Customs and Practices Surrounding Holy Communion* (Kampen: Kok Pharos 1995), pp. 87–90.

unworthy reception of Communion being the eating and drinking of divine judgement upon oneself was taken literally; and intellectually, some theologians, such as the English Franciscan Alexander of Hales, pressed towards insisting that worthy communicants had some cognitive understanding of the paradox of Christ's sacramental presence in the eucharistic bread and cup.[54]

In terms of practice, there is evidence that frequent reception of the sacrament had long been regarded as desirable, but the prerequisite conditions for an individual made it quite impracticable.[55] As well as questions about the individual's spiritual health, there was also an unease about the physical act of receiving the sacrament. For some it felt almost sacrilegious to receive God in the mouth. Given this complex religious sensibility, it is no wonder that the kind of 'spiritual communion' afforded by gazing at the consecrated host was popularly considered the safer option when, as it was believed, the divine encountered the worshipper through the consecrated species of the sacrament of Christ's body.

We have already said that such seeing of the holy was also regarded as a kind of receiving too, but a little more needs to be said about how this was experienced and conceived. The devout gazing at the consecrated host was both an active and a passive act on the part of the worshipper. As the elevation became more common, it came to be accompanied by the ringing of the so-called sacring bell. This ringing of the bell was intended to draw the attention of members of the congregation from their parallel devotion,[56] and their looking up to see the host was a deliberate, and one may also say expectant, moment. For the very act of seeing was not only a looking but was also a receiving of the reality in their field of vision. And so it came to be understood that in some sense the perceiving subject received what he or she saw when looking at the host in the context of the celebration of the Mass. So was this a kind of ocular communion, and if it was, how did it compare with actually receiving the consecrated host in the act of Communion?

---

54 See Kumler, *Translating Truth*, pp. 147–9.
55 A good case in point is the eighth-century Bede who, as Donald Bullough shows, actively urged a more frequent receiving of Communion. See 'The Carolingian Liturgical Experience' in R. N. Swanson (ed.), *Continuity and Change in Christian Worship*, Studies in Church History, vol. 35 (Woodbridge: Boydell Press 1999), p. 33.
56 Robert N. Swanson, 'Medieval English Liturgy: What's the Use?' *Studia Liturgica*, vol. 29, no. 2, 1999, p. 175.

These are complex questions, and it is important to recognize that clear distinctions were actually drawn and need to be carefully unpacked. Simply looking at the consecrated host was not regarded as the equivalent of actually receiving Communion and sharing the eucharistic gifts of Christ's body and blood. Indeed, since the time of scholastic theologians the official teaching of the Western Church had consistently been that ocular communion did not convey the same grace as was received in the actual reception of the sacrament. Nevertheless, grace was understood to be conveyed in what today we may well call a 'graced encounter' between Christ and the worshipper. For when we take the iconographical evidence together with the contemporary theoretical understandings of perception, there is a strong suggestion that seeing the host was experienced as, and understood to be, a communicative moment for the worshipper. It was, in other words, a moment when the possibility of an encounter with the divine in the architectural space of the church was at its most intense, in and through the visible sign of Christ's invisible sacramental presence.

Visual devotion to the 'sacrament of sacraments' was given further impetus by the feast of Corpus Christi, a kind of inverse of the commemoration of the Last Supper, the institution of the Eucharist, on Maundy Thursday in Holy Week. The feast originated around 1246 as a local celebration in Liège and was endorsed and promoted in Rome by Pope Urban IV in 1264 because of his connections with Liège.[57] It fell to Pope Urban's successor to promulgate the feast effectively. Corpus Christi entered the Calendar of the Western Church, and so came to be universally observed by the wider Church early in the fourteenth century.

At the heart of the celebration of Corpus Christi, observed on the Thursday following Trinity Sunday, was the carrying of the sacrament in procession and its exposition. This exposition or public display of the consecrated host effectively extended the moment of the elevation in the celebration of the Mass. For the host was exposed to sight in a glass container, the monstrance. The displaying of the host in a container deliberately designed to make it visible is not without an element of paradox. For as is stated by the text of the Sequence *Lauda, Syon,*

---

[57] On the origins and gradual spread of the feast, see Rubin, *Corpus Christi*, pp. 164–85; M. R. Dudley, 'Liturgy and Doctrine: Corpus Christi', in *Worship*, vol. 66, no. 5, 1992, pp. 417–26.

Salvatorem, written for the Mass of Corpus Christi, and questionably attributed to Thomas Aquinas, the sacramental reality of Christ's presence in the host was perceived by faith, not by naked physical sight:

> Doth it pass thy comprehending?
> Yet by faith, thy sight transcending,
> Wondrous things are understood.
>
> Yea, beneath these signs are hidden
> Glorious things to sight forbidden:
> Look not on the outward sign.[58]

Look not on the outward sign, and yet look they did! The host needed to be seen, particularly when the Mass was celebrated. In England during the later fourteenth and early fifteenth centuries, squint holes were made in the panels of chancel rood screens so that even in the nave lay people could press forward on a Sunday to gain a sight of the eucharistic host.[59] The conspicuous rood – a polychrome painted crucifix, usually with the figures of Mary and John on either side – was generally set up in English churches at the chancel crossing, and the screen, with its lower painted panels of the saints, provided a frame that functioned to heighten the sense of mystery, the encounter with the holy, that occurred at the altar, the locus of the liturgical action. In this way the screen functioned as a kind of window through which one may glimpse heavenly realities.[60] For the laity, the climactic moment in the celebration of the Mass was the visual spectacle of the ritual of

---

58 As rendered in a contemporary hymn book, *The New English Hymnal* (Norwich: Canterbury Press 1987), no. 521.

59 Eamon Duffy has marshalled evidence of screens with squint holes and sculpture showing that the elevation was the iconic moment of the Eucharist; see illustrations 44 and 45, and for a sculpted Mass scene showing the elevation at the sacring, see illustration 42, in *The Stripping of the Altars*. See also Rubin, *Corpus Christi*, pp. 290, 293. On screens as material evidence of lay investment and as a visual backdrop to side altars for votive and requiem Masses, see Eamon Duffy, *Saints, Sacrilege and Sedition: Religion and Conflict in the Tudor Reformation* (London: Bloomsbury 2012), chs 3 and 5.

60 In this sense, the rood screen functioned as a lens to focus attention on the mystery being made visible at the altar, rather as the later templon screen, or iconostasis, in the Orthodox Church. See Pavel Florensky, *Iconostasis* (Crestwood, NY: St Vladimir's Seminary Press 1996), p. 62.

the elevation, when the priest raised the host – and also the chalice, for reasons of ritual symmetry[61] – high above his head.

Low Masses were a different experience. They were invariably celebrated at side altars in the nave of the church dedicated to a particular saint, whose image would be represented in an altarpiece or stained glass behind the altar. At a low Mass there was a closer proximity between the faithful crowding around and the priest at the altar.[62] This gave rise to the increasingly popular practice of going round from altar to altar or church to church, even on the same day, to gain health, success or a blessing in one's quotidian life through seeing 'one's maker' at the elevation during the celebration of the Mass.[63] An architectural feature of fifteenth-century churches that relates to this practice is the often sizeable opening made in the walls, a so-called squint, giving a view of the altar.

Until the Fourth Lateran Council the expectation had been that the laity should receive Communion three times a year, at Christmas, Easter and Pentecost, but the Council reduced this expectation, and decreed that each faithful Christian should receive the Eucharist at Easter.[64] The receiving of Communion at Easter was expected as a sign of one's belonging to the Church, and as such was a public and social act of the individual's good standing within the community.[65] But as the effects of Communion were long lasting and, as Innocent himself had taught,[66] Christ was received spiritually by the faithful, there were no

---

61 The elevation of the chalice had been promoted by William Durandus (1230–96) but was largely resisted for fear of spillage. Benjamin Gordon-Taylor has observed that it was the elevation of the chalice that attracted the acclamation *mysterium fidei*, and suggested that as the content of the chalice was not seen, so the 'precious blood' attracted to itself a numinosity and greater sense of sacramental mystery.

62 Artistic evidence suggests that there could be a real jostling for position at side and private altars. See Swanson, 'Medieval English Liturgy', p. 179; Kumler, *Translating Truth*, ch. 3, esp. figs 28, 31.

63 'Petitions and requests were made at the elevation in a pandemonium of vernacular prayers and salutations, exchanging faith and acceptance of the host as God, for a large variety of benefits' – Rubin, *Corpus Christi*, p. 155.

64 This essentially ecclesial understanding of the Eucharist was expounded by scholastic theologians including Peter Lombard and Peter Abelard, and came in the late twelfth and early thirteenth centuries. See Macy, *The Theologies of the Eucharist in the Early Scholastic Period*, p. 138.

65 Macy, *Treasures from the Storeroom*, p. 158.

66 In his description of the Papal Mass, *De missarum mysteriis*. See Macy, *Treasures from the Storeroom*, p. 154.

calls for an increase in the frequency with which the faithful Christian should receive Communion.[67]

Once Easter Communion was established as the norm, and the visual seeing of the consecrated host at the elevation was by far the most frequent mode of popular participation in the Mass, the faithful went to church, 'the sacring to see',[68] right up to the eve of the Reformation in England. From then on, official changes in attitude and understanding vacillated greatly. In a manuscript on the ceremonies of the Church[69] that was written by someone apparently close to Henry VIII and his new Archbishop, Thomas Cranmer, but never published, the author offered an explanation of the elevation of the bread and the cup. They were lifted up so that the people 'with all reverence and honour may worship the same' and to signify how Christ was lifted up on the cross and then exalted by God. This double signification is explicitly said to combine the mysteries of Christ's suffering and death, and his resurrection and Ascension, in language reminiscent of the 'Christ hymn' in Philippians 2.1–11. However, only a few years after this manuscript was written, the reforming Thomas Cranmer peevishly described the practice in derogatory terms as the 'peeping, tooting, and gazing at that thing which the priest held up'.[70] Unsurprisingly, although the German reformer Martin Luther (1483–1546) retained the elevation in his German Mass, Thomas Cranmer proscribed the practice of 'shewing the Sacrament to the people' in his first English Prayer Book of 1549, and the direction inserted after the institution narrative in the Holy Communion service is unequivocal: 'These words before rehearsed are to be said, turning still to the altar, without any elevation or showing the sacrament to the people.'

---

67 Caspers, 'Augenkommunion or Popular Mysticism?', pp. 91ff.

68 As described in the fourteenth-century English rhyming form of *The Lay Folks' Mass Book*.

69 The MS entitled *Book Concerning Ceremonies to be used in the Church of England* (c. 1539) was edited by Cyril S. Cobb as *The Rationale of Ceremonial* and published as the Alcuin Collections 18 (London: Longmans, Green and Co. 1910). For the relevant section see pp. 3–43.

70 Thomas Cranmer, *Defence* (1550), p. 442 (cited by Dix, *The Shape of the Liturgy*, p. 620). Diarmaid MacCulloch draws attention to a close resemblance between Cranmer and his literary assistant, his evangelical chaplain Thomas Becon, who vehemently opposed the practice of the elevation. See Diarmaid MacCulloch, *Thomas Cranmer: A Life* (New Haven, CT and London: Yale University Press 1996), p. 386, n. 125.

Although Cranmer repeatedly warns against receiving Communion unworthily, his aim, more fully realized in the Order in the 1552 Prayer Book of Edward VI, was to promote the practice of Communion. In his mature understanding of the Eucharist, Communion was a sacramental eating and drinking in remembrance of Christ, an eating and drinking that was an effective spiritual feeding through faith on Christ, the Bread of Life.[71] This spiritual Communion was also a physical act, but now one involving the sense of taste rather than of sight. Cranmer's Communion Office was in one sense a victory of word over image. It consequently erased a doctrine of 'real presence' in the sacrament of the Eucharist and led inexorably to a wholesale devaluing of the visual in the arena of worship. By the time of Elizabeth I, the break with the 'old religion' was final, and it was unequivocally asserted in the *Articles of Religion* of 1562 that the 'sacraments were not ordained of Christ to be gazed upon' (Article 25) – further evidence, if any were required, of the 'blinding' of devotion that occurred through the consecutive phases of the English Reformation. Indeed, the abandoning of the altar and the setting up of a table in the chancel, as directed by the Communion Office of the Edwardine Prayer Book of 1552, fractured the visual connections and interplay between the priest and worshippers and the reredos, cross and altarpiece.

In this fracturing of ritual from its complex visual setting, something was lost in terms of the interplay between the worshipper and the visible artefacts above and behind the altar at which the Mass was celebrated. This interaction may well have been a key factor in how the Mass was experienced and understood by the worshipper, and so the loss of the highly visual setting and mode of the Mass at the Reformation would have restricted the worshipper's experience and understanding. To recover what was lost and gain a deeper appreciation of the interplay between the worshipper, ritual and setting, we could profitably return again to the subject of the altarpiece.

As we have seen, the altarpiece and its placing were critical to its function and the ways in which it may have been read. And we know that both the artist and the ecclesiastical body responsible for the commissioning of the altarpiece would in each case have intended the

---

71 For a full and critical treatment of Cranmer's thinking on the Eucharist, see Jeanes, *Signs of God's Promise*.

worshipper to interact with the artwork in specific and conventional ways.[72] One of these intended ways of interacting with the altarpiece occurred at the elevation, when the viewer, as worshipper, would have seen the large priest's host aligned with the painted figure of Jesus, either presented by his mother or portrayed on the cross. Beside this fusion of objects of the sacramental and the painted body, another intended interplay would, in some if not all cases, have occurred as the worshipper was drawn into the *sacra conversazione* between the figures of the saints depicted in the altarpiece.

How viewers receive and respond to works of art has been a key question since the publication of David Freedberg's seminal study, *The Power of Images*.[73] Freedberg attributes the power of images to their capacity to elicit a psychological response, but there is no reason to restrict their power to their potential to elicit certain behavioural and emotional responses. The way a painting such as an altarpiece works cannot be limited to postulations, however plausible, of psychological responses alone. In broader terms, we should acknowledge that it is extremely difficult to predict, or indeed to delimit, the behavioural, cognitive and affective responses of the viewer to a work of art. But given the original setting and liturgical context in which an altarpiece was seen by the worshipper, the worshipper's responses would have been bound up with a whole nexus of doctrinal understandings, patterns of learnt devotion and ritual enactment that would have focused the multiple ways in which the art was received and responded to. Indeed, I would contend that the reception of an altarpiece depended as much on the viewer's sense of the sacrality of the zone in which it was placed as on the seeing of it as being integral to the liturgical action that occurred in what was designated as 'holy space'.

Given the original context and setting of the altarpiece, how then would it have been originally read, and how might we recover its meaning today? To recapitulate the argument so far, we know that what we *see* is

---

72 One might consider Cimabue's mural of the crucifixion in the Upper Church of the Basilica of St Francis, Assisi, in which Mary Magdalene's arms are raised in despair and even the angels avert their grieving faces from the calamity of the death of the Son of God.

73 See David Freedberg, *The Power of Images: Studies in the History and Theory of Response* (Chicago: University of Chicago Press 1989). For a more recent study of later seventeenth-century altarpieces in Rome, see Pamela M. Jones, *Altarpieces and their Viewers in the Churches of Rome from Caravaggio to Guido Reni* (Aldershot: Ashgate 2008).

largely refracted through what we bring to an image, and the particular cultural lenses through which we view the world around us depend to some extent on what we expect to see, and what we expect to see is in turn influenced by the place in which an object is seen. In the particular case of an altarpiece, we could say that how the artwork was received was coloured by a whole complex set of ingrained religious beliefs and devotional practices. Regarding the artwork itself, we have already said that it is entirely likely that particular theological conventions influenced the choice of subject, but the interesting feature to emerge from our present survey of altarpieces is that the choice of subject and the way it was artistically rendered provided a clear trajectory between what we might call the visual image and the ritual action at the altar. Indeed, in terms of both its making and its perceived meaning, we may propose a kind of triumvirate:

1 the patron and the artist
2 the altarpiece
3 the viewer as priest/worshipper.

And as we begin to trace the possible interactions between the three points of this dynamic triangular relationship, we can begin to plot the meaning of an altarpiece in its original setting by reference to three more specific triangulation points:

1 the understanding of the Mass
2 the rite, that is, both the text of the service and the ritual actions of the priest
3 the interactive field between the image and celebrant and people.

This proposed triangulation extends the likely meaning of the visual image beyond its psychological reception and response by the viewer. It takes full cognizance of the setting in which the artwork is placed, seen and responded to in its ecclesial setting, and within the context of the performance of the liturgy, we can see that far from being mere decoration or even a devotional backdrop, the altarpiece had a performative function. What was seen was what is happening in the celebration of the rite, the 'making present' of Christ's sacramental body. For, as the unfolding medieval rite reached its climax, the embodied worshipper – as viewer – was caught up in a devotionally appropriate way to the mystery of the depicted fleshly body that was the body believed to be sacramentally conveyed to the worshipper in Communion.

Bearing in mind its original context and function as an altarpiece of the high Renaissance, let me conclude this chapter with a reading of a finely accomplished painted altarpiece, *Crucifixion with the Virgin Mary, Saints and Angels*, also known as the Mond Crucifixion. This work was painted around 1503 for a merchant-banker donor by the young Raphael (Raffaello di Giovanni Santi) for a side chapel in the church of San Domenico in the Città di Castello, and can now be viewed in the National Gallery in London.[74]

The gentle undulating hills of the Umbrian landscape form the background of this perfectly symmetrical composition of the crucifixion. The painting is not perhaps as dramatic as a Luca Signorelli, but has all the dynamism of a Perugino, an artist with whom Raphael was closely associated during his career as a painter. The dreadful pain of crucifixion is visible in the bowed head still wearing the crown of thorns, and yet the figure of the Crucified is gracefully muscular and proportioned, and hangs on a rather tall cross, evoking those words from John's Gospel (12.32) in which Jesus foretells: 'And I, when I am lifted up from the earth, will draw all people to myself.' On either side are two balletic angels standing tip-toe on wisps of cloud, who gather the blood from Christ's wounded hands and side in three ornate chalices.

Two penitential saints, Jerome and Mary Magdalene, kneel with their attention fixed on the cross. By contrast, the composed and sad faces of Mary the mother of the Lord, and John the beloved disciple look out towards the viewer, seeking to catch the eye and thereby draw him or her into the scene presented pictorially. And so in this painting the placing and composition of the figures of John and Jerome, and Mary and Mary Magdalene, link the event of the cross with the contemporary viewing audience. Jerome's open left hand, for instance, can be read as both a supplicatory gesture and an invitation to the viewer to stand before the Crucified in an attitude of prayerful attention. When we look at this painting, with its distinct eucharistic reference and its gentle invitation to the viewer to contemplate the cross, we can begin

---

74 Hugo Chapman, Tom Henry and Carol Plazzotta, *Raphael: From Urbino to Rome* (London: National Gallery 2004), pp. 120–4.

to see that it does not simply picture a scene but intentionally draws the viewer into the scene portrayed in a way that includes the viewer as worshipper in the company of those gathered around the cross. For the painting is not simply an invitation to meditate upon an image or pictorial scene but to enter and to interact, through the eyes of devotion,[75] *with* the scene, a scene that in some more narrative style of paintings of the crucifixion can be full of dramatic incident.

If this is the case, then something more, and more specific, can be said about *Crucifixion with the Virgin Mary, Saints and Angels*. For when we register the landscape background and the anachronistic inclusion of a saint who was not present on the actual occasion of Christ's crucifixion, and reflect on the original placing of this painting and the context in which it would have been seen, we can see that the visual image of the crucifixion is a transposition of both time and space, corresponding to the transposition of the Eucharist, in which the significance of what happened then – Christ's Passion and death – was understood to be made present for the participants in the actual liturgical performance of the Mass.

This conviction resonates with earlier patristic teaching, specifically that of Leo the Great (440–61), who in one sermon declared that 'that which was visible in our Redeemer has passed over into the sacraments' (sermon 74). To reiterate the conviction in more contemporary terms, it could be said that the significance of what happened there and then was applied here and now, and that this was grounded in the belief that in the eucharistic offering, the fruits of Christ's Passion were given to those for whom the Mass was offered – the benefactors, the gathered faithful, the living and the departed. Communion may not have been given and received, but in the late medieval mentality each Mass was an occasion of *communitas*, of that which sustained and strengthened a sense of a particular community, present and past, bound and held together in Christ.

---

75 The Renaissance also saw a return to the classic sources of Christian thought and reflection, such as the writings of Augustine. In a commentary on the book of Genesis, Augustine elaborated three ways of seeing: the corporeal (physical perception), spiritual seeing (the imagining of a holy scene or person) and intellectual (the receiving of the divine gift of contemplation). Franciscan writers in the fourteenth century, such as Bonaventure, again emphasized the importance of the faculty of sympathetic imagination as a way of apprehending religious truth.

With this example we again see that the meaning of the painting was, in part, determined by its placing – the setting in which it was placed and the context in which it was responded to. The placing of a painting of a crucifixion behind an altar put it into a particular frame of reference. In the high Middle Ages, the Eucharist was seen primarily as the commemoration of the atoning sacrifice of Christ to the Father. The eucharistic sacrifice was offered on the altar, and so a direct visual correspondence was drawn between the sacrifice of Christ and the offering of the bread and the cup in the Mass that was, above all, a commemoration of Christ's self-giving to the Father, a fact graphically shown in the priest's missal, where an illustration of the crucifixion quite often faced the *Te igitur* section of the Canon of the Mass. In this instance, prayer text and image were complementary, and worship combining visual art and ritual enactment was experienced as being directly and dramatically visual.

During a celebration of the Mass, in other words, the art was integral to the perceived meaning of the rite. Two key aspects of what was communicated through art and ritual are explored in more detail in the following chapter.

Chapter 3

The cross in blood and in bloom

A symbolic connection between the cross and the Eucharist was pictorially established in the Carolingian era, with the inclusion of a eucharistic chalice placed at the foot of the cross. A number of examples are to be seen in the illustrations in Carolingian and Ottonian liturgical books, such as the Sacramentary.[1] In this period the official policy regarding the place of art in churches was set out by Charlemagne's theological adviser, Theodulf of Orleans, in his tightly argued and polemical *Libri Carolini*. Here, Theodulf endorsed Pope Gregory's well-known letters on the use of art in churches. Pictures were permitted to aid the unlettered, but there was little here in the way of encouragement for the production of art in churches. In this treatise Theodulf argued that the resolutions of the Council of Nicea II (787), which had been hastily convened after the first wave of intermittent iconoclasm in the East, were based on a misreading of Scripture, and so he was unequivocal in his denunciation of the veneration of icons in the liturgy and the devotional practice of the East generally.[2] Faith could not come from what was *seen* but only from what was read. Such a premise gave priority to text over images and secured Scripture as the primary source for the gaining of knowledge of Christian truth.[3]

---

1 Barbara C. Raw, *Anglo-Saxon Crucifixion Iconography and the Art of the Monastic Revival* (Cambridge: Cambridge University Press 1990), p. 118.

2 For a full discussion, see Thomas F. X. Noble, *Images, Iconoclasm and the Carolingians* (Philadelphia: University of Pennsylvania Press 2009), ch. 4.

3 For a thorough discussion of these issues, see Henry Mayr-Harting, 'Charlemagne as a Patron of the Arts' in Diana Wood (ed.), *The Church and the Arts* (Oxford: Blackwell 1995), pp. 43–75.

And yet despite Theodulf's call for restraint in the placing and use of figural artworks in church, artists, including some recruited from Ravenna, the Western Byzantine centre, came to be employed in the artistic workshops of the imperial palace of the Emperor Charlemagne (*c.* 742–814) at Aachen, and produced striking decorated Gospel and other liturgical books. The arts deployed in the making of books, with painted illustrations and covers worked in ivory, metal and precious stones, became typical and prolific through the major centres of the Holy Roman Empire, in which Charlemagne intended to rival the architectural and creative glories of both Rome and Byzantium. So what transpired was the making of fine liturgical books at Aachen and in the later centres of the new empire such as Metz and Trier, in which pictorial art was harnessed to serve the word.[4] The rich and multiple connotations of what was denoted in the texts, written either for liturgical use or for study purposes in monastic schools, provided what Herbert L. Kessler has described as 'spiritual seeing'.[5] And so the artwork in these books was neither simply decorative nor straightforward illustration but highlighted particular words that were sounded in liturgical chant and prayer and that, literally, showed and extended the meaning of the written text.

A perfect illustration of this is to be found in the *Drogo Sacramentary*. This Sacramentary, a book containing all the prayers used by a bishop, the chief liturgical minster, in the celebration of the sacraments, was named after an illegitimate son of Charlemagne who became Bishop of Metz. The book was probably made in the last decade of Drogo's episcopacy (845–55) to enhance his standing as a bishop. The innovative element in the illustrations of such liturgical books as the *Drogo Sacramentary* is the miniatures painted in enlarged capital letters, which art historians call historiated capitals. The lettering follows an antique Roman style, and the small paintings set within selected capital letters are delicately colour-washed small figures and scenes that effectively extend the meaning of the words. A particular example is the painting in the capital letter 'O' of the first word of the collect for Palm Sunday in the *Drogo Sacramentary*. This collect speaks of how the omnipotent and eternal God made Christ to be an example to the human race

---

4 For a fuller discussion of this point, see William J. Diebold, *Word and Image: An Introduction to Early Medieval Art* (Boulder, CO: Westview Press 2000), ch. 2.
5 See Herbert L. Kessler, *Spiritual Seeing: Picturing God's Invisibility in Medieval Art* (Philadelphia: University of Pennsylvania Press 2000), ch. 7.

through his Incarnation and the cross, and asks that those who pray may be 'made worthy to see the tokens of his passion and be made partakers of his resurrection'.

Compressed within the comparatively small space of this enlarged opening letter is a composite picture of the crucifixion scene. The first observation to be made is that this scene does not occur in the material for Good Friday. Its position is deliberate and signals a message about the whole of Holy Week, the commemoration of the Lord's Supper on Maundy Thursday, as well as the events around Christ's death and Passion solemnly commemorated on Good Friday. In this way a direct link is made between the cross and the Eucharist, but to explore this further we need to describe the illustration in a little more detail.

The pictures of the historiated capital letters in the Sacramentary are framed by intertwining gold-painted acanthus leaves and tendrils in the shape of the particular letter. The choice of this repeated decorative feature could simply be a borrowing from a common Hellenistic decorative motif, but it could equally signal that the sacred event framed by the decoration is to be read in relation to the natural world and its renewal. The composition of the capital illustration is interesting, and a number of figures crowd the small scene. At the centre is the crucified Christ and on either side stand the figures of Mary and John. Two angels hover above the cross, and seated to its left is an enigmatic figure of an old man. The most intriguing figure is that of a woman standing on the right side of the cross, placing her at the very centre of the drama. She reaches up with a cup to catch the spurting blood of the Crucified. The figure of Jesus is slightly turned and his head bent, not in death but to engage the woman who gathers the flowing lifeblood of the Christ. The figure is evidently *Ecclesia*, the personification of the Church, who was first depicted in the art of the catacombs in second-century Rome and occasionally was figured beside the cross in illustrations of the *Te igitur* in missals up to and including the eleventh century.[6] The figure of *Ecclesia* represented the guardian of the sacraments and the one who guaranteed that the faithful received the benefits of the incarnate Christ's saving work on the cross.

---

6 For example, a tenth-century Reims Missal, possibly written and illustrated by scribes in Canterbury, which is now in the Carnegie Library in Reims.

The interplay between the written word and the image in this instance both intensifies and extends the meaning for the reader of this liturgical book. The collect begins with a double statement of what God has done in Christ: he has 'assumed our flesh' and 'suffered on the cross', and both of these aspects of the saving story are shown visually in the rendering of the figure of Christ in the initial illustration. Here the painted figure of Christ is shown wearing a *perizoma* (a loin cloth) rather than a long *colobium*, thereby exposing more of his incarnate fleshly body. The Christ figure hangs on the cross, a direct visual representation of the Passion that was celebrated in the Mass for Palm Sunday. But a connection is made both visually and textually that goes well beyond any straightforward illustration. For having stated what God has done, the collect moves into a petitionary clause, which asks that the gathered community may be made worthy to see the evidence of Christ's patience – or suffering – and to share his resurrection. The connection made through the inclusion of the figure of *Ecclesia* is how this 'seeing' of Christ's suffering and this 'sharing' of the resurrection are actually mediated to the praying community, namely, through the celebration of the Church's Eucharist, represented by the figure of *Ecclesia* shown collecting Christ's life-blood in her chalice.[7]

A further point may be teased out of this contextualized reading of the image of the cross in this initial illustration, and one that may have reflected the controversy regarding the mode of Christ's presence in the Eucharist. The controversy hinged on whether Christ's sacramental presence in the Eucharist was to be conceived in spiritual or in more realistic terms. Writers who deployed more realistic vocabulary in their writing on the Eucharist often identified the elements with the physical flesh and blood of Christ, as pictorially shown in the initial illustration, so that the body of Christ received in Communion was regarded as the same (physical) body of the one who was crucified. The contents of the cup were premised on this identification and expressed in the most extreme realistic language. Fulgentius of Ruspe, for instance, described the contents of the eucharistic chalice as 'the cup of the bodily Passion',[8]

---

7 The figure of *Ecclesia* holding a chalice features in the sumptuous painting of the crucifixion in the thirteenth-century *Amesbury Psalter*, which is referred to below.

8 Cited by Henri de Lubac in his exhaustive study, *Corpus Mysticum: The Eucharist and the Church in the Middle Ages*, trans. Gemma Simmonds and Richard Price (London: SCM Press 2006), p. 61.

and Paschasius Radbertus cited an Augustinian formula in his treatise *De Corpore et Sanguine Domini* (drafted in 831) that urged the communicant to 'take in the chalice that which poured from [Christ's] side'.[9]

The gathering of the blood flowing from Christ's physical body in a eucharistic cup may be seen in a number of artworks painted in close proximity to an altar, but in these cases the figure of *Ecclesia* has been replaced by those of angels.

A couple of thirteenth-century examples of crucifixion frescoes painted on the wall directly behind an altar in the basilica of St Francis in Assisi come to mind. Reference has already been made in the previous chapter to the fresco attributed to Giotto in the north transept, and the second example is Cimabue's dramatic crucifixion fresco in the south transept. In this fresco, angels gather the blood from the punctured hands of Christ on the cross into finely wrought ecclesiastical chalices. A later example is in the densely dramatic crucifixion scene painted by Bernardo Daddi (1280–1348) as part of his polyptych altarpiece, *Crucifixion and Saints*, that was originally painted for the Church of San Giorgio in Florence and can now be viewed as part of the Gamber Parry Bequest at the Courtauld Gallery in London. Here again angels gather the blood of Christ in goblets. This became a common motif in paintings of the crucifixion throughout the whole of Europe during the Renaissance and into the Gothic period of art.[10]

The high Middle Ages saw an increasingly popular devotion to the 'precious blood', and we may recall the devotional prayer poem *Anima Christi*, in which the supplicant asks that he or she may be 'inebriated' by Christ's blood. Such sentiments were influenced by an earlier eleventh-century affective devotion. In one of his devotional prayers, the monk theologian Anselm of Canterbury prayed that if only he had been present at Calvary, and had himself then seen and felt Christ's bloody

---

9 De Lubac, *Corpus Mysticum*, p. 62.
10 The motif is seen in the work of Giotto, in his crucifixion fresco (*c.* 1305) in the Scrovegni Chapel, Padua, in fourteenth-century manuscript illuminations and liturgical books. A later mid fifteenth-century example is Giovanni Bellini, *The Blood of the Redeemer*, a panel originally painted for the door of a sacrament house (now in the National Gallery, London), in which a kneeling angel catches the blood flowing from the crucified Christ shown in the pose of a Gothic 'Man of Sorrows' holding his cross. An example from northern Europe is the oil on wood crucifixion of the Rhenish School, *c.* 1470–80, now in the Städelsches Kunstinstitut, Frankfurt am Main, which shows four angels collecting blood from the crucified Christ on the cross.

agony on the cross.[11] The affective sentiment expressed here is more often associated with later Cistercian spirituality, and it was the Cistercian monk Aelred of Rievaulx (d. 1167) who counselled a recluse nun to imagine graphically the blood flowing down the corpus, the figure of Christ on a crucifix, as she prayed. Two centuries later, and following her own meditations on a crucifix, Julian of Norwich received a series of some 14 revelations or visions. In one of these, Julian records that she sees the blood oozing from Christ's flesh punctured by the thorns in the crown of thorns: 'And at once I saw the red blood trickling down from under the garland, hot, fresh, and plentiful, just as it did at the time of his passion.'[12]

Caroline Walker Bynum has convincingly demonstrated that the appropriation of the symbol of Christ's blood in mystical prayer and the proliferation of blood relics, such as miraculously bleeding hosts, became detached from the actual celebration of the Mass.[13] However, although such devotion took on a life of its own, such sensory personal prayer does seem to be logically grounded in eucharistic faith and practice. Indeed, the images of Christ's Passion that gave rise to such devotion – the popular images of the Man of Sorrows, or the Instruments of the Passion produced in sculpture, glass, painting and later as woodprints for example – were regarded and promoted as a way of preparing the pious individual to receive the eucharistic gift of Communion.[14] In the final analysis, such devotion ultimately emerged from and in some instances led into liturgical experience, and so it could be claimed that these fourteenth-century images evoking Christ's death and Passion provided the visual hinterland of the Eucharist.

---

11 Anselm, 'Prayer to Christ'. See *The Prayers and Meditations of Saint Anselm with the Proslogion*, trans. Sister Benedicta Ward SLG (London: Penguin 1973), pp. 91–9; G. R. Evans, *Saint Anselm of Canterbury* (London and New York: Continuum 2001), p. 30.
12 Julian of Norwich, *Revelations of Divine Love*, trans. Clifton Wolters (Harmondsworth: Penguin 1966), p. 66.
13 Caroline Walker Bynum, 'The Blood of Christ in the Later Middle Ages', *Church History*, vol. 71, no. 4, December 2002, pp. 691ff. Caroline Walker Bynum's more recent publication, *Wonderful Blood: Theology and Practice in Late Medieval Northern Germany and Beyond* (Philadelphia: University of Pennsylvania Press 2007) is an expanded and detailed study of devotion to the miraculous bleeding eucharistic hosts and popular devotion to the precious blood in the north-eastern town of Wilsnack, Germany.
14 Charles Caspers, 'Augenkommunion or Popular Mysticism?' in Charles Caspers, Gerard Lukken and Gerard Rouwhorst (eds), *Bread of Heaven: Customs and Practices Surrounding Holy Communion* (Kampen: Kok Pharos 1995), p. 95.

Given the focus upon Christ's Passion and death in both the definition of the sacrament as a sacrament of that Passion and in popular devotional practice, it is not surprising that blood emerged as a dominant symbol. The devotional focus on the blood may have been reinforced by the prohibition from receiving the chalice and the perceived holiness of its contents. Many were inhibited from receiving Communion even at Easter, when it was allowed, because of feelings of unworthiness, but apparently there were exceptions and examples of those who wanted to receive more frequently. A recent study well illustrates the connection between the Eucharist and a vivid devotion to Christ's Passion. It concerns a text that tells the story of an anonymous married woman in Basel at the turn of the fifteenth century who sought to live a devoted life like a beguine. Known as 'the holy Schererin', she apparently felt drawn to make frequent Communion but was persuaded by her Franciscan spiritual director only to receive the sacrament on Sundays, and on other days to meditate on the Passion of Christ as she attended the offering of the Mass. The account of the eucharistic visions of the holy Schererin curiously concerns the receiving of Christ's blood and is told in the most graphic terms: 'As she felt the feeling and taste of the blood in her mouth, [she] was very much strengthened from this drink of love.'[15] In actual Communion, of course, this woman, as all communicants except the priest, would only have received the host, the consecrated eucharistic bread. Nevertheless, it was the image of blood that most directly linked the eucharistic sacrifice with the cross, and thereby became the most prominent image in the holy Schererin's devotional imagination.

As we have noted, such an affective devotion to Christ's bloody sacrifice on the cross was promoted in the twelfth century, but it was the Cistercian exemplar of an interior devotion to Christ's Passion, Bernard of Clairvaux (d. 1253), who averred that ultimate and full sanctification could only come from being splattered with the blood of the cross.[16] Being smothered in blood is a dense metaphor for both

---

15 Cited by Hans-Jochen Schiewer, 'Preaching and Pastoral Care of a Devout Woman (*deo devota*) in Fifteenth-Century Basel' in Miri Rubin (ed.), *Medieval Christianity in Practice* (Princeton, NJ: Princeton University Press 2009), pp. 126–31.
16 There are a number of fourteenth-century German and Bohemian book illustrations and paintings of the crucifixion inspired by the devotional writings of Anselm and Bernard, such as the crucifixion panel attributed to the Master of the Vyssi Brod altarpiece, which shows a swooning Mary by the cross with her white veil literally spattered with Christ's blood flowing from his wounded side, in St Agatha's Convent Museum in Prague.

redemptive cleansing and Communion, and would have undoubtedly recalled the imagery in Revelation of God's chosen ones whose robes have been washed in the blood of Christ (see Revelation 5.12; 7.14; 12.11).

The image of being sprinkled with blood carries a distant echo of the blood ritual of the Jewish temple on the feast of Yom Kippur, the Day of Atonement. On that day, and on that day alone, the high priest entered into the most sacred zone of the temple in Jerusalem, the Holy of Holies, to make expiation for the sins of the people as prescribed in Leviticus 16. The high priest first filled the Holy of Holies with incense, presumably as a visual symbol of the invisible presence of YHWH, believed to be 'enthroned between the cherubim' carved on either side of the sacred Ark and the mercy seat. He took a bowl of the blood of a bull and a bowl of the blood of a goat into the Holy of Holies and this, in turn, was vigorously sprinkled and smeared around the sanctuary. According to the Mishnah, the remainder of the blood was then poured out before the great altar in the courtyard of the temple. What is interesting is that this blood ritual of the Day of Atonement only involved the high priest, and only once a year, and that it was the *place* rather than the people that was sprinkled with the blood. This annual ritual action was not directly to cleanse the people but to restore a place whose symbolic function was understood to be impeded in some way by human sin and transgression. The place, in other words, was paramount, and as Margaret Barker has repeatedly asserted,[17] the reason was that the temple was regarded as a microcosm of creation. And if this is the case, then the purpose of the annual cleansing of the Holy of Holies on Yom Kippur was effectively the ritual restoration and renewal of creation itself.[18]

Whether there was a connection between the blood ritual of the feast of Yom Kippur and creation, as Margaret Barker claims, there is certainly a strand of iconographical tradition of the cross that seems

---

17 See, for instance, Margaret Barker, *The Great High Priest: The Temple Roots of Christian Liturgy* (London: T. & T. Clark 2003), pp. 49–51, 82–3; *Temple Theology: An Introduction* (London: SPCK 2004), pp. 62–3; *Creation: A Biblical Vision for the Environment* (London: T. & T. Clark 2010), pp. 154–60.

18 The function of sacrifice in the reordering of life in creation as much as in relation to God was at least acknowledged in a systematic exposition of the Christian doctrine of atonement by Colin Gunton in *The Actuality of Atonement* (Edinburgh: T. & T. Clark 1988), p. 118.

to draw a connection between the bloody body of Jesus on the cross and the renewing and restoration of creation. In a scholarly discussion of medieval iconography of the cross, Jennifer O'Reilly discusses the sumptuous crucifixion illustration in the thirteenth-century *Amesbury Psalter*, now at All Souls College, Oxford.[19] Here the dead Christ is nailed to what looks like a freshly lopped tree, significantly painted green to evoke the paradisal tree of life,[20] with blood running down and being caught by three bodies of the dead depicted below the base of the cross.[21] This image of a living cross 'drenched with blood' has its antecedents in the relief carving of eighth-century stone crosses and in Anglo-Saxon poetry.[22]

In case the reader might think this was a peculiarly Western pre-dilection, one may also look to the very different cultural context of Ethiopian Christianity. Here, in church wall paintings and in icons of the crucifixion, streaks of blood are shown to run down the cross on to the skull of Adam, resting at its base.[23]

A literal picturing of blood sacrifice may not be compatible with our refined sensibilities and may well induce in us a feeling of repulsion. But it must be seen that these images and their associated rituals belong to the realm of symbolic ordering, and to understand that, the imagery may need to be transposed into a more symbolic key. In part this transposition may entail the suspension of some our own reactions and culturally conditioned responses, and require of us the kind of imaginative sympathy that may enable us to apprehend a world view, or way of seeing,

---

19 Jennifer O'Reilly, 'The Trees of Eden in Medieval Iconography' in Paul Morris and Deborah Sawyer (eds), *A Walk in the Garden: Biblical, Iconographical and Literary Images of Eden* (Sheffield: Sheffield Academic Press 1992), p. 186.
20 Christopher Irvine, 'The Iconography of the Cross as a Green Tree' in Stephen Prickett (ed.), *The Edinburgh Companion to the Bible and the Arts* (Edinburgh: Edinburgh University Press 2013).
21 Jennifer O'Reilly, 'Signs of the Cross: Medieval Religious Images and the Interpretation of Scripture' in Tim Ayers (ed.), *The History of British Art*, vol. 1, *600–1600* (London: Tate Publishing 2008), p. 189, fig. 106.
22 The same expression, 'drenched with blood', echoes the Anglo-Saxon heroic poetry of the cross, and is also found inscribed on an eleventh-century processional cross known as the Brussels Cross, which was probably crafted in a Benedictine monastery in the south of England. The cross contained a relic of the true cross and its central decoration is the *Agnus Dei*, the Lamb of God, and so is closely associated with the sacrifice of the Mass. See Ayers (ed.), *The History of British Art*, 2008, pp. 182–4.
23 Stanislaw Chojnacki, *Ethiopian Crosses: A Cultural History and Chronology* (Milan: Skira 2006), p. 86.

very different from what we are accustomed to. Quite simply, we need to see blood imagery at the symbolic rather than the literal level. For it was precisely a symbolic reading of blood that enabled the ancient writers of the Hebrew Scriptures to see blood as the very life-force. Killing was literally the spilling of blood, and in most religious belief systems the killing of animals for food is strictly regulated. In the holiness code in Leviticus, the spilling of blood was prohibited because blood was the natural symbol of the precious and often fragile gift of life itself. 'The life . . . is in the blood' (Leviticus 17.11; cf. the priestly text of Genesis 9.4), and so the shedding of blood in the killing of life was strictly prohibited. Sacrifice, however, was a different category (see 1 Samuel 14.31–35). In the case of sacrifice, the releasing of blood from a domestic animal was not regarded as a killing but as a life-giving or restorative ritual act because the living animal had first been offered to God.[24]

The modern reader may well consider the category of sacrificial blood as belonging to the more primitive element of religion. But far from being a medieval fetish, the trope of blood resurfaces and becomes visible again in contemporary art and culture. In his poem, 'Canticle for Good Friday', the modernist poet Geoffrey Hill places the Apostle Thomas on a cliff top to observe the crucifixion from a distance. What Thomas sees in this scene of horror is a deliberate spattering of blood on a stone pavement, poignantly described by the poet as 'Creation's issue congealing'.

The blood of the cross becomes visible again in the crucifixion paintings of the British artist Craigie Aitchison, who died in December 2009. In every decade from 1958 onwards, Aitchison painted a number of distinctive and simple crucifixions.[25] While he was an art student at the Slade School of Fine Art in London, Craigie was asked by his tutor why he was attempting to paint such a 'serious subject' when he painted a copy of a Rouault crucifixion. He took this as a criticism of his ability but did not allow it to undermine his confidence. On the contrary, it strengthened his resolve to continue painting the cross until he found his own style and got 'the colours and the shapes right'.[26] This

24 Mary Douglas, *Leviticus as Literature* (Oxford: Oxford University Press 1999), pp. 66–9.
25 For further discussion, see Graham Howes, *The Art of the Sacred* (London and New York: I. B. Tauris 2007), pp. 142–7.
26 Accounted by Craigie Aitchison in conversation with the author on 5 October 2009.

he achieved in a number of distinctive and simple crucifixions. In some of these paintings the figure of the Crucified seems to stand against a solitary cross, and there is little to distract the eye. In some Craigie has included one of his beloved Bedlington terriers looking up at the figure on the cross, perhaps to add a note of pathos. In others there is a bird or two, which sometimes seem to morph into angels on either side of the cross. But generally speaking the Crucified stands alone as a marginal figure, pared down to a symbol. Occasionally a conical shape hill, inspired by the Tuscan landscape, is in the background, but otherwise both foreground and background are an empty simple band of single, unmixed and tranquil colour. Against this is placed the cross and its figure, looking to all intents and purposes like a question mark that gently teases the question of the meaning of human life and death. Just what is this life, this death, for? The very posing of the question in visual form evokes the ambiguity of this life in death, an ambiguity that can only be answered or, as is more likely, be *shown* in the realm of symbolic meaning and ritual enactment.[27]

One may look, for example, at Aitchison's painting entitled *Small Crucifixion* (2007). This shows the figure of the Crucified hung on the cross against a dark background. A yellow halo surrounds the head of this focal figure, and the lack of any close detail or decoration makes the red stream of blood from the wounded side rather striking. The life-blood runs down to the groin. And yet this is not a painting of a figure mangled by the pain of torture. The subtle detail, the vibrant colouring and the very fullness of the figure painted against the narrow cross all suggest a kind of sacrificial bloodletting, a sort of release. Indeed, the simple visual language here speaks more of a passing on than of a draining away of life. Some life-force is being released, is being given over.

Another striking example is Aitchison's larger canvas known as the *Pink Crucifixion* (2004). This painting, owned by the Timothy Taylor Gallery in London, is on loan to the impressive Methodist Art Collection that was exhibited at Wallspace, All Hallows on the Wall, London, in July 2010. In this painting, as in other Craigie crucifixions, the details are pared down to such an extent that they symbolically highlight the

---

27 For a discussion of symbol as action within a religious context, see Christopher Irvine, 'The Language of Symbols' in Christopher Irvine (ed.), *The Use of Symbols in Worship* (London: SPCK 2007), pp. 1–18.

release of blood from the pierced side of the figure on the cross, and once more make that a prominent visual feature of the painting. But again, how is this symbol to be understood?

The anthropologist Mary Douglas has argued that the natural symbol of blood is an extremely ambiguous one, and one that is both powerful and dangerous at the same time. When blood seeps from the body, it can both pollute what is deemed to be clean and, paradoxically, increase fertility, vitality and life. It is messy and difficult to contain, and that is why rituals have their social counterpart. For as the skin of the body was seen to contain the blood, so religious rituals were seen to be necessary for the integrity of the social body – they maintained its social structures and set boundaries within and between social and tribal groups.[28] The religious strictures on what a people have to do when they touch blood are set out and codified in the ritual law. What was deemed to be unclean, a danger to the good ordering of creation, was not allowed in the temple, with the exception of blood – and that, as we have seen, was strictly restricted to blood shed in sacrifice.[29] The ritual roots of this understanding of sacrificial blood are found in the complex sacrificial system detailed in Leviticus. According to Mary Douglas's reading of Leviticus, the purpose of offering animal sacrifice, involving the loss of blood, was to maintain the good ordering of creation, to safeguard its sustainability and guarantee its flourishing.[30]

Following the trajectory of this interpretation, we can more confidently assert that the symbol of blood is closely associated with the maintenance of the order of creation, for it alone is seen to give form and vitality to disordered formlessness. The emission of bodily fluids, such as menstrual blood, saliva and semen, is strictly regularized in a variety of religious systems of belief and practice. To lose blood was the gravest danger, for if a living being loses its blood it is at risk of death, and death leads inevitably to the dissolution of form and a return to dust. For a living thing to turn to dust is, of course, a reversion to formlessness. It is as though the highly regulated and prescribed rituals

28 See the classical works of the anthropologist Mary Douglas, *Natural Symbols* (Harmondsworth: Penguin 1973); *Purity and Danger* (London: Routledge & Kegan Paul 1966). The symbolic ambiguity of blood surfaced in the early discussions around the ordination of women. See, for instance, Ali Green, *A Theology of Women's Priesthood* (London: SPCK 2009).
29 See also Douglas, *Purity and Danger*, p. 159.
30 See Douglas, *Leviticus as Literature*, pp. 137, 174.

involving blood confound the inexorable movement of the physical world towards entropy, disintegration and decay. The rush of blood reinvigorates, provides social cohesion and renews creation itself.

Given this complex ritual symbolism of blood, how are we to read the visual images of angels gathering blood from the wounds of Christ, and what significance can be assigned to the blood shed on the cross? First, we could say that the shedding of Christ's blood on the cross is not the draining away of a life but an intentional giving over – one might almost say transfusion – to counter the 'bad blood' of human relationships within a disordered world. Such a reading was not lost on the early Christian writer, the author of the epistle to the Hebrews. This writer deliberately set out to rewrite the Hebrew religious heritage in the light of his understanding of who Jesus was and of what had been achieved through his life, death and vindication by God.

According to the Old Testament, humankind is held accountable for every drop of blood spilled on the earth, whether by accident or act of violence. The life is in the blood (Leviticus 17.11), and in the first biblical incidence of murder, of Abel by his brother Cain, God tells Cain that his brother's blood is crying out from the ground (Genesis 4.10). This reference was taken up by the writer of the epistle to the Hebrews, and used to set up a contrast between the blood of Abel (crying out for vengeance) and the sprinkled blood of Christ that 'speaks a better word than the blood of Abel' (Hebrews 12.24), namely the word of divine forgiveness. In Hebrews too there is an explicit linking of the blood of Christ shed on the cross, back to the blood covenant ritual performed by Moses and the yearly atonement ritual – Yom Kippur – of the high priest in the Holy of Holies (Hebrews 9.18–22). The passage concludes with the assertion that 'without the shedding of blood there is no forgiveness of sins' (Hebrews 9.22).

The themes of the shedding of Christ's blood and forgiveness are conflated in Matthew's account of the words spoken by Jesus over the cup at the last supper: 'Then he took a cup, and after giving thanks he gave it to them, saying, "Drink from it all of you; for this is my blood of the covenant, which is poured out for many for the forgiveness of sins"' (Matthew 26.27–28). The word 'covenant' in this sentence is theologically loaded, evoking the account of the sealing of the old covenant with the sprinkling of blood on the people of Israel (Exodus 24.6–8), as well as resonating with the foundational Passover story in Exodus that tells how the people of God marked the lintels of their homes with the blood of the sacrificed Passover lambs. Of the four accounts of the so-called institution narrative in the New Testament (that is, Matthew, Mark, Luke and Paul in 1 Corinthians 11), Matthew alone identifies the fruit of the vine with Christ's blood shed for the forgiveness of sins. And it is interesting to note that this single mention of forgiveness as a specific benefit of Christ's suffering and death in Matthew's Gospel was appropriated and written into the major Eucharistic Prayers and anaphoral traditions of the Christian Church, both East and West.[31]

The words spoken by the celebrant over the cup in the Roman Canon are closely associated with the *mysterium fidei*, the mystery of faith in the *Qui pridie*, or conflated institution narrative that structurally forms the hinge of the prayer: 'this is the cup of my blood of the new and eternal covenant, the mystery of faith, which will be shed for you and for many for the forgiveness of sins.' The close conjunction of 'blood' and 'mystery' probably accounts, at least in part, for the reserving of the eucharistic chalice to the priest in the celebration of the Mass in the Western Church. The eucharistic offering, using the figures or elements of bread and wine, was again universally described in early fourth-century euchological sources as an 'unbloody sacrifice',[32] and its effect was understood in terms of making peace between God and humanity and restoring harmony between heaven and earth. The question of how this occurred, and how the relationship between the historic sacrifice of Christ and the sacramental sacrifice was conceived, became the most contentious issue in the theological controversies of the fifteenth and sixteenth centuries.

The logical relationship between the language of the atonement and the Mass was taken by the Reformers as given, and so it was natural to see the benefits of Communion as flowing from the cross of Jesus. The cross was central to the theology of the German reformer Martin Luther (1483–1546), and his whole account of salvation was constructed upon

---

31 For the texts of the Roman Canon, the Gallican Liturgy, the Liturgies of Basil and St John Chrysostom, the Liturgy of St Mark, and the Liturgy of St James, see R. C. D. Jasper and G. J. Cuming, *Prayers of the Eucharist: Early and Reformed* (Oxford: Oxford University Press, 1980, revised edn).

32 For a positive assessment and account of the origins of this expression, see Kenneth Stevenson, '"The Unbloody Sacrifice": The Origins and Development of a Description of the Eucharist' in Gerard Austen OP (ed.), *Fountain of Life* (Washington, DC: Pastoral Press 1991), pp. 103–30.

a *theologia crucis*, a theology of the cross. The cross, he claimed, was God's hiding place, and there Christ secured our salvation. The cross to which Luther points from his pulpit in the famous Wittenberg altarpiece functions more as a depiction of the content of Luther's proclamation of the cross than as a visual depiction of a material object. For, although the cross was proclaimed in the present, the event itself belonged to the past, and because of this, Luther came to the conclusion that the Mass had to be distanced and distinguished from the sacrifice.

But what was it that eventually led Luther to rethink his understanding of the Mass? He first took up the pen on this subject in response to the publication of a treatise by an Italian Dominican who had set out to justify the practice of receiving Communion in one kind and of reserving the chalice to the priest.[33] In his riposte Luther insisted that all Christians should be invited to receive the chalice. Although this conviction was driven in part by a reconsideration of the nature of priesthood, it was firmly grounded in his reading of the Last Supper, which was to become the main narrative frame through which he understood the nature of the Eucharist. This was presaged in his two Catechisms, a shorter form for the laity and a longer for the clergy, in which he asserted that the Last Supper constituted the pattern and the meaning of the Mass.

At first Luther was conservative in his liturgical reform of the Mass, but as time and controversies flared with Catholics on the one side and Anabaptists on the other, he became increasingly convinced that the more distant the liturgy becomes from the pattern of the Last Supper, the more distorted becomes the view of the Mass. For Luther, the words of institution were a condensed summary of the meaning of the Eucharist, and it was the words of Christ in this narrative – 'this is my body', 'this is my blood' – that consecrated the elements and not any power conveyed to the priest at ordination. These words were regarded as being performative – 'doing words' that activated the divine promise, the promise that Christ would be present with his faithful people and confer upon them his gift of forgiveness, life and salvation.[34] This was Christ's testament, his will, guaranteed by his death on the cross of Calvary.

---

33 Bernard Lohse, *Martin Luther's Theology: Its Historical and Systematic Development*, trans. and ed. Roy A. Harrisville (Minneapolis, MN: Fortress Press 1999), p. 134.
34 Luther set out these benefits of Communion, guaranteed by the very death of Christ, in his *Small Catechism*.

From his reading of the Last Supper narratives in the Synoptic Gospels and St Paul's account of the tradition of the Lord's Supper in 1 Corinthians 11, Luther understood that Christ offered the chalice to all (*omnes*) as he did with the broken bread. And it was on this basis that Luther launched his full reforming agenda in the publication of *The Babylonish Captivity of the Church* (1520). Here he carefully set out a case to support his earlier recommendation that the cup should be restored to the laity. To withhold the chalice from Christian people would be to deny Christ's gifts to those whom he had called his own.[35] And so Communion in both kinds became the accepted practice in the diverse family of what may be called Lutheran liturgies.[36]

In England, Thomas Cranmer followed Luther's lead. His intention of restoring the cup was made clear in his *Order of Communion* of 1548, which made provision for the giving of the chalice to the laity, 'giving everyone to drink once and no more', with the accompanying words of administration: 'the blood of our Lord Jesus Christ, which was shed for thee, preserve thy soul unto everlasting life'.[37] In these words the 'sacrament of the blood' is designated as being 'life-giving'. The chalice

---

35 See *Luther's Works*, vol. 2, 742, 24–31, for the sermon in which he calls for the restoration of the Chalice, and vol. 36 for his scholarly attack on the Church's captivity of the chalice.

36 For specific examples, see Lee Palmer Wandel, *The Eucharist in the Reformation: Incarnation and Liturgy* (Cambridge: Cambridge University Press 2006), pp. 117ff.

37 H. A. Wilson (ed.), *The Order of the Communion, 1548* (London: Henry Bradshaw Society 1907). It is instructive to trace the development of the words spoken at the giving of the Cup at the Communion in Anglican rites. The Order in the 1559 Book of Common Prayer combined the words of 1552 and 1549, and this was carried through into the 1662 Order: 'The blood of our Lord Jesus Christ, which was shed for thee, preserve thy body and soul unto everlasting life. Drink this in remembrance that Christ's Blood was shed for thee, and be thankful.' Following a series of revisions, the words of administration in *The Alternative Service Book* of 1980 was radically simplified to 'The Blood of Christ', whereas Order One allows some variation within the rubric of 'authorised words', including 'The Blood of Christ, shed for you' and the fifth and final option omitting any reference to blood, 'The cup of life in Christ Jesus'. Meanwhile, the words 'The Blood of Christ, the cup of salvation' appeared in *The Book of Common Prayer* (1977) of the Episcopal Church of the United States of America. The Anglican Church of Australia, in its Third Order for Holy Communion (1995), simply has: 'The Blood of Christ keep you in eternal life.' An objection to the reference to blood in the words of administration was forcefully raised by John Fenton, entitled 'Eating People', in which he thoughtfully asked how the words may be heard, received and responded to by the contemporary communicant. See *Theology*, vol. 94, no. 762, November/December 1991, p. 414.

was the life-giving 'sacrament of blood', and as such, what was held out to the communicant as the cup conveying sacrifice (see Mark 10.38b and 14.36) was received as 'the cup of salvation' (Psalm 116.13). In the short-lived English Prayer Book of 1552, Cranmer undoubtedly worked with a weak sense of anamnesis as memorial, but in continuity with later medieval piety, the focus remained on the Passion and death of Christ. Cranmer's radical achievement was in restoring Communion to the laity with a clear understanding that what was received here and now in the cup of Communion flowed from what happened there and then on Calvary. Apart from the stated logical connection between there and then and here and now, the anamnesis was reduced to little more than a mental act on the part of the communicant, of recalling the death and Passion of Christ in the act of eating the bread and drinking the cup.[38]

However, Cranmer's view of anamnesis need not be taken as being definitive for an Anglican understanding of sacramental celebration, at least in relation to the development of Anglican theological reflection. Indeed, it could be argued that Anglicanism itself was not forged until the reign of Elizabeth I, and that it was classically formulated by the theologian Richard Hooker. Hooker, in turn, had been influenced by Bishop John Jewel, who in 1562 was the first to write an apology or defining account of the English Church. Although this was a polemically charged anti-Tridentine piece, Jewel's aim was to demonstrate that the English Church was grounded in Scripture and the teachings of the church catholic. A more focused account of Jewel's understanding of the sacraments is to be found in a posthumous work, *Treatise on the Sacraments* (1583), that was compiled from sermons he had preached in Salisbury Cathedral.[39] Here a more dynamic understanding of anamnesis surfaces as Jewel attempts to articulate how the effects of the cross are effectively played out in the celebration of the Eucharist. Interestingly, he speaks of this in terms borrowed from Matthew's

---

38 For further discussion, see Colin O. Buchanan, *An Evangelical Among the Anglican Liturgists*, Alcuin Club Collections 84 (London: SPCK 2009), ch. 5, 'What did Cranmer think he was doing?', pp. 71–113; Peter Atkins, *Memory and Liturgy: The Place of Memory in the Composition and Practice of Liturgy* (Aldershot: Ashgate 2004).

39 See Geoffrey Rowell, Kenneth Stevenson and Rowan Williams (compilers), *Love's Redeeming Work: The Anglican Quest for Holiness* (Oxford: Oxford University Press 2003), p. 69.

dramatic account of Christ's death on the cross (Matthew 27.51–53). This narrative speaks of the cosmic effect of Christ's death as an unlocking of the creative power of resurrection, the breaking open of the tombs of the dead. It is this same resurrection power of the cross that Jewel suggests is present and at work in the celebration of the Eucharist: 'In this supper lieth a hidden mystery,' he writes. 'There may we see the shame of the cross, the darkness over the world, the earth to quake, the stones to cleave asunder, the graves to open, and the dead to rise. These things may we see in the supper: this is the meaning of these holy mysteries.'[40]

Wherever readers may place themselves on the scale of an understanding of anamnesis and sacramental presence, we can return to our suggestion of a transposition from the cup of suffering to the cup of salvation for a more adequate appreciation of the historic view of anamnesis.[41] My contention is that such a view presupposes a more dynamic appreciation of the liturgical rite as the unfolding in time and space of the mystery of Christ's saving work, and one that finds its ultimate and unifying reference in the symbol of the blood of Christ. For in the Eucharist, what becomes the 'unbloody sacrifice' is the setting forth, or the application in time and space, whenever and wherever the Eucharist is celebrated, of that single and bloody sacrifice of Jesus on the cross, offered 'once and for all' (Hebrews 7.27b, 9.26). The anaphoral language of 'setting forth' echoes the Pauline language of Christ's crucifixion that speaks of 'the putting forward' of Christ as 'a sacrifice by his blood' (Romans 3.25; see also Ephesians 2.13–14a and Colossians 1.20) and therefore places the 'unbloody sacrifice' of the Eucharist in a relationship of logical dependence upon that blood that was shed upon the cross of Calvary.

---

40 John Jewel, 'A Treatise of the Sacraments' in J. Ayre (ed.), *Works of Bishop Jewel* (Cambridge: Parker Society 1845), p. 1123.

41 In the following pages I am using the term *anamnesis* in its more general sense as a core characteristic of liturgical celebration, rather than specifically referring to that element of the Eucharistic Prayer conventionally known as 'the anamnesis', which follows the so-called Institution narrative and specifically mentions the suffering, death, resurrection and Ascension of Christ. The more general sense is rooted in some of the Psalms, such as Psalm 136, and the Old Testament memorial sacrifices, such as the Passover. Regarding the eucharistic anamnesis, the ecumenical consensus in the ARCIC and the World Council of Churches documents was cast in terms of past events being effective in the present, but more recent reflection has tended to see the anamnesis as the articulation of the whole Christ, incarnate, crucified and glorified being present in the celebration.

At this juncture we may return to the artwork in crucifixion altar-pieces and reiterate the point that even in artistic depictions of the cru-cifixion the intended and perceived meaning of the painting is closely related to its setting, to the site in which it is displayed and to the context of the story that is repeatedly acted out when Christians gather in a church building to remember the very source of their Christian life in the celebration of the Eucharist. For as I have attempted to illus-trate, the crucifixion altarpiece intentionally carried a freight of sym-bolic meanings, associations and intimations of the benefits of Christ's Passion, of what is understood to be effected by that single, historical sacrifice on the cross during the reign of Pontius Pilate. But how is the historical distance between the past event of Christ's crucifixion and the present circumstances of the viewer as worshipper to be bridged? In seeking an answer to this question we can come to see a happy conflu-ence in both art and liturgical theology around the respective key areas of perception and anamnesis, or 'making present'.

In artistic terms we could reflect on Velazquez's exquisite painting, *Kitchen Scene with Christ in the House of Mary and Martha* (1618), which can be seen in the National Gallery. Taking up the whole left side of the visual field of the painting is a contemporary interior scene in which an old woman prods a young frowning kitchen maid engaged in a culinary chore. Above the table at which the maid works, close to tears, is a square depiction of the scene of Christ with Mary and Martha (see Luke 10.38–42). The perceptual puzzle is whether this depiction of the Lucan story is a painting hung on the wall – as a pictorial juxtaposi-tion of scenes – or a serving hatch opening into a further room in which Christ is actually present, thereby relating the two frames and enabling the reading of one pictorial space in terms of the other.[42] The painting, in other words, can be seen in two ways. But perhaps there is a third and more sacramental way we may see its parallel composition, namely as a kind of double picture – a frame within a frame – of a historical within a contemporary scene. What I am suggesting is that the artist may delib-erately be using a pictorial device whereby the viewer is presented with two events – the old woman chiding the kitchen maid; Jesus addressing

---

42 See John Drury, *Painting the Word: Christian Pictures and their Meaning* (New Haven, CT and London: Yale University Press 1999), pp. 156–60, for a reading of the painting in terms of words exchanged and a vocation to attend to the Word being resisted.

Martha – as though they were both occurring simultaneously. Seeing the painting as representing the two scenes within a single timeframe may explain the use of the preposition 'with' in what may at first reading seem a rather cumbersome title for Velazquez's painting, a kitchen scene *with* Christ. This way of seeing the painting as a visual presentation of a past encounter occurring in the time of the contemporary kitchen scene brings us close to a stronger sense of presence, and of liturgical anamnesis as the dynamic pressing of the past into the present.

A sufficient and strong sense of anamnesis will also include the aspect of the future impinging on the present,[43] and is rooted in the Hebrew remembering of YHWH's past saving events, like the Passover, in the present. But even here there is a dynamic sense of remembering, a sense that is best conceived as the effective carrying forward of a past action. This is recalled when God is said to 'remember' or act graciously towards his people. Looking at altarpieces in churches and paintings of the Last Supper in the refectories of monastic communities, one is frequently struck by the way artists placed contemporary or exemplary figures back into the frame of the past event. This painting into the past of the present recalls how Jews celebrating the Seder meal at the Passover feast are urged to imagine that they themselves were present at the time of the first Passover in Egypt.[44] We have seen a pictorial example of what we may call a backward projection in the inclusion of the figure of Jerome in Raphael's Mond Crucifixion. In an obvious sense this is plainly anachronistic. Jerome was not born until some 300 years after the event. But art and its meaning are not constrained by such literal historicism, and it is therefore an apt vehicle for conveying that the outcome of a past event, such as Christ's crucifixion, is not locked in time past but is available for all people and in every place in which God's forgiveness is proclaimed and celebrated. The picture works, in other words, as a visual form of anamnesis, combining the three dimensions of time – past, present and future – within the single surface of the painted board or canvas. For as within the arena of the liturgical celebration, time itself is condensed within a single frame, and

---

43 For an account of the future aspect of remembering, see Louis Weil, '"Remembering the Future": Reflections on Liturgy and Ecclesiology' in Christopher Irvine (ed.), *Anglican Liturgical Identity*, Joint Liturgical Studies 65 (Norwich: Canterbury Press 2008).
44 The Mishnah directed that in each generation a man should look on himself as if he had been liberated from Egypt.

the past presses itself upon the present in a way that simultaneously opens up for the worshipper the possibility of God's future. The liturgical act of anamnesis, the commemoration of time past in the rehearsal of saving history, and the orientation of worship to the dawning of a new light upon the world, is analogous to the way in which some paintings function in inviting viewers to enter and place themselves in a new landscape – a world, that is, of new possibilities, forms and expressions of life. As in liturgy, so it is often the case in art that what we are shown is the transposition of time and place, and that what happened then is shown now, and what happened there occurs here.

The analogy between the anamnetic aspect of liturgical celebration and art cannot be pressed too far. Nevertheless, it is possible to recognize some congruence between the visual experience of an altarpiece in which the frame holds together a past event (the crucifixion) and a contemporary element (such as the figure of the patron) and the liturgical dynamic of the past being made present. In this sense it is possible to speak of the saving work of Christ being ritually made present, and for that sacramental making present to be presented visually within the frame of an altarpiece.

The memorial or anamnetic aspect of the liturgy has its visual counterpart in a great many artworks commissioned for churches and convents, and the work of one particular mid-fifteenth-century artist, Guido di Pietro, the Dominican priest-painter Fra Giovanni who came to be known as Fra Angelico, is a particular example that repays attention.[45] Fra Angelico (*c.* 1400–55), the most popular artist of the Dominican Order of contemplative preachers, was commissioned by Cosimo de' Medici to paint the frescoes and a magnificent altarpiece for the newly restored and enlarged convent and church that was to be the new home of the reformed Observant branch of the Order of Dominicans at San Marco in Florence. The building had formerly been the convent of the

---

45 According to Giorgio Vasari's biography, Fra Angelico gained the reputation of being an artist whose very life was grounded in Christ, and the claim that 'to paint the things of Christ, one must live with Christ' is attributed to him by Vasari in *The Lives of the Artists*, trans. Julia Conaway Bondanella and Peter Bondanella (Oxford: Oxford University Press 1991). Whether or not this is a historically reliable report, there are good grounds for asserting that Fra Angelico's art is essentially *participatory*; for as the artist expressed his engagement in the spiritual realities of his subject through light, colour and form, so the original intended viewer was not a detached spectator but a person who was called to engage with the invisible reality made visible in the artwork.

Silvestrine monks (a reformed branch of the Benedictine Order), and when the reformed group of Dominicans took possession of the house and church in February 1436, it was in a fairly ruinous state and in need of considerable rebuilding.

If the record of Giorgio Vasari in *The Lives of the Artists* is to be believed, Fra Angelico was associated with the reformed or Observant Order of Preachers when they lived in Foligno. A recent monograph catalogue of the artist's work revises Vasari's chronology on documentary grounds, and concludes that Fra Angelico, who had established himself as a painter in Florence, entered the reformed Dominican Order between 1419 and 1422.[46] And at some time between 1438 and 1443, he and the assistants working under his direction[47] painted frescoes on the walls of the corporate, shared spaces, such as the chapter house, refectory and cloisters, as well as a fresco for each individual cell in the so-called dormitory at San Marco. The work, it seems, progressed in stages. A crucifixion fresco, incorporating the figure of St Dominic at prayer, was also painted in each corridor, providing what has been described as a spiritual topography of the whole convent complex.[48] The intention of painting a single fresco in each brother's cell, some 44 in total, was to provide a visual focus for sustained individual contemplative meditation.

The placing of these artworks was critical for the vocation of the Dominicans, who as the Order of Preachers lived a mixed life of contemplation and action. They were encouraged to picture in their minds the saving mystery of Christ, which they were called to proclaim in their active roles as preachers and teachers. Although the placing of an individual fresco as a kind of 'spiritual window' in each brother's cell was innovative, it fitted the established meditative technique of focusing one's attention upon a single figure or scene – such as the Annunciation or the cross – in order to interiorize the plot of the Christian story of salvation. The artwork undoubtedly enabled a more sustained reflection

---

46 Laurence Kanter and Pia Palladino, *Fra Angelico* (New York: Metropolitan Museum of Art 2005).

47 It is thought that Zanobi Strozzi, noted for his illustrations in liturgical books, and Benozzo Gozzoli, were among Angelico's assistants. See Kanter and Palladino, *Fra Angelico*, pp. 177–83.

48 See William Hood, 'Fra Angelico and the Liturgy of Cloistered Life' in Timothy Verdon and John Henderson (eds), *Christianity and the Renaissance: Image and Religious Imagination in the Quattrocento* (New York: Syracuse University Press 1990).

on a single image, and functioned as a visual cue for the individual friar to recall the whole narrative of salvation in his mind, memory and imagination.[49] Each fresco painting provided a pictorial image for rational reflection, inviting the viewer to deepen his appreciation of the significance of the single figure or scene depicted in the painting and, further, to live with these images as icons of divine presence.[50] Alongside the exemplary figures of Dominican saints, the figure of Mary frequently figures in Angelico's art – she typifies that attentive reception of the Word that the Dominican friar was called to bring to expression in his preaching and life.

The paintings themselves are bathed in a gentle light and the colour tones are characteristically warm. In each fresco the expressive figures draw the eye and dominate the visual field. They were often shown within an architectural space, but with little other background detail or decorative ornamentation. The exception is that in two prominently placed pictures, space is given to natural forms. Such naturalism is found in Angelico's earlier altarpiece of the Annunciation painted for the church of San Domenico in Fiesole around 1425. Here, to the right of the angel addressing Mary within the architectural frame of a portico, is a lush, verdant garden from which two disconsolate grey figures, Adam and Eve, are being expelled by an angel.

At San Marco there are two further examples of Angelico's naturalism. The first is the fresco of the Annunciation painted in the north corridor of the convent, which again includes a lush garden. The second is the resurrection fresco, *Noli me Tangere*, in which the risen Christ reveals himself to Mary Magdalene in what is shown to be a green and blooming garden.

---

49 Sources for this teaching are cited by Richard Viladesau, *The Triumph of the Cross: The Passion of Christ in Theology and the Arts, from the Renaissance to the Counter-Reformation* (Oxford: Oxford University Press 2008), pp. 51–2.

50 In Gerard de Frachet's history of the first Dominicans, written in the 1260s, he refers to Dominican friars looking on images and in doing so, of being held in the loving gaze of God through the pictorial image. He wrote: 'In their cells they had before their eyes images of the Virgin and of her crucified Son so that while reading, praying and sleeping, they could look upon them and be looked upon by them with the eyes of compassion.' Cited by Hans Belting, *The Image and its Public in the Middle Ages: Form and Function of Early Paintings of the Passion*, trans. Mark Bartusis and Raymond Meyer (New Rochelle, NY: Aristide D. Caratzas 1990), p. 57, quoted in Gabriele Finaldi, *The Image of Christ* (London: National Gallery 2000), pp. 106–7.

To complete the story, mention should be made of Angelico's final work at San Marco, a single-panelled altarpiece commissioned by the Medici family for the rebuilt choir and apse of the conventual church. The enlarged and newly decorated church was consecrated on the feast of the Epiphany, 6 January 1443, just following the Council of Florence, which had brought together leaders of the Eastern and Western Church and secured a precarious peace between Constantinople and Rome.

This monumental altarpiece of the Virgin and Child, enthroned and attended by angels and saints, is described as one of Angelico's most poetic creations[51] and has long drawn the attention of art historians as representing a decisive development from the Gothic polyptych or multi-panelled arrangement that was set behind the altar. But what is significant for our line of enquiry is the original central panel of the predella (the horizontal structure immediately below the altarpiece), now to be seen in the Alte Pinakothek in Munich. The painting, *The Entombment of Christ*, shows the final episode of the story of the Passion. But again, Angelico is not simply a narrative painter here, because both the choice of subject and its composition would suggest a direct link with what was ritually enacted at the altar: the celebration of the Mass. The painted figure of Christ was directly level with the eyes of the celebrant offering the Mass at the altar, and at the taking of the host into his hands, the eucharistic bread would have been at the exact same level as the painted figure of Christ's body held before the tomb. So what came to be made present through the words 'this is my body' and was ritually presented to the Father, was visibly shown in the artwork. The correspondences between the composition and rendering of this painted panel and the ritual actions are even more pronounced when we look further at the details.

In this composite scene of the placing of the dead Jesus in the tomb, Jesus is not a horizontal dead cadaver but is held upright by Joseph of Arimathea. The vertical positioning of the body may well be read as a prefiguring of the resurrection. Further, the figures of Mary and John painted on either side of Christ tenderly lean forward to take his hands in theirs, and this gesture may well be seen to mimic the ritual actual of the priest: first, in taking the host into his hands at the words of the

---

51 Kanter and Palladino, *Fra Angelico*, p. 192.

Canon: '*Qui pridie quam pateretur accepit panem in sanctas ac uenerabi-
les manus*' ('Who, on the day before he suffered, took bread in his holy
and venerable hands'), which corresponded to the action of Jesus at the
Last Supper when he took bread; and then, at the elevation of the host
after the rehearsal of dominical words.

But there is yet another feature in this painted panel of the predella
that is a key and vital element in the trajectory of this exploration. For
here again we see a mixed carpet of delicate flowers in the foreground of
the painting of the entombment, an intimation of resurrection and of
God's ultimate purpose to renew creation.

These examples of naturalism in Fra Angelico's painting are in
marked contrast to the crucifixion frescoes at San Marco, where the
cross is invariably painted set in bare, dry ground. Further, they always
include a Dominican figure at prayer. In these instances it would be
reasonable to infer that the original intention was to elicit a devotional
response on the part of the original viewers, the contemplative Dominican friars. But what precisely were the friars being asked to respond to
in these bare images of the crucifixion? They certainly depict the stark
and bloody reality of the cross, but how would the heart and mind
be engaged in contemplating such an image lead? Such contemplation
undoubtedly involved an affective element, of the viewer coming to
feel, for instance, the dereliction that Mary experienced as she stood by
the cross. But contemplation also demanded a sustained sticking with
the image and a resolve to follow the questions the image presented.
The consideration of these questions may well have gone beyond asking
how it actually was to asking why and to what end and purpose Christ
suffered and died. This latter question returns us to my earlier remark
about the stark contrast between Fra Angelico's crucifixion frescoes and
paintings such as the *Entombment*. This contrast leads us, as the process
of close consideration led the contemplative friar, to see that the point
of this bloody sacrifice on the cross was not only to effect humanity's
reconciliation with God but to change the blasted and bare earth so that
it may blossom and be green.

Looking at Fra Angelico's work as a whole, the impression given is
that we can see salvation rendered in colour and naturalistic form. As
we have shown, a vision of salvation as the renewal of creation and the
burgeoning of nature is first intimated in his frescoes of the Annunciation and the Resurrection. It appears in the painting of the entombment, but it finds its fullest and most lyrical expression in his large

painted panel of the *Last Judgement*, originally painted for the church of Santa Maria degli Angeli but now to be seen in the Pilgrims' Hall at San Marco. This painting, begun by Lorenzo Monoco and completed by Fra Angelico after his death in 1423, has an ingenious lateral composition showing the graceful figures of the elect being drawn by the angels on the viewer's left side of the painting into a circular dance on a grassy plateau where flowers of every hue are in bloom. So here, God's final purpose for his creation is enchantingly shown to be the restoration of paradise.

But the reader may object that the kind of reading I am proposing here rather overlooks or, worse, softens the stark reality of the death of Christ on the cross. Further, it could plausibly be argued that the kind of realism that artists in the high Renaissance aspired to achieve in their painting is precisely what is required in treating such a 'serious subject' as the crucifixion. And yet a painting that aimed to portray solely in anatomical and bloody detail 'what it was like' would be too restrictive a view, and would effectively truncate the full narrative of Christian salvation. There are moments when the Christian should reflect on the figure of Christ disfigured by the agonizing pain on the cross of Calvary, but as I have attempted to chart here, there are a range of hints and intimations in both liturgy and sacred art that take us beyond the question of what it was like, to a glimpse of something of its outcome and what it was for. After all, this is the perspective of the New Testament witness, as well as being the anamnetic supposition of all doxology and liturgical celebration.

The seeing, rehearsing and ritual enacting of the full story of salvation that I am alluding to here is again illustrated in the composition of the Isenheim altarpiece. Here the horrific portrayal of the Cross in the crucifixion panel is most certainly realistic. And yet it is, as we have seen, integral to a whole series of related painted panels, and so should not be read in isolation from the images of the other paintings of this multi-panelled altarpiece, including the resurrection. The iconography of the cross in the visual field of its liturgical setting is invariably more nuanced, and takes us beyond the visual representation of God's solidarity with human pain and suffering to the whole saving mystery of God, in Christ and through the Spirit.

As a final reflection on this point, we may consider a painting that many would reckon to be as realistic a portrayal of the sacrifice of Christ on the cross as one could imagine. This is a canvas painting, *Crucifixion with Mary Magdalene,* now in the Uffizi Gallery in Florence, attributed to the artist Luca Signorelli (*c.* 1441–1523) from Cortona. In *The Lives of the Artists,* Vasari described Signorelli as an excellent painter and one whose rendering of the human body made the figure look as though it were alive.[52] His *Crucifixion* is an unusual and remarkable painting in a number of ways. Canvas altarpieces were rare in central Italy at this time, and for this reason some art historians have suggested that it was originally painted as a processional banner. Current scholarly opinion, however, argues that the weight of evidence suggests that the canvas was intended and painted as an altarpiece.[53]

The composition of this picture is perfectly symmetrical, with two imposing rockscapes on either side of the cross. On the right-hand side, Signorelli has painted the scene of the deposition, of the figure of Christ being taken down from the cross, and below this, along a winding road, the body of Christ is being carried to the place of burial on the left-hand side of the picture. Here a small painted figure, possibly of St Peter, holds an urn containing the bitter ointment for burial. Perched on the top of this dramatic outcrop, Signorelli has painted a series of buildings possibly representing the now ruined Temple and the Holy Rotunda. In the centre of the painting, and dominating the pictorial space, is the cross, and its vertical bar runs almost the whole length of the canvas.

So in terms of the composition of this dramatic painting, what is presented here is a kind of triple exposure, the rendering of the three temporally distinct scenes of the Passion, the cross, the death and the burial all combined in a single visual field. Unusually, there is just one figure beside the cross, Mary Magdalene, and not the usual group scene including Mary the Lord's mother and the beloved disciple John. The artist deliberately brings the two figures of Mary Magdalene and the crucified Christ into close focus and visibility. In this respect, the canvas is reminiscent of the meditative frescoes of Fra Angelica in San Marco. The reason why the figure of Mary Magdalene is so prominent in this painting may well be found in the circumstances of its commission. In a recent monograph, the art historian Tom Henry has argued that

---

52 Vasari, *The Lives of the Artists,* p. 268.
53 See the complete catalogue compiled by Tom Henry in Laurence B. Kanter, *Luca Signorelli: The Complete Paintings* (London: Thames & Hudson 2002), p. 175.

this Signorelli altarpiece was probably commissioned in the late 1490s for the chapel of the Dominican convent of St Stephen and Vincent Ferrer in Florence. This convent had been founded by Annalena Malatesta, and she apparently shared the popular fifteenth-century Florentine devotion to Mary Magdalene,[54] traditionally the saint of penitents and often painted in the group of figures around the cross.[55] But perhaps we might also recall in looking at this particular painting that it was this Mary who was first met by the risen Christ in the garden at the dawn of the first Easter morning.

In Signorelli's painting, Mary Magdalene looks intently at the crucified figure of Christ as she reaches up to hold the cross with her left hand and extends her right arm and hand as if beckoning the viewer not simply to see but to behold and to ponder the composed and muscular figure of Christ crucified on the wood of the cross. At the foot of the cross is the signature human skull, indicating that the place where Christ was crucified was Golgotha, 'the place of the skull' (John 19.17), which in later literary elaboration was identified as the site of Adam's burial, the darkest domain of death.

A clue as to how we might read this composite painting of the Passion is in the figure of the Magdalene. The body language speaks volumes, but it is Mary's face, shown in profile, that is most telling. It is not the face of a person who is distraught with grief or overcome by a sense of sorrow for past sin, rather, as the high brow indicates, the face of a person who thinks and considers things deeply. Bending on one knee beside the cross, Mary Magdalene focuses her full attention on the body of the crucified, and the tilted angle of her arms invites the viewer likewise to focus on the cross that she resolutely holds with the hand of her raised left arm as it comes to yield its hidden meaning.

The figure of Mary Magdalene in this painting is neither that of a person distressed at what she sees nor one diminished by her own pain and loss. On the contrary, she appears as a robust person, one determined to stay with the cross, to hold on to it until its meaning, its mystery, are revealed to her and to the invited viewer who stands before

---

54 Tom Henry, *The Life and Art of Luca Signorelli* (New Haven, CT and London: Yale University Press 2012), pp. 147–50.
55 For an extensive discussion of the composite figure of Mary Magdalene in Christian art and literature, see David Brown, *Discipleship and Imagination: Christian Tradition and Truth* (Oxford and New York: Oxford University Press 2000), esp. pp. 43–56.

the painting. Indeed, the expressive rendering of Mary's face suggests that she is indeed struck by the enormity of the event, contemplating the image of Christ's crucified body with such intensity as she puzzles over the enigma of what the outcome of such a sacrifice could possibly be. Of course, both the artist and those who viewed this altarpiece in its original setting knew well that there was an outcome of this sacrifice of Christ, and they believed that its benefits were conveyed sacramentally in the Mass. But there is a wider outcome beyond the rite, and an intimation of what this might be is provided by Signorelli in a particular element in the foreground of this painting that, I believe, cannot be regarded as mere decorative ornamentation. The striking element I refer to is a circle of delicate spring flowers, including violas, forget-me-nots, buttercups, wood sorrel and strawberries, painted around the base of the cross.[56] I would contend that this feature is not decorative but is intentionally symbolic, and evokes a sense of the image of the cross as a kind of planting, a certain sign of the burgeoning of life, like the flowering of the crocus in the barren desert.

In the Christian imagination the cross was often regarded as the counterpoint of the Incarnation, and we can adduce evidence for this view from both liturgical and artistic sources. From the liturgical perspective, we may reflect on the shaping of the Christian calendar, particularly the early Western tradition possibly dating back to third-century Rome, which calculated that the day in the year – 14 Nisan – when Jesus was crucified fell on 25 March. In the Julian calendar this was the day when the angel appeared to Mary and announced that she would bear a son.[57] The coincidence of the dates of the Passion and the Annunciation provided a richly suggestive theological theme for some early Christian writers. It came to be articulated in some of the liturgical texts composed for the celebration of the feast of the Annunciation of the Lord, in Rome,[58] and was shown in later monumental Christian

---

56 In Renaissance paintings these flowers symbolized a remembrance of sorrow, death and paradisal joy. See Mirella Levi D'Ancona, *The Garden of the Renaissance: Botanical Symbolism in Italian Painting* (Florence: Leo S. Olschki 1977).

57 See Susan K. Roll, *Towards the Origin of Christmas* (Kampen: Kok Pharos 1995), pp. 73, 80.

58 For a discussion of the Roman and North African sources that correlate the date of the Annunciation of the Lord to the last day of Christ's earthly life, see Thomas J. Talley, *The Origins of the Liturgical Year* (New York: Pueblo 1986), pp. 91–9.

art, such as the late seventh- or early eighth-century Ruthwell Cross, with its prominent relief sculpture of the Annunciation. It has been suggested that the positioning of this Annunciation relief directly above the crucifixion scene on the south side of the Cross was an intentional artistic articulation of the tradition of the coincidence of the Annunciation and the crucifixion.[59]

Although the exact origins of this feast are unknown,[60] it is likely that the Annunciation to Mary was celebrated as a separate feast in the mid sixth century, and was established in Rome by the Eastern Pope, Pope Sergius I (687–701). In Rome the Mass of the Annunciation of the Lord was peculiar to the Papal liturgy, and its opening collect, *Gratiam tuam*, though focusing on the Incarnation, economically compressed together the Incarnation, crucifixion and resurrection, and thereby articulated the whole saving mystery: 'as the incarnation was made known by the message of an angel, so by his Passion and Cross we may be brought to the glory of the resurrection.' Here was a stroke of sheer theological brilliance that presented new life in the Cross of the incarnate Son. Apart from being celebrated as a separate feast, the Annunciation was also marked in the season of Advent, as indeed it continues to be in the West. Passages in the book of the prophet Isaiah that speak of the promise of divine redemption being presaged by the appearing of spring flowers in bloom in the arid desert, and of new growth from the stump of Jesse, were appropriated into the cycle of readings and chants for the Advent season. The readings of the Roman Vigil Mass for Advent IV, effectively a summation of the major Advent themes, focused on the Annunciation and included a reading of Isaiah 35.1–2, the appearing of the crocus in the desert, and Isaiah 45.8,[61] the sprouting of salvation from the opened earth. In the multi-layered themes of the season of Advent and the feast of the Annunciation of the Lord, Christ's coming

59 Éamonn Ó Carragáin demonstrates how the iconography of the Ruthwell Cross faithfully represents the themes of the feast of the Annunciation of the Lord as it developed after 650 at St Peter's in Rome. See his *Ritual and the Rood: Liturgical Images and the Old English Poems of the Dream of the Rood Tradition* (London: British Library and University of Toronto Press 2005), pp. 83–106.

60 See Paul F. Bradshaw and Maxwell E. Johnson, *The Origins of Feasts, Fasts and Seasons in Early Christianity* (London: SPCK 2011), pp. 159, 210.

61 See Martin Dudley, '*Vox clara*: The Liturgical Voice in Advent and Christmas' in Martin Dudley (ed.), *Like a Two-Edged Sword: The Word of God in Liturgy and History* (Norwich: Canterbury Press 1995), p. 80.

and the Cross were fused and their significance signalled by the burgeoning of nature, in fulfilment of the divine promise that the desolate places would become a garden of delights (Isaiah 51.3).

Returning to the work of the artist Signorelli, we may likewise switch from a portrayal of the cross to the birth of the Christ, and trace a correspondence in pictorial terms between the appearing of the incarnate Christ and his sacrifice on Calvary. In Signorelli's Nativity painting, *The Adoration of the Shepherds*, which was probably painted around the same time as his *Crucifixion with Mary Magdalene*, three beds of delicate blooming flowers appear in the foreground. This painting, which can be viewed now in the National Gallery in London, is thought to be the one referred to by Vasari in 1550 that was originally painted as an altarpiece for the church of San Francesco in Citta di Castello.[62]

In Signorelli's paintings the natural world blooms at the appearing of God incarnate, and again is seen around the cross. And this is a visual representation of the unfolding of the same mystery of salvation. Although the crucifixion is dramatically rendered by Signorelli, with the bold gestural movement of Mary Magdalene, her outstretched arms expressing the incomprehensible calamity of Christ's death, the mystery of creation being renewed shows in the appearing of spring flowers. So what we note pictorially is fully commensurate with the combining of conception and death in liturgical time, and we see in this altarpiece a clear intimation of something growing from this particular death, a hint that life burgeons from the cross itself. The promise of new life announced by the angel Gabriel to Mary, and shown in the particularity of the birth at Bethlehem, is seen to be fully and universally realized through the Passion, death and resurrection of Christ, the firstborn of the dead and the guarantor of a creation being made new.

What I have attempted to sketch out in this chapter is something about the reception of images within a liturgical setting and, more precisely, within the context of a liturgical celebration of the Mass. The images we have considered reinforce the view that the Eucharist is inextricably bound up with the sacrifice of the cross, and suggest that the gift of Communion is the fruit of the cross. Further, as we see the cross

---

62 I am grateful to Susanna Avery-Quash for drawing my attention to Signorelli's *Adoration of the Shepherds*.

not only in blood but also in bloom, we would venture to say that the eucharistic gift is also, to appropriate a phrase of Irenaeus of Lyons, the first fruits of [a new] creation,[63] and therefore, a sacramental sign of God's ultimate purpose to re-order, renew and redeem the natural order of creation from its 'bondage to decay'.

We have seen that the varied range of images presented in a liturgical context are richly suggestive, and together present a view of the crucifixion that is beyond an image of human physical suffering and opens up before our eyes the divine promise of a future flourishing of life. This whole mystery ultimately relates back to the primal symbol of blood – the blood of human birth and the blood shed by the God incarnate on the cross of Calvary. And in our reflections on the iconography of the cross, we have repeatedly seen the vital connection between the blood that was shed on the cross and the eucharistic cup. The imagery of the blood of the Crucified is presented as having the power both to purify and revivify, and this power was understood to be released and conveyed in the symbolic exchange of the Eucharist. For the eucharistic cup, as Paul unequivocally said, is a participation in the blood of Christ (1 Corinthians 10.16a). We may be rightly cautious in spelling out how this may happen, and wise to turn to the poet whose words evoke the mystery of that which eludes explanation. In 'The Agony', the priest-poet George Herbert (1593–1633) said that when we receive the chalice at Communion we receive that 'Which my God feels as blood; but I, as wine'. On the cross, Jesus literally felt the warm drops of blood oozing from his fleshly wounds. But what is offered in the eucharistic cup is the life of Christ, a cup that is received so that divine life may pulse through the veins of the communicant and make him or her alive with the very life of God.

Following the arc of our exploration of the theme of blood in relation to the cross and the Eucharist, we may observe by way of conclusion that although the natural symbol of blood resonates with a variety of both scriptural and liturgical texts, a particular association is drawn between blood and creation in Revelation, that most dramatic book of the New Testament. The final chapter of Revelation presents an intriguing juxtaposition of images: the image of blood and the image of the tree of life. In this text it is those who are washed [in the blood] of Christ who

---

63 Irenaeus, *Against Heresies* 4.17.5.

are given access to the tree of life (Revelation 22.14). This motif of the tree of life will emerge from our treatment of a variety of sources, both liturgical and artistic, and will repeatedly return us to that persistent but often understated view of salvation as the renewal of creation itself.

Chapter 4

The noble tree

The question of how the cross came to occupy such a prominent place in churches as the focus for Christian prayer is an intriguing one, and reflecting on what the cross represented in both Roman and Jewish society in the first century of the Christian era, the fact that it did so is not a little surprising. For in the Roman world, crucifixion was an ignominious end. It was a shameful, publicly humiliating and excruciatingly painful way to die – a slow, agonizing form of execution reserved for those who were violent thieves or political criminals. And so as a form of execution, the cross stood as a deterrent to safeguard the ordered *Pax Romana*.[1]

However, in the earliest written sources of Christianity, the reference to the end of Jesus' life on a cross was evidently seen to anchor the Christian story of salvation in human history. Echoing what may well have been a primitive hymn of Christ as saviour, Paul makes a specific reference to the cross as he rehearses the mystery of salvation: 'being found in human form, [Christ] humbled himself and became obedient to the point of death – even death on a *cross*' (Philippians 2.7–8). Elsewhere Paul claims with all the rhetorical force he can muster that when he came to Corinth he had decided not to know anything, except Christ, and Christ crucified (1 Corinthians 2.2). And yet Paul does seem to recognize the difficulty of talking about the cross, and we can trace a distinct element of ambiguity and unease about the subject in his writings. He acknowledges that the cross was a scandal for the Jews, folly for the educated citizens of the Roman Empire (1 Corinthians 1.23). This ambiguous view of the cross led Paul to write to his Gentile readers, in

---

1 See Martin Hengel, *Crucifixion* (London: SCM 1977).

paradoxical terms, of the divine folly being wiser than human wisdom and of God's power being perfected in human weakness. What the cross means, in other words, was seen by the author to go beyond what the cross as an instrument of death actually denotes.

This unease in speaking about the cross persisted in the urban centres of early Christianity. Justin Martyr, writing in the middle of the second century in Rome and aiming to correct the misunderstanding and gossip about Christian beliefs and practices, fully acknowledged the scandal of the cross. To claim a crucified man as God was considered 'madness'. In some circles this view apparently persisted, as illustrated by a derisory cartoon scrawled on a wall of a classroom on the Palatine in Rome that showed a scratched figure with arms raised and graffiti that read: 'Alexamenos worships his god'. Here was a crudely rendered figure of the crucified with an ass's head. The cartoon was undoubtedly intended to mock the Christian, Alexamenos, and would have struck the Christian as a blasphemous parody of the crucified Jesus. The ambivalence towards the cross in the earliest Christian witness in the very first centuries of the Christian era undoubtedly gave rise to a reticence in artistically portraying Jesus as crucified.

As the cross was 'folly to the Gentiles' so it was a scandal for the Jewish believer. The very thought of God's Son being crucified was abhorrent and offensive. Indeed, the Law stated unequivocally that the person who suffered such a shameful end was considered to be cursed by God (Deuteronomy 21.23). This required the rabbinically trained Paul to construct the most complex argument to demonstrate that Christians were no longer bound by the Law but were heirs of the promise of life given by God to faithful Abraham (Galatians 3.13–14). Paradoxically, in this passage the figure of the accursed becomes the source of blessing, and in this way it tacitly acknowledged the life-power of what had previously been regarded as being taboo and impure.

But there is another aspect in the earliest Christian witness that is often overlooked by our contemporary cultural preoccupation with the view of God, who in the Passion of Jesus entered into, and became present within, the suffering and brokenness of the human world.[2] This

---

2 This popular modern view, which all to easily leads us to seeing the figure of the Crucified as a victim, is characterized by von Balthasar as the 'solidarity model'. See Hans Urs von Balthasar, *Theo-Drama: Theological Dramatic Theory*, vol. 4, *The Action* (San Francisco: Ignatius Press 1994), pp. 267–72.

often neglected aspect is the view of the cross that relates the saving work of Christ's suffering, death and resurrection to creation. This relationship has not always been lost to view, and may well be implicit in one of the earliest foundation documents of the Christian movement, the letter of St Paul to the Galatians. In a section of the letter where Paul argues against those who evidently insisted that Gentile Christians should follow the requirements of Jewish Law, Paul speaks of the cross, as opposed to any human achievement or marking, as being the basis of his claim to having been placed in a right relationship with God: 'May I never boast of anything except the cross'(Galatians 6.14). For Paul, the cross provided the very ground from which he dared hope for a new future, a future that was already breaking over the horizon of the closed-in world of human making. The specific subject of this passage – the question of circumcision and its logic – is not of immediate concern here, but the language, the vocabulary he uses, certainly is. For here he speaks of the cross in relation to a *new creation*, a creation being newly made. This is what matters, and matters above and beyond all else: 'a new creation is everything!' (Galatians 6.15b; cf. 2 Corinthians 5.17).

A relation to something similar may be detected in one of the traditions that informed the shaping of the Gospel story of Christ's suffering, death and burial. It may underlie the incongruous conjunction of 'glory' and the 'cross' in John's Gospel, and of an agonizing 'death' and the promise of 'paradise' in Luke's. This juxtaposition of cross and garden, suffering and glory may well have suggested the kind of paradoxical language that served to point to the wider meaning of Christ's suffering, death and burial beyond the merely historical. It was effectively a shift, as illustrated in the previous chapter, from the perspective of 'this is how it was' to 'what it is about'. It is the framing of the cross within the wider perspective of God's purpose of restoring humankind, and of seeing the natural world as the hinterland into which redeemed humanity is placed. The figuring of the crucified in such paradoxical ways resulted in speaking of the end of Jesus in terms of a divine drama played out in part as a human tragedy. This drama of Christ's Passion is probably best conveyed and communicated by the poet and through the ritual actions that developed from the Christian's devotion to the cross, and for an example of a poetic telling of the cross we could probably do no better than turn to the writing of Ephrem the Syrian, born around 306. In a hymn entitled 'Crucifixion', Ephrem speaks of the living wood of the cross as a sword whereby Christ slew death; and, moreover, as Christ was pierced by the lance, so the way to paradise was opened:

> Happy are you, living wood of the Cross,
> for you proved to be a hidden sword to Death,
> for with the sword which smote Him,
> the Son slew Death, when He Himself was struck by it.
> The sword that pierced Christ removed the sword guarding
> Paradise . . .[3]

These words from the poet theologian, rich in typology and full of paradox, are a forceful reminder of how the worship of the primitive church was indivisible. Here the Passion, death and resurrection of Christ form a thematic unity; and being held in tension rather than separated out in distinct episodes, they present the paschal mystery of Christ as a single event. This is not to deny, as evidenced by this literary citation, a specific and deliberate focus upon the cross as the site of God's saving work in Christian prayer and devotion. This there certainly was, but always celebrated in the light of the resurrection. It was integral to the Christian celebration of the *Pasch* long before there was a separate time or even day of the week set aside to focus on the cross. The Eucharist was not celebrated on weekdays, and originally Friday had no particular liturgical significance.

Our earliest Church Order from the second century, the so-called *Didache*, designates Wednesdays and Fridays as fast days, days on which there was to be no celebration of the liturgy. In other words, Friday is a non-liturgical day. A later Church Order, giving directions regarding the ordering of the Christian life and corporate worship, the so-called *Didascalia Apostolorum* (literally, 'the teaching of the Apostles'), gives an even firmer directive in stating that unlike the fast observed during the first three days of what we now call Holy Week, a complete fast had to be observed on the Friday and Saturday. In some regions of the early Christian world, this observance apparently persisted right into the fifth century. A letter of Pope Innocent I (402–17) to Decentius, the Bishop

---

3 Translation Sebastian Brock. See Brock, *The Luminous Eye: The Spiritual World Vision of Saint Ephrem the Syrian*, Cistercian Studies Series 124 (Kalamazoo, MI: Cistercian Publications, 1992, revised edn), p. 81. On Ephrem the Syrian, see further Chapter 5, n. 46 below.

of Gubbio, seeks to justify the practice of a two-day fast by referring back to the alleged practice of the Apostles : 'It is clear that the Apostles during these two days [that is, Friday and Saturday] both were in mourning and also hid themselves for fear of the Jews.' And further, he adds, 'there is no doubt that the tradition of the Church requires entire abstinence from the celebration of the sacrament on these two days.'[4]

Nevertheless, numbers of travellers from the ancient Christian world, despite hazardous and long journeys, made their way to Jerusalem, the city in which the saving events of Christ's death and resurrection occurred. The needs of these travelling pilgrims may well have contributed to the shift from an eschatological sense of salvation to a more historical approach to Christianity, with its episodic view of what happened where and when. But this supposed shift in perspective should not be exaggerated. Fourth-century pilgrims may well have been attracted by the opportunities to commemorate the events of Christ's Passion, death and resurrection on the day, at the time and in the location of the events recorded in the Gospels. And yet the evidence suggests that far from visiting all the sites that feature in the Passion story, such as the Upper Room and the house of Pontius Pilate, pilgrims tended to focus on the site of Jesus' crucifixion and burial. The itinerary was selective.[5]

What we can reasonably infer from the evidence of the fifth-century Armenian Lectionary that lists the scriptural readings for what came to be known as the Great Week, is that although the Passion story from all four Gospels was extensively read and heard, the Gospel of Matthew, the most Jewish of the four Gospels, was the most prominent.[6] Undoubtedly the familiar stories from the Passion narratives would have had a particular resonance for pilgrims in the city in which the recorded events took place. Admittedly, while the Gospels, such as that of St Mark, give the place names in the narrative of Christ's Passion, exact locations, such as the site of the crucifixion, are not actually given. The omission of detail may reflect an ambiguity towards such things, but

---

4 Martin F. Connell, *Church and Worship in Fifth-Century Rome*, Joint Liturgical Studies 52 (Cambridge: Grove Books 2002), p. 34.
5 Paul Bradshaw, in line with the research of Robert Taft and John Baldovin, qualifies the historicizing tendency suggested by Gregory Dix. See Paul F. Bradshaw, *The Search for the Origins of Christian Worship: Sources and Methods for the Study of Early Liturgy* (London: SPCK 2002, 2nd edn), p. 186.
6 See *Egeria's Travels*, trans. John Wilkinson (Warminster: Aris & Phillips 1981, revised edn), pp. 253–77.

what is more certain is that in the period between the final destruction of the Jewish city of Jerusalem and the fourth century, Christian thinkers and writers were more concerned to emphasize the universal application of Christianity and the fact that its practice was not geographically bound to particular places.

For example, Melito of Sardis, in his homily for the *Pasch*, the unified celebration of Christ's death and resurrection, was quite explicit in saying that the historical city of Jerusalem was insignificant in the light of the heavenly Jerusalem.[7] Nevertheless, Jerusalem had been a significant centre of early Christianity, and certainly within its own community, memories of places and what was recorded as having occurred there would undoubtedly have been treasured. Further, alongside what we might call this historic interest was the religious need, particularly for Christians travelling from other parts of the eastern Mediterranean region, for symbolic places that would serve the Christian memory. The place where Christ had died and been raised from the dead increased in significance, particularly at the time when Christianity became a tolerated religion, and its adherents, like the senatorial women from Rome, had both the freedom and the resources to travel. But this was some time after a deliberate and drastic attempt to suppress the Jewish religious memory by the demolition of the city's landmark sites.

Following the destruction of the temple and the Jewish wars, the Emperor Hadrian, between AD 70 and 135, radically altered the city and renamed it Aelia as a Hellenic city or *polis*. But two centuries later, following his victory over Licinius, Constantine annexed the eastern part of the Empire, and apparently had ambitions to establish Jerusalem as a Christian centre. A key source mentioning this ambition only survives as a citation in Eusebius' *Life of Constantine*, the Bishop of Caesarea's rather flattering account of the Emperor's achievements, which purports to be from a letter sent by Constantine to Macarius, the Bishop of Jerusalem. In this letter, which would seem to have been written shortly after the Council of Nicea (325), which Bishop Macarius had attended,[8] Constantine expressed his desire to recover and mark the significant Christian sites in Jerusalem, and indeed elsewhere in Palestine,

---

7 See Stuart George Hall (ed.), *Melito of Sardis: On the Pascha* (Oxford: Oxford University Press 1979), p. 23, sec. 45.

8 See Colin Morris, *The Sepulchre of Christ and the Medieval West: From the Beginning to 1600* (Oxford: Oxford University Press 2005), pp. 10, 16, 18–19.

that were associated with the Christian story. The city had been the focal point and goal of Jesus' earthly ministry (see Luke 9.51 and 13.33), and so the Emperor's ambition was consistent with the Gospel story. This is especially the case with the writings of the evangelist Luke, who seems to have been as much concerned with sacred geography as with history, presenting Jerusalem as the site of Christ's 'exodus' and exultation. In one of Luke's most familiar resurrection narratives, it is Cleopas, one of the two journeying disciples, who exclaims to the stranger who joined him and his companion on the road to Emmaus: 'Are you the only stranger in Jerusalem who does not know the things that have taken place there in these days?' (Luke 24.18).

And so after the peace of Constantine in 313 it was inevitable that Jerusalem would become the primary centre of pilgrimage, and as such a crucible for the future development of Christianity and its liturgical 'rememorative' celebrations.[9] Indeed, the importance of Jerusalem as a place of pilgrimage cannot be overstated. For it was here that Christians, Eastern and Western, met, experienced new ways of prayer, exchanged ideas and practices and where the cross, which was to become the most ubiquitous and defining symbol of Christianity, came first to be venerated.

Perhaps the most celebrated of the earliest pilgrims to Jerusalem was the Emperor Constantine's mother, Helena (255–c. 330). What is curious is that the story of Helena's pilgrimage, which in time spawned a literary tradition that found its fullest expression in England in the second half of the eighth century in the poem *Elene*, is not recorded in Eusebius' *Life*. This poem may have been written by Cynewulf, the Bishop of Lindisfarne, and elaborates the story of the finding of the true cross. Here it is Helena who is portrayed as the one who initiated the expedition to Jerusalem and who oversaw the discovery of the cross. The poem tells how she extracted an old story of where the cross had been buried from the Bishop of Jerusalem, and then made the arrangements for its recovery. In this long poem, the cross is frequently referred to as a tree and is variously designated as the 'tree of Triumph', the 'holy

---

9 The term 'rememorative' was appropriated by Kenneth Stevenson to distinguish between the liturgical celebrations in contradistinction from the simple historical commemoration of past events, and dramatic re-enactment. See Stevenson, *Jerusalem Revisited: The Liturgical Meaning of Holy Week*, a series of lectures delivered at the College of the Resurrection, Mirfield, Holy Week 1984 (Washington: Pastoral Press 1988), p. 9.

tree', the 'Victor tree', the 'tree of glory' and the 'tree of life'. As we shall see, the imagery of the poem echoes the deep themes of the developing liturgical veneration of the cross, which sees the wood of the cross as a 'token of triumph' within the wider frame of creation, provided by the recurrent references to the 'tree'. But does the story of Helena told in this early English poem have any historical veracity?

The evidence is fragmentary, and the fact that neither Egeria (see below) nor Eusebius of Caesarea make any mention of Helena's being the one who discovered the true cross would suggest that the purpose of the legend was to secure an imperial association to the practice of the veneration of the cross, and through this association enhance the status of the holy city in which it was first practised. The association between Helena and the finding of the cross was known in Italy in the fourth century and was referred to by Ambrose, the Bishop of Milan, in the sermon that he preached at the funeral of the Emperor Theodosius in 395. The story is told more fully by a contemporary of Ambrose, Rufinus of Aquileia, in his *Ecclesiastical History*. Rufinus (*c.* 345–410) had stayed in Jerusalem, possibly shortly after Egeria's pilgrimage, and his account of the discovery of the true cross by Helena differs from the later poetic tradition in stating that the wood of the cross had been verified as being the cross upon which Jesus was crucified because of its efficacy in healing a sick woman.[10]

Our earliest account of the veneration of the cross comes from a fourth-century pilgrim, Egeria. She was a woman of some financial means and evidently had the freedom to travel, and possibly had some association with a religious community in her native Spain.[11] Egeria wrote from the perspective of a pilgrim and provided a detailed account of the religious observances in Jerusalem as they had been developed by its bishop, the renowned teacher Cyril of Jerusalem (*c.* 348–86), in the church complex built by Constantine following the Council of Nicea. A tantalizingly brief reference to what had been achieved in this extensive building project by the year 333 is provided by an anonymous traveller from Bordeaux. He or she records the two sacred sites of Golgotha and the tomb, and refers to the basilica – which he or she also calls

10 *Hist. Eccl.* 1.7; *Patrologia Latina* 21.475.
11 See Hagith Sivan, 'Who was Egeria? Piety and Pilgrimage in the Age of Gratian', *Harvard Theological Review*, vol. 81, no. 1, January 1988, pp. 68–72.

a *dominicum*, a Latin term literally meaning 'a house for the Lord' – and an adjacent baptistery.[12] It may be that although Golgotha and the tomb were visible shrines on the perimeter of the building, only what came to be known as the Martyrium church, on the alleged site of the discovery of the true cross,[13] had in fact been built by that stage.

In the catechetical instructions that Cyril delivered to those preparing for baptism at Easter, the bishop took full advantage of the topography of the Jerusalem church complex and impressed upon his hearers how they literally stood in close physical proximity to the sacred sites where Christ had died and been buried (see below, Chapter 7). One can imagine him pointing with his finger to add to the rhetorical fact: 'There, the cross was erected, and over there, Christ's body was laid to rest.' What is clear is that Cyril reinforced what he said by drawing his hearers' attention to the site of the crucifixion and to the tomb, and made specific reference to 'the holy wood of the cross', which he says 'is seen among us to this day'.[14] But when exactly was this holy wood seen, and on what occasion? To answer this question we need to look to Egeria and to read her pilgrim's record alongside other contemporary and near contemporary sources.

Although our primary source for knowing what happened on Good Friday in fourth-century Jerusalem is Egeria's *Journal*, her record, though thoroughly detailed in parts, is far from being a full description of each of the services on that day. As a pilgrim, Egeria was especially concerned to note those things that differed from the practice of her native church and what she was accustomed to in the local worshipping community to which she belonged. What she records in her pilgrim's diary took place in a large church complex, with its imposing courtyards and churches incorporating some smaller chapels, which had been built under the patronage of the Emperor Constantine to accommodate the large number of pilgrims who journeyed to Jerusalem. The church complex encompassed Calvary, the site of the crucifixion, as well as the site of Christ's burial. Tradition has it that the basilica church was dedicated on the very day that commemorated the discovery of the true cross. In later centuries, as we shall see, the cross was exhibited or shown

---

12 *Egeria's Travels*, p. 158.
13 John F. Baldovin sj, *Liturgy in Ancient Jerusalem*, Alcuin/GROW Liturgical Study 9 (Nottingham: Grove Books 1989), p. 7.
14 *Catechesis* 10.19.

to the people in the basilica on the second day, 14 September, of an eight-day dedication festival of the church.[15]

Egeria called the church adjacent to Calvary – or Golgotha as it is sometimes called – 'the Martyrium', and the rotunda church built over Christ's tomb was called 'the Anastasis' (the Church of the Resurrection). This rotunda was built on a large and impressive scale, and at its centre was the sepulchre or cave in which Christ had reputedly been buried. Twelve pillars delineated the sacred site, which measured some 12 metres in diameter. It is understood that the tomb was discovered under the rubble that formed the foundations of the Forum of Hadrian.[16] Eusebius, eager to present Constantine in a heroic light and wanting to emphasize the victory of Christianity over pagan religions, gives us the further detail that the church had been built over a Roman temple of the pagan goddess Venus,[17] thereby asserting Christ's supremacy over the pagan cult. Although the *Life of Constantine* is a rather rambling and incomplete account of the building and decoration of the church complex in Jerusalem, it is interesting to note that Eusebius placed the emphasis on the resurrection rather than on the crucifixion itself, and this emphasis he attributes to Constantine. According to Eusebius, Constantine's expressed aim in this monumental building project was indeed 'to honour the Saviour's resurrection'.

A large cross was erected in a courtyard in front of the rotunda, but according to Egeria's description of events in Holy Week, the veneration of a relic of the 'sacred wood of the cross' on Good Friday took place in a modest chapel, measuring some 45 by 35 metres, which the pilgrim referred to as the *post Crucem*, 'the chapel behind the cross'. John Wilkinson places this chapel within the Martyrium at the eastern end of the south aisle, with 'the cross' located in the open court leading to the round church.[18] Curiously, the actual site of the crucifixion is not recorded in the earliest accounts of the church complex, but we know that by the third quarter of the fourth century the alleged site was marked by a large jewelled cross.[19] Egeria tells us that on Good Friday

---

15 Thomas J. Talley, *The Origins of the Liturgical Year* (New York: Pueblo 1986), p. 47.

16 Talley, *The Origins of the Liturgical Year*, p. 40.

17 *VC* III.26–28.

18 *Egeria's Travels*, p. 45.

19 Barbara C. Raw, *Anglo-Saxon Crucifixion Iconography and the Art of the Monastic Revival* (Cambridge: Cambridge University Press 1990), p. 43.

the wood of the cross was venerated by a large number of people. But given the time taken for this to happen, from 8 a.m. to noon, and the size of this small chapel, it seems probable that the veneration involved a steady stream of people. These were local people of all ages and included catechumens as well as visiting pilgrims, who came in great numbers. They formed a winding queue making their way through the chapel rather than an ordered assembly gathered in a single space.[20] The veneration of the cross, in other words, was an informal popular devotion rather than a liturgical celebration with a structured order of service. There was such a service, and it seems this followed the popular veneration of the cross at noon. It lasted some three hours and consisted of biblical readings interspersed with prayers and appropriate psalmody, culminating with the reading of the Passion in John's Gospel.[21]

The circulation of legends of the discovery of the true cross undoubtedly drew pilgrims to Jerusalem, and what happened there on Good Friday may indeed be the origin of the liturgical Veneration of the Cross that gradually came to be adopted across the Christian world.[22] But how exactly did it happen in Jerusalem? To begin to answer this question we need to return to our primary source.

Egeria begins her description of the veneration of the wood of the cross by setting the scene as follows:

> The bishop's chair is placed on Golgotha behind the Cross (the cross there now), and he takes his seat. A table is placed before him with a cloth on it, the deacons stand round, and there is brought to him a gold and silver box containing the holy Wood of the Cross. It is opened and the Wood of the Cross and the Title are taken out and placed on the table.[23]

Egeria then spells out precisely how the relic of the true cross was venerated, and as this is recorded in such detail we may safely assume

---

20 See Louis van Tongeren, 'A Sign of Resurrection on Good Friday' in Charles Caspers and Marc Schneiders (eds), *Omnes Circumadstantes: Contributions Towards a History of the Role of the People in the Liturgy: Presented to Herman Wegman . . .* (Kampen: Kok Pharos 1990), pp. 105–7.
21 *Egeria's Travels*, p. 137.
22 See Paul F. Bradshaw and Maxwell E. Johnson, *The Origins of Feasts, Fasts and Seasons in* Early Christianity (London: SPCK 2011), p. 63.
23 *Egeria's Travels*, 1981, pp. 136–7.

that this devotional practice was something she had never previously experienced before her pilgrimage to the holy city. Her account continues:

> As long as the holy Wood is on the table, the bishop sits with his hands resting on either end of it and holds it down, and the deacons round him keep watch over it. They guard it like this because what happens now is that all the people, catechumens as well as faithful, come up one by one to the table.[24]

In what might strike the modern reader with some wry amusement, Egeria recounts a story that was evidently circulating at the time of her pilgrimage to Jerusalem, explaining why the wood of the cross was so guarded. The story told how someone was so carried away in his – or her – devotion on one Good Friday, and so much wanted a relic of the cross for himself, that he bit into the wood as he was venerating it. The manner of how the wood of the cross was venerated is again told in detail by Egeria. People, she tells us, took their turn in the queue and went past the relic one by one. When each person stood before the relic, he or she would bend down, touch the holy Wood, first with their forehead then with their eyes, and finally kiss it and move on. To reinforce the point, Egeria adds that people were not allowed to reach out and physically touch it with their hands.

At the time of Egeria's visit to the holy land, the popular devotional focus on Good Friday was different in Constantinople, the old Byzantium that Constantine had expanded to be the second Rome. This imperial city, now known as Istanbul, was strategically placed, for both military and commercial purposes, on the Bosporus. It seems that in comparison with fourth-century Jerusalem, the liturgy for Good Friday had little to distinguish it from any other celebration on Fridays in Lent.[25] According to Robert Taft, who has charted the development of the Byzantine Holy Week ceremonies in the first millennium, the only distinctive devotional practice on Good Friday in Hagia Sophia was the veneration of Constantinople's relic of the Passion, the lance that had

---

24 *Egeria's Travels*, 1981, p. 137.
25 See Robert Taft sj, 'A Tale of Two Cities: The Byzantine Holy Week Triduum as a Paradigm of Liturgical History' in J. Neil Alexander (ed.), *Time and Community* (Washington, DC: Pastoral Press 1990).

pierced Christ's side (John 19.34). Apparently the veneration of this relic of Christ's Passion took place before the morning Office known as Orthros,[26] and attracted large numbers of people to Hagia Sophia on Good Friday. This prized relic and its use on Good Friday soon came to influence both the iconography and the devotion to the cross in Byzantine liturgy. Longinus, the name given to the Roman soldier who pierced Jesus with his lance in the apocryphal *Gospel of Nicodemus*, came to feature on the Eastern icon of the crucifixion. And again, a reference to the sacred lance came to feature in the liturgical poetry of the Byzantine liturgy for Good Friday. And this, interestingly, suggests that the act of venerating the Passion of the incarnate Christ on Good Friday was the occasion when the faithful asked Christ to manifest his resurrection:

> The Son of the Virgin is pierced with a spear.
> We venerate Thy Passion, O Christ.
> Show us Thy glorious Resurrection.[27]

In this sense, devotion to the Passion, to Christ's suffering, death and burial, pointed ahead to the resurrection, the *anastasis*, the victory of Christ's triumph over sin and death. In this perspective, the cross was again seen and understood in the light of the resurrection. This was not a conscious flinching away from the physical pain and agony suffered by Jesus on the cross or, worse, a denial of his bloody agony and the reality of his death – this devotional approach was too dependent on John's account of the Passion for that. Rather, what we see here is a conscious drawing out, and a deepening, of the theological perspective of what God was doing in the drama of salvation. God was 'in Christ' (cf. 2 Corinthians 5.19) even at that point when, from the human point of view, God seemed to have abandoned Jesus on the cross.

In order to catch the mood and the tone of the paradoxical view of the Passion seen in the light of the resurrection as it crystallized in liturgical texts, let me cite two short examples drawn from sixth- and seventh-century Byzantine liturgical poetry. Both examples are from

---

26 Taft, 'A Tale of Two Cities', p. 24.
27 From the stichera at the Ninth Hour in *The Lenten Triodion*, trans. Mother Mary and Kallistos Ware (London: Faber & Faber 1978), p. 609.

verses of hymns sung at the Liturgy on Good Friday, and both under-
line Christ's divinity by identifying the Crucified as the creator God of
the cosmos:

> Today He who hung the earth upon the waters is hung on the Cross.
> He who clothes himself in light as in a garment stood naked at the
> judgement.
>
> He who is King of the angels is arrayed in a crown of thorns.
> He who wraps the heavens in clouds is wrapped in the purple of
> mockery.[28]

Relics of what was considered to be the true cross were highly treasured
by those who were unable to make the arduous and often dangerous
journey to Jerusalem itself. Documentary evidence tells how fragments
of the wood of the true cross were taken by pilgrims from Jerusalem
around the Christian world. A relic of the wood of the cross was
publicly venerated on Good Friday in Antioch,[29] and the evidence is
that this practice spread fairly rapidly in the fourth century. Cyril of
Jerusalem alludes to this in one of his addresses to candidates preparing
for baptism when he mentions that fragments from the wood of the
cross are 'distributed piecemeal from Jerusalem all over the world'. The
picture of relics of the true cross being given by the Bishop of Jerusalem
and taken to the major centres of the Christian world is corroborated by
the early fifth-century Paulinus of Nola, who in a letter accompanying a
gift of the 'holy wood' explains how tiny fragments of the sacred wood
from Jerusalem were to be found in many churches, so that others may
'win great graces, and faith, and blessings'.[30]

We know that as early as the sixth century, requests for relics of the
cross were being sought after by the patrons of major churches and religious communities, and the reliquaries were often exquisitely wrought
objects. One well-documented example, to which we shall return, is
the request made by Radegunda (see below) to Justin II, the Emperor

---

28 *The Lenten Triodion*, pp. 582, 587.

29 Patrick Regan OSB, 'Veneration of the Cross', in Maxwell E. Johnson (ed.), *Between
Memory and Hope: Readings on the Liturgical Year* (Collegeville, MN: Liturgical Press
2000), p. 145.

30 Letter 31.6 cited in Regan, 'Veneration of the Cross', p. 144.

in Constantinople, for a fragment of the true cross for the convent she had founded and dedicated to the holy cross near Poitiers in France.[31]

The church in Constantinople had obtained a relic of the wood of the cross from Apamea in Syria in 578,[32] and presumably it was from this date, or soon after, that this relic of the true cross was venerated throughout the triduum in Constantinople.[33] The precious relic of the true cross had been taken captive with the invasion and sack of Jerusalem by the Persians in 614. But against all the odds, in 628 a new Byzantine Emperor, Heraclius (610–41), was successful in driving the Persian forces back to their own lands, and the cross soon thereafter found a secure home in Constantinople. Despite his best intention to restore a replica of the true cross to Jerusalem, the Emperor was thwarted by the invasion of the holy city by a new enemy, the Muslim Arabs.[34] And so it came about that Constantinople held the remains of the true cross from the time of Heraclius, and around that time fragments of it, presented in decorated reliquaries, became prized imperial gifts that considerably enhanced the prestige of the churches that received them.

The artwork in the decoration of these reliquaries, which is theologically significant and represents a specific way of liturgical seeing, tells us something of the intended and received meaning of the cross. A stunning example of the decorated cross reliquary is the famous Fieschi Morgan *Staurotheke*, which may be seen in the Metropolitan Museum of Art in New York. At one time this reliquary belonged to the collection of Pope Innocent IV (1243–54) and was part of the booty brought back by the Crusaders after the sack of Constantinople in 1204. The provenance and dating of this fine object have been extensively debated – although it could be as early as the seventh century, it is generally thought to have been made early in the ninth century.[35] This small

---

31 For detail of sources, see David Buckton, 'Early Enamel in France' in Pamela Armstrong (ed.), *Ritual and Art: Byzantine Essays for Christopher Walter* (London: Pindar Press 2006), p. 97, n. 15.

32 Anna Kartsonis, 'The Responding Icon' in Linda Safran (ed.), *Heaven on Earth: Art and the Church in Byzantium* (University Park, PA: Pennsylvania State University Press 1998), p. 64.

33 Regan, 'Veneration of the Cross', p. 145.

34 Cyril Mango, 'Byzantium: A Historical Introduction' in Robin Cormack and Maria Vassilaki (eds), *Byzantium 330–1453* (London: Royal Academy of Arts 2008), p. 27.

35 Helen C. Evans and William D. Wixom (eds), *The Glory of Byzantium: Art and Culture of the Middle Byzantine Era A.D. 843–1261* (New York: Metropolitan Museum of Art 1997), p. 74.

rectangular box, measuring 10.2 × 7.4 cm, is wrought in silver-gilt. It is decorated with cloisonné enamel, possibly the work of an artisan from the West working in Constantinople. The inside of the lid is divided into four panels, showing the Annunciation to Mary, the nativity, the crucifixion and the *anastasis* or resurrection, a feature that suggests that the material of the wood of the cross was taken to represent the *whole* saving work of God in Christ. The lid has a crucifixion scene, and on the sides of the box are 28 busts of saints with their names inscribed in Greek. The crucifixion scene shows Christ wearing the *colobium*,[36] a full-length priestly robe. His arms are outstretched against a blue horizontal bar, and on either side of the figure of the Crucified are the attending figures of Mary and John, and a rough inscription citing John 19.26 and 27, the text in which Jesus, hanging on the cross, says to the beloved disciple, 'Here is your mother', and to Mary, 'Here is your son'.

So what we see in this material object, as in later illuminated manuscripts, is pictorial art combined with text in order that the word and the image may interpret and illuminate each other. In this instance, the selection and combination of the different decorative elements suggest, as noted, that the cross was regarded as a sign that made visible the *whole* mystery of Christ.[37] But what did this complex sign signify, and how might we read it? In answer, I would say that what was presented in this reliquary was a sign of the Christ who, on the cross, reconfigured

---

36 The earliest surviving depictions of the crucifixion tend to show Christ with outstretched arms and wearing the *colobium*, a garment that may have been inspired by a visionary passage describing Christ the high priest 'clothed with a long robe and with a golden girdle round his breast' (Revelation 1.13b RSV). Examples of images of the crucified wearing a *colobium* include the eighth-century fresco in the Church of Santa Maria Antiqua in Rome, the famous eighth-century larger than life-size figure of the crucified, known as the *Volto Santo*, at Lucca in Tuscany, on the Via Francigena pilgrimage route from Canterbury to Rome. For an Eastern example, one may consider the more realistic eighth-century crucifixion icon in the monastery of St Catherine on Mount Sinai. Part of the humiliation of crucifixion in the ancient world was being crucified naked, a point that is emphasized in John's account of the Passion. Showing Christ on the cross dressed in the *colobium* may well have served the purpose of indicating the priestly aspect of Christ's work of salvation as expressed in the Letter to the Hebrews that has featured in the liturgy for Good Friday at least, according to the Armenian lectionary, since the fifth century.

37 Another example is a Syrian cross-shaped reliquary of the true cross, now in the Vatican, which is decorated with scenes from the Christmas cycle, from the Annunciation to the Baptism. See David R. Cartlidge and J. Keith Elliott, *Art and the Christian Apocrypha* (London and New York: Routledge 2001), pp. 74–5.

human relationships, one with another, and who drew humankind, as members of the *communio sanctorum*, to participate in the life of God. If this reading of the reliquary and the sacred relic it contained is feasible, then we have further reason to say that the cross was seen as a tangible sign of the new life into which Christ draws humanity. Further, in taking the whole decorative pattern and the significance of the relic itself into account, I would say that the cross was seen as a sign of resurrection and, as such, a pledge of creation healed, restored and made new. But can this same complex meaning be transferred and assigned to the fragment of the cross that was used for the veneration on Good Friday?

The development of the Good Friday liturgy was intermittent, and it varied from one geographical region to another. For those communities that held a relic of the wood of the cross, the relic provided a focus for Christians in their devotion on Good Friday. The origins of a Good Friday devotion in Rome are rather hazy, but they too seem to depend upon a tradition regarding a relic of the cross. However, the sources do not provide either a full or a complete picture. Between, let us say, the fifth and the seventh centuries, it would seem that the main liturgy in Rome on Good Friday was a Service of the Word, and that this service consisted of readings, psalmody and solemn prayers. By the seventh century, Rome had adopted the devotional practice of venerating the wood of the cross, which was probably made possible by a gift of a fragment from Constantinople or perhaps from pilgrims returning from Jerusalem. Once the practice had entered into the liturgical life of the city, the early development of the ceremonial was restrained and simple, involving the Pope, the bishop of that cosmopolitan city. Our earliest sources, ironically dating from the time when the Good Friday veneration of the 'holy wood of the cross' no longer occurred in Jerusalem, are twofold. The first is the diary of an anonymous eighth-century Frankish pilgrim to Rome, the other is from a collection of ceremonial directives for the rites celebrated by the Pope that came to be known as *Ordo Romanus* XXIII. From these two sources it is possible to build up a fairly reliable picture of how the papal Good Friday ceremony was celebrated in Rome by the end of the seventh century.

Egeria repeatedly remarked on how the particular Holy Week and Easter devotions and services she experienced in Jerusalem were appropriate to both the time and the place, and the sources describing what happened in Rome on Good Friday suggest that the liturgical celebration also occurred at the appropriate time, and in its movement seemed to reproduce the itinerary of the Jerusalem pilgrim in his or her own locale. For at 2 p.m. on that solemn day, the time when Jesus had hung on the cross at Golgotha, a light was lit from an oil lamp to precede the Pope as he left his church, the basilica of St John Lateran, and slowly walked, barefoot, the comparatively short distance to the Sessorian basilica, which was known as Santa Croce in Gerusalemme (literally, the holy cross in Jerusalem).[38] This basilica, built on to the Sessorian Palace on the imperial estate, was once owned by Helena herself. Within was a small chapel which, according to a late fourth-century legend, was the shrine for a relic of the true cross that Helena had brought back from Jerusalem. The design of the church had been inspired by, if not exactly modelled on, the ground plan of the fourth-century basilica in Jerusalem, and thereby facilitated a circular flow of pilgrims moving around the building.[39] The veracity of the provision of a symbolic pilgrimage to Jerusalem in Rome itself is difficult to establish with absolute certainty, but later arrangements for Good Friday do seem to suggest that this intention fuelled, at least in part, the development of the Good Friday liturgy in Rome.

What we can say, then, is that the papal liturgy in Rome in the late seventh or early eighth century was intended to be a symbolic pilgrimage to Jerusalem. The description of the rite tells us that the Pope, ably assisted by an archdeacon who supported his left arm, led the procession swinging a smoking thurible. (The reference to the Pope carrying the censer is unusual for Rome, and may well be a vestige of Byzantine influence from Constantinople.) Whatever the influence, the action certainly evokes the biblical image of the high priest entering the Holy of Holies on the Day of Atonement.[40] In the procession, a deacon carrying the relic of the true cross in a richly decorated box walked immediately behind the Pope. As the procession made its way, the cantors sang Psalm 119: 'Happy are those whose way is blameless, who walk in the law of the Lord.' On arrival at Santa Croce, the deacon immediately

---

38 John Baldovin sj, *The Urban Character of Christian Worship: The Origins, Development, and Meaning of Stational Liturgy*, Orientalia Christiana Analecta 228 (Rome: Pont. Institutum Studiorum Orientalium 1987), p. 136.

39 Matilda Webb, *The Churches and Catacombs of Early Christian Rome* (Brighton: Sussex Academic Press 2001), pp. 52–4.

40 Regan, 'Veneration of the Cross', p. 151.

placed the reliquary on the altar and the Pope opened it. The Pope then
prostrated himself in silent prayer before the altar and immediately rose
to venerate the wood of the cross by kissing it. Once he had venerated
the relic he moved to his chair, and then the relic was venerated by the
worshipping community, each in their order – first the bishops, then
the presbyters, deacons, other clergy, and finally the congregation, after
the relic had been brought down to the sanctuary step.[41]

As this papal liturgy was being celebrated it is possible, as Patrick
Regan has suggested, that those smaller suburban churches – *tituli*,
'titular' – that possessed a relic of the wood of the cross exposed the
relic on Good Friday, and that it was venerated by the clergy and the
people at 3 p.m.[42] A fuller picture of what came to happen on Good
Friday in these smaller churches is provided by a later source known as
the *Gelasian Sacramentary*. Again, the ceremonial directions are sparse,
and the impression given is that the Service of the Word reached a devotional climax with the adoration of the cross – but in this case, it seems,
a convenient wooden cross, rather than a relic, could have been the
focus of devotion.[43] In these churches there was no processional movement, and apparently the cross was simply placed on the altar at the
beginning of the service and venerated at the end, following the solemn
prayers of intercession. But what, we may ask, was being commemorated on this occasion? It is impossible to say exactly, but for those
who came to 'adore the holy cross' the focus of their devotion may well
have recalled the physical sufferings and cruel death of Jesus. However,
both the context of the action and the prayer texts that preceded it
would suggest that on this occasion the cross had a wider symbolic
connotation. The devotional exercise of venerating the cross connected
the worshipper to the whole mystery of Christ; that is, to his suffering
and death, certainly, but also to his victory over sin and death and to
the hope of his appearing in glory. This sense of the cross's being a sign

---

41 Gordon P. Jeanes, *The Origins of the Roman Rite*, vol. 2, Joint Liturgical Studies 42
(Cambridge: Grove Books 1998), p. 6.
42 Regan, 'Veneration of the Cross', p. 146.
43 As the practice spread over time it became fairly common for a wooden cross to be
used for the Veneration on Good Friday in those churches that did not possess a relic of
the true cross. By the ninth century, the hugely influential Amalarius of Metz conceded
that the power of Christ's holy cross would not be lacking in a likeness of that cross. The
relevant text is cited by Regan in 'Veneration of the Cross', p. 153.

of Christ's appearing is corroborated by the iconographical representations of it in some of the late fifth- and early sixth-century apse mosaic crosses, such as those seen in St Apollinare in Classe (near Ravenna), St Pudenziana in Rome and St Felix in Nola (east of Naples). The visual evidence certainly suggests that the cross was regarded pre-eminently as a sign of Christ's appearing, and that it represented the whole Christ, crucified and glorified, the coming one who had come and who even now was present with his people.

Later descriptions of the performance of the Good Friday liturgy in Rome seem to confirm this understanding of the cross as a sign of Christ, and a good example of these is *Ordo Romanus* XXIV. This *Ordo* is thought by Andrieu to reflect the performance of the liturgy in a smaller neighbouring city under the control of Rome, and includes in its provision for Good Friday an antiphon that had presumably been written particularly for the occasion: 'Behold the wood of the cross on which the salvation of the world hung: Come, let us adore him.'[44] Regan has demonstrated that the vocabulary of this antiphon, presumably sung between verses of Psalm 119 during the adoration of the cross, was drawn from the earliest literary source of the legend of the discovery of the true cross by Helena in Jerusalem. Rufinus tells how in looking for the cross, Helena had prayed that God would lead her to discover 'the blessed wood on which hung our salvation'.[45] The correspondence of language between the antiphon and the earliest account of the finding of the true cross not only reveals a close association between the liturgical practice on Good Friday and the true cross tradition of Jerusalem, but also sheds light on what the cross was taken to signify at that time and on that occasion. The words 'Behold the wood of the cross on which the salvation of the world hung: Come, let us adore him' indicate that the material object of the cross revealed Christ, the source of salvation, and represented his life-giving and restoring presence among the people; hence, the invitatory clause: 'Come, let us adore *him*' rather than 'it'. Again, the cross is presented as a sign of the presence of the whole Christ, crucified and glorified. The sense of the cross as a sign of Christ's presence in the Veneration on Good Friday is heightened by developments in the ritual action reflected in

---

44 Jeanes, *The Origins of the Roman Rite*, p. 12.
45 Cited by Regan, 'Veneration of the Cross', p. 147.

later liturgical books. In *Ordo* XXXI, for instance, dated around the second half of the ninth century, the directions indicate that a veiled cross was processed through the church, and at three stational points, the *trisagion*, 'Holy God, Holy and strong, Holy and immortal, have mercy upon us', was sung, and then the people were directed to bow in adoration. The dramatic tension is held until the final station, when the presiding bishop finally unveiled the cross and sang the antiphon as an acclamation: 'Behold the wood of the cross . . .'.

Having reviewed the evidence, it seems reasonable to assert that this rite of adoring the cross on Good Friday was not simply an exercise in the recalling of a historic event, the actual Passion and death of Jesus, but the liturgical making present of the whole saving mystery of Christ for the worshipper. At this time, and on this occasion, the cross was a condensed symbol of Christ, holding together his incarnate life, his suffering and death, and his resurrection and glorification. And in its ritual performance, the action of venerating the cross was a sacramental way of allowing oneself to be caught up in the whole drama of salvation, rather than being simply a cathartic exercise that would cast Christ in the role of a victim. This wider sense of being connected to the whole Christ through the adoration of the cross was reinforced by the provision that was made for the local clergy and people to receive Communion at the *tituli* churches on Good Friday.

In the Good Friday liturgy the Eucharist was not celebrated, but Communion was offered from the sacramental bread that was reserved from what today is known as the Mass of the Lord's Supper on Maundy Thursday. This was an unusual practice in the West. Known as the Mass of the Pre-Sanctified, it possibly originated in Constantinople and is practised today in Orthodox churches on Wednesdays and Fridays throughout Lent. On Good Friday in Rome the cup was consecrated by placing the *fermentum* – a fragment of eucharistic bread from the Maundy Thursday celebration – in the chalice. The *Gelasian Sacramentary*, which originated in the dioceses and parishes around Rome, mentions the adoration of the cross and the receiving of Communion in a single descriptive sentence, suggesting that as each worshipper came forward to venerate the cross, he or she then received Communion: 'all adore the holy cross and communicate'.

The gift of Communion was the precious food of the one who had died, who was raised from the dead and who would come again in glory, and so the two ritual acts – of venerating the cross and of receiving Communion – thereby set the former in the context of the embracing of the whole event of salvation. According to the description in the *Gelasian Sacramentary*, the double ritual action followed the solemn chanting by a deacon of the Passion narrative of John's Gospel, which places the moment of Christ's death at the time when the sacrificial Passover lambs were being sacrificed in the temple in Jerusalem. The identification of Jesus as the Lamb of God, signalled by John the Baptist early in John's Gospel, was reinforced by the choice of the first Old Testament reading at this service, namely Exodus 12.1–14. This recounts the foundational story of the slaughter of the Passover lambs. The focus on the theme of sacrifice is matched by the prophetic voice in the choice of the second reading, Hosea 6.1–6. This prophetic passage was deliberately chosen because it sounded a distinct note of future hope and restoration and, as such, set the tenor of the liturgical observance of Good Friday. For the mood of Good Friday was both sorrowful and hopeful, and was about penitence and the opening of a new horizon. For the very ritual action of venerating the cross impressed upon the faithful the Passion and death of the incarnate Christ and opened their hearts and minds to God's promise of restoration and the dawning brilliance of Easter. This reference to Easter was signalled at the very beginning of the rite in a collect for the day. This collect includes a concisely constructed petitionary clause that asks that God grant and bestow the grace of Christ's resurrection upon the worshippers: *resurrectionis sue gratium largiatur.*[46]

Over time, particular texts came to be sung during the veneration of the cross. Some of these developed the themes we have already identified; others, such as the so-called Reproaches (see below), heightened a more individual and emotional response to the suffering and death of Christ. It is my contention that this later devotional focus has rather obstructed the reception of the meaning of the cross as a sign of the life of the risen Crucified Lord. But first, let us look at some of the earliest poetic compositions associated with the cross that present it as a life-giving sign of the crucified and risen Lord.

The first classic composition is the work of Venantius Honorius Fortunatus. Fortunatus was born around 530, educated in Ravenna, and after a rather wandering life eventually settled in Poitiers in France,

---

46 H. A. Wilson (ed.), *The Gelasian Sacramentary* (Oxford: Clarendon Press 1894), p. 75.

where he became bishop and is believed to have died in 609. Among his surviving hymns, which belong within the tradition of Latin hymnody exemplified by Ambrose of Milan and Prudentius, three treat the subject of the cross. The circumstances that led Fortunatus to write the hymn *Vexilla regis prodeunt*, 'The royal banners forward go, the Cross shines forth in mystic glow', are rather colourful and deserve some mention here. The story tells how Fortunatus befriended the Princess Radegunda, who was married to the violent Merovingian king Clotar I. Fortunatus supported the Princess when she separated from her husband and set up a convent in Poitiers with her adopted daughter Agnes. Fortunatus was regarded as an accomplished poet, and when Radegunda was given a relic of the true cross for her convent by the Emperor Justin II (565–78) and his wife the Empress Sophia, she asked Fortunatus to write some triumphant verses with which to ceremoniously greet the relic and carry it in procession to the convent, which was dedicated to the holy cross. These verses, which are still found in the Passiontide section of contemporary hymn books, albeit in shortened forms, were first sung on 19 November in 569. From then on they only gradually made their way into liturgical books as the Office hymn for Holy Week, from Palm Sunday to Maundy Thursday. The hymn slowly became attached to services on particular days designated to commemorate and honour the cross, especially on Good Friday, and then on the feast of the Invention of the Cross, designated as a celebration of the discovery of the true cross on 3 May, and by the late eighth century, as evidenced in some Frankish liturgical books, on the feast of the Exaltation of the Cross celebrated on 14 September.[47]

---

47 In the tenth century the hymn is only intermittently included in liturgical collections both south and north of the Alps as a Passiontide Office hymn. In a Trier monastic hymnary, the hymn was included in the material for the feast of the Exaltation of the Cross, celebrated on 14 September. See D. A. Bullough, *Carolingian Renewal: Sources and Heritage* (Manchester: Manchester University Press 1991), p. 250. Liturgical provision for both feasts was first made in the old *Gelasian Sacramentary* and gradually came to be included in liturgical books north of the Alps. Though popular throughout the Middle Ages, both of these feasts were excised from the English Calendar by Thomas Cranmer. They were reinstated in the Calendar of the 1662 Prayer Book and, in the present Calendar and Lectionary of the Church of England, 14 September is designated as a festival. Full liturgical provision is made for Holy Cross Day (14 September) in *Common Worship: Festivals* (London: Church House Publishing 2008), pp. 102–7.

Because of the scant documentary evidence, scholars are wary of giving precise dates to the incorporation of Fortunatus' hymns, but the consensus is that the *Pange Lingua* was a constituent part of the service of the Veneration of the Cross on Good Friday on the Continent by at least the ninth century, and that it came later, and in a truncated form, to Anglo-Saxon England.[48]

At the Veneration of the Cross on Good Friday, the *Pange Lingua* verses 'Sing, my tongue, the glorious battle' came to be sung, with the stanza *Crux Fidelis*, 'O Faithful Cross! Above all other, one and only noble tree', as a refrain between the verses.[49] The hymn was written in the same metre as Roman military marching songs, and so it aptly fits the triumphant tone of the whole composition celebrating the victory of heaven's King. Here the Passion of Christ is presented as a recapitulation, casting Jesus as the new Adam and the cross as the tree placed in the centre of the garden. For Christ, the incarnate Son, came to restore what humanity had lost in Eden, and his cross-tree (*lignum*) undid the curse that had resulted from eating the fruit of the tree (*lignum*) of knowledge (Genesis 3.1–7). In paradise, Eve had been tricked by the cunning serpent, but on the cross, as the third stanza claims, Jesus outwitted the Devil himself and thereby fulfilled the divine plan to bring salvation to humankind. This final motif has antecedents in fourth-century patristic writing, and also featured in a hymn that is ascribed to Ambrose of Milan.[50]

Although the hymn rehearses the actual physical suffering of Christ on the cross, specifically mentioning the nails, the vinegar and spear, the cross emerges as a throne from which the royal Christ reigns as the one who was victorious over the destructive and distorting power of sin and evil. So again the cross is presented as an emblem of victory, the standard of the heavenly King. This poetic trope of the unfurling banners of the King provided the imagery in which Christians throughout the first

---

48 The hymn was included in the hymnal known as the Leofric Collector, which was compiled by four scribes working in Exeter in the mid eleventh century. See Sarah Larratt Keefer, 'The Veneration of the Cross in Anglo-Saxon England' in Helen Gittos and M. Bradford Bedingfield (eds), *The Liturgy of the Late Anglo-Saxon Church* (Woodbridge: Henry Bradshaw Society 2005), p. 152; Richard W. Pfaff, *The Liturgy in Medieval England: A History* (Oxford: Oxford University Press 2009), p. 133.

49 A. S. Walpole, *Early Latin Hymns* (Cambridge: Cambridge University Press 1922).

50 Louis van Tongeren, *Exaltation of the Cross: Towards the Origin of the Feast of the Cross and the Meaning of the Cross in Early Medieval Liturgy* (Leuven: Peeters 2000), p. 231.

Plate 1: The Isenheim altarpiece, the Unterlinden Museum, Colmar
(photograph: SuperStock)

Plate 2: The ritual action of the taking of bread, showing alignment of the host with
the altarpiece (photograph: reproduced by permission of Canterbury Cathedral)

Plate 3: The Tree of Life nave altar at Lichfield Cathedral
(photograph: reproduced by permission of the Chapter of Lichfield Cathedral)

Plate 4: The Crucifixion panel, Redemption Window, the Corona, Canterbury Cathedral
(photograph: reproduced by permission of Canterbury Cathedral)

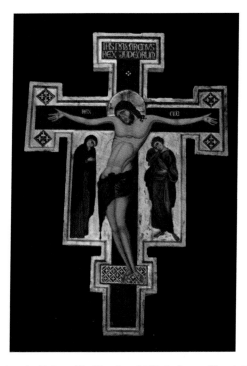

Plate 5: Jennifer Holmes, *The Blue Cross*, 2007, the Lower Church, Mirfield
(photograph: reproduced by permission of the College of the Resurrection, Mirfield)

Plate 6: The Kelibia font, the Bardo Museum, Tunis, sixth century
(photograph: Robin Margaret Jensen)

Plate 7: Roger Wagner, the *Tree of Life* window, St Mary's Church, Iffley, Oxford
(photograph: Rupert Martin)

millennium visualized the cross, and made it an apt hymn to sing in procession. The heroic imagery of the victorious King recurs in a spectacular early English poem of the late eighth or early ninth century, the so-called *Dream of the Rood*. In this poem, as in the verses of Fortunatus, the victorious Christ appears to mount the cross, as a warrior would mount his war horse, in order to plunder hell and ride triumphantly into heaven. The *Dream*, possibly written by a Northumbrian monk, is full of scriptural allusions and echoes of liturgical texts and hymnody, and presents the cross as a shimmering, jewelled and wondrous tree of glory. The poet twice alludes to what may well be a liturgical adoration of the cross, possibly to the veneration on Good Friday, and speaks of its power to make whole those who venerate it: 'I tower / High and mighty beneath the skies, having power to heal / Whosoever shall bow to me.'[51]

Because the cross in this Old English poem represents the bloody scene of Christ's victory, so it is transmuted into a tree of beauty, a tree that bore the king in his dazzling splendour. Here again we can trace the imagery back to the cross hymnody of Fortunatus, particularly to the fifth stanza of the *Vexilla Regis* that speaks of the cross as the tree of dazzling beauty (*arbour decora et fulgida*). This may echo the record of Adomnan, the seventh-century Irish monk of Iona who, relating the observations of a Frankish pilgrim to the holy sites in Jerusalem, described a shimmering gold and silver cross that was placed above the sepulchre within the Anastasis church in Jerusalem.[52] Whether Fortunatus knew of this cross or not, he had spent his formative years in Ravenna, and so it is very likely that he would have known the dazzling early sixth-century mosaic jewelled cross in the apse of St Apollinare in Classe, and that it was this glorious image of the cross that may have inspired some of the imagery in his verses.

As we have seen, the cross in the *Pange Lingua* is presented as the anti-type of that tree in Eden, whose fruit Adam and Eve were expressly

51 J. A. W. Bennett, *Poetry of the Passion: Studies in Twelve Centuries of English Verse* (Oxford: Clarendon Press 1982), p. 31.
52 'The entrance of this small building faces east. Its whole exterior is covered with choice marble, and the roof is decorated on the outside with gold, and supports a large gold cross.' Adomnan, *The Holy Places*, Bk 1, 2.7, translation from John Wilkinson, *Jerusalem Pilgrims Before the Crusades* (Warminster: Aris & Phillips 2002), p. 171. A blood-jewelled cross, known as a *crux gemmate*, is shown above the sepulchre in the much-restored apse mosaic dating back to the mid fifth century at St Pudenziana in Rome.

commanded not to eat. Pitying the fate of fallen humanity, God chooses another tree according to the second stanza, 'to repair the injury of the forbidden tree'. It seemed fitting, in other words, that the medium that had brought about humanity's downfall should become the medium whereby the injury was repaired. And in doing this, something is achieved that is beyond the simple rescuing of humankind from the destroying vortex of death and decay.[53] And as the fate of humanity was linked by Fortunatus to the wider created world, so a further stanza widens the application of the saving significance of Christ's suffering to a wider cosmic scope. The blood and water that flowed from Christ's pierced side as he hung on the cross is said to cleanse the whole created order: 'washing the earth, the sea, the stars, and the world' (stanza 7). Indeed, the overall thrust of what is said in these verses is that as the fate of humankind hinged upon the tree planted in Eden, so the cross-tree of Christ is central to God's intention to restore humanity and renew creation.

The motif of the cross as the tree of life, however, finds its fullest expression in the *Crux Fidelis* stanza, and at this point the poet addresses the tree directly. Here the cross is greeted as the most noble of all trees. This noble tree is hailed as the fullest, most verdant and productive of all other trees, as no other wood has ever borne such foliage, blossom and fruit. The immediate reference here is to the sacrificed body of Christ nailed to the wood of the cross and, as such, invites the reader to consider the Eucharist as being the fruit of the cross. Such a connection is only implicit in this stanza, but a more explicit link between the Eucharist and the cross is drawn by Fortunatus elsewhere in his verses on the cross.

One may consider, for example, the seventh stanza of the *Vexilla Regis*. Here the poet speaks of the fragrant spice that issues from the bark of the tree, and tellingly adds a line about its taste being more delicious than nectar. The meaning of this tightly constructed Latin verse is not immediate, and one can understand why it has been excised in more modern liturgical versifications. However, given the implicit

---

53 This typology of the tree of the fall and the cross-tree has parallels in the Byzantine hymnody, and Regan cites the Stichera of the Cross 4, which is set for Vespers on the Third Sunday of Lent: 'O you first-created Couple, fallen from heavenly status . . . through the bitter pleasure from the olden tree: Come! See here the true and more revered Tree' – 'Veneration of the Cross', p. 145.

identification of the wood of the cross with the figure of the Crucified in the hymn, and the use of the word 'taste', it is clear that what we have here is a distinct allusion to the heavenly food of the Eucharist, to wisdom's banquet in the Church's 'sacrifice of praise' (see Proverbs 9.1–6; Wisdom 16.20–21).

The fruit of the noble tree recurs in another and lesser known composition of Fortunatus, the *Crux Benedicta*. This hymn on the cross speaks splendidly of the powerful fecundity of the cross-tree. In the penultimate stanza (stanza 8), there is an allusion to Psalm 1.3 with its reference to a tree planted by water, and the imagery of this stanza evokes the figure of the tree of life extending its branches and being adorned with fresh flowers. In the final stanza, a direct allusion is made to Christ the true vine (John 15), who is explicitly identified as the source of the eucharistic cup: 'Among your branches hangs the vine / from which blood-red sweet wine flows.'[54]

The motif of the 'noble tree' evokes the priestly and the kingly character of Christ as he willingly undertook the work of God on the cross, and it is this dominant metaphor of Christ's saving work that is paralleled in the earliest Christian iconography of the cross. Indeed, most of the earliest depictions of the Crucified in liturgical art and sacred book and manuscript illustrations, such as the sixth-century Rabbula Gospel Book, depicted Christ robed on the cross. This image of the Crucified was embellished with a crown during the Carolingian period, but this did not detract from the priestly character of the image. The priestly image of Christ was repristinated and actively promoted a century or so later by the liturgical developments at Cluny in Burgundy. Certainly by the tenth century the increasing influence of the Cluniac monastic reform and renewal had reinforced the view of the cross as a sign of Christ's victory, and had led to developed liturgical forms and services, especially for the feasts of the Invention, celebrated on 3 May, and the Exaltation of the Cross, celebrated on 14 September, as well as the liturgy of Good Friday. The image of Christ reigning from the cross, dressed in a red tunic with a girdle tied around his waist, persisted in the large polychrome painted crosses and rood figures painted in northern Italy, in parts of Spain and in northern France up until the late thirteenth century.

---

54 Van Tongeren, *Exaltation of the Cross*, p. 247.

The shift from a presentation of a 'heroic Christ' to a more sentimental piety of the cross focusing on the suffering borne by Christ has
often been attributed to Anselm of Canterbury (1033–1109), but again
it is advisable to exercise some caution in attributing a definitive break
from earlier ways of presenting and responding to the cross in Christian
prayer, the liturgical arts and in personal piety.

Even before Anselm there had been those like Peter Damian who
had written prayers on Christ's Passion in a more emotional key. In
these prayers the authors expressed the wish that they themselves had
seen the unspeakable bloody agony of Christ's death on the cross and
had felt its shame. This sentiment was reinforced by the lines in the
Improperia (Reproaches) that were sung during the veneration of the
cross in the Good Friday liturgy. These verses are framed as a direct
and emotionally charged accusation, and are sung by the deacon who,
mimicking the voice of the Crucified, asks: 'What have I done to you?
Why are you treating me in such a brutal and agonizing way? It was I
who delivered you. I who planted you as a choice vine.' Anselm's contemporary, John of Fécamp (990–1078), the abbot of a neighbouring
Norman monastery on the Channel coast of Anselm's monastery at Bec
Hellouin, had written a collection of prayers for a royal widow in a style
that deliberately engaged both the imagination and the emotions. But
in this case the aim of such affective prayer, particularly that reflecting
on Christ's Passion, was not so much to inculcate a sense of sympathy,
of feeling for oneself the physical agony of Christ crucified, but to gain
a greater appreciation of God's overflowing mercy. It was this divine
mercy that led to the Incarnation and to Christ's being brought to the
very limits of what is humanly bearable.[55] These were the theological
issues that also exercised the considerable intellect of Anselm and found
their fullest expression in his *Cur Deus Homo* ('Why did God become
Man?'), which was completed during a period of exile in his latter days
as Archbishop of Canterbury. In this substantial book, Anselm sought
to address, through the literary contrivance of a dialogue with Boso, a
fellow monk, the question, keenly pressed by both Jews and Muslims,
as to why God had to suffer – a view, of course, that was and still is
repugnant to both religious traditions.

---

55 See Rachel Fulton, *From Judgment to Passion: Devotion to Christ and the Virgin, 800–
1200* (New York: Columbia University Press 2002), pp. 146–70.

During his time as a monk at Bec Hellouin, Anselm also wrote a series of prayers and meditations, including a prayer to the holy cross. This was effectively composed as a reflective personal prayer on the cross, and in its language we can detect a distinct echo of some of the themes of the prayers and chants of the Good Friday liturgy. The use of the verbs 'venerate' and 'adore', for instance, links the prayer directly to the central ritual act of the Good Friday liturgy, when the cross is presented as a devotional focus for the individual worshippers. In this prayer, Christ is presented as freely choosing to take up the cross, and Anselm speaks of his death in the paradoxical language that resists any single, one-dimensional meaning. The crucifixion is spoken of in this way: sinful humanity conspired to kill life, yet Christ destroys death; and so through the cross, life is brought to the dead. These lines of the prayer are undoubtedly inspired by the liturgy of the cross, and so the cross itself is repeatedly said to signify God's mercy and to carry and convey the significance of God's gift of salvation, life and resurrection. The vocabulary Anselm uses here directly parallels the words of the Introit chant that was sung at the Mass on the feast of the Holy Cross (14 September): 'We should glory in the cross of our Lord Jesus Christ: in whom is our salvation, life and resurrection: by whom we were chosen and set free.'[56] And so even in regard to Anselm it could be said that the cross was a sign of life, its significance considered to be of cosmic scope. For the excessive divine economy of mercy and grace was seen by Anselm not only to override human sin and to restore the divine honour but finally to renew and beautify the created order: 'By you the world is renewed and made beautiful with truth.'[57]

We know that the image of the cross was present in church buildings in a number of different ways. In some the cross was part of the permanent decoration of the building as a mosaic or a wall painting on the east wall or apse, and thereby became the focal symbol of

---

56 These words have now been appropriated for the Introit for the Mass of the Lord's Supper, which is the first liturgical celebration of the triduum in the revised Roman Rite (revised 1955 and 1970), and are incorporated into a Post-Communion Prayer for the feast of the Holy Cross (14 September) in the Church of England's recent provision of liturgical texts for festivals. See *Common Worship: Festivals* (London: Church House Publishing 2008), p. 106.

57 'Prayer to the Holy Cross', line 50, *The Prayers and Meditations of Saint Anselm with the Proslogion*, trans. Benedicta Ward SLG (London: Penguin Books 1973).

the worshipping space.[58] Less common in the early centuries was the placing of the cross upon an altar, but this became customary in late Anglo-Saxon England. An illustration in the royal charter, the *Liber vitae* for New Minster, the new Anglo-Saxon monastic community at Winchester, shows King Cnut (d. 1032) and Queen Aelfgifu presenting a large silver altar cross for the high altar of the church.[59] In the later Norman church it became common for a large cross to be erected on a rood screen above the entrance to the choir, and these crosses were often highly decorated. In the twelfth century, Henry de Blois gave the community at Cluny a life-size silver gilt sculpted figure of Christ with a gold crown for the large rood cross in the abbey church. Both the examples I have cited here were royal benefactions to monastic foundations and were undoubtedly bound up with a desire to sacralize a view of kingship. But alongside this political motive was an increasing custom to place a cross, and later a crucifix, on the altar for the celebration of the Mass. The practice was certainly promoted by Innocent III who, even before his elevation to the papacy in 1198, had written a tract on the desirability of a cross and candles being placed on the altar for the celebration of the Mass.[60]

The arrangement of altars within the architectural space of a church, particularly in monastic churches, returns us to Jerusalem and specifically to the architectural arrangements of the Martyrium and Anastasis. As we have seen, this church complex became a topographical map of the foundational narrative of Christ's death and resurrection, which was ritually enacted morning and evening each day and with particular drama and devotion on Good Friday and the evening of Holy Saturday. We know that by the beginning of the fifth century the Jerusalem model influenced the design and building of churches and baptisteries in the Christian world, both East and West. Reference has already been made to the fifth-century apse mosaic at St Pudenziana in Rome, and this well illustrates the impact that Jerusalem had on the Christian imagination and the desire to reproduce it elsewhere. In this glittering mosaic

---

58 E. Peterson, 'La croce e la preghiera verso oriente', *Ephemerides Liturgicae*, vol. 59, 1945, pp. 52–66.

59 Raw, *Anglo-Saxon Crucifixion Iconography*, p. 26; Richard Gameson, *The Role of Art in the Late Anglo-Saxon Church* (Oxford: Clarendon Press 1995), p. 130. This manuscript was exhibited in the Royal Manuscripts exhibition at the British Library, January–March 2012.

60 *De sacro altaris mysterio* PL 217:811.

Christ is depicted as sitting on a throne above which is the mound of Golgotha, from which rises a towering jewelled cross as described by pilgrims to Jerusalem.[61] Images of the holy places in Jerusalem were dispersed throughout the Christian world. From the fifth century, large numbers of pilgrims would return home with small *ampullae*, flasks for holy oil or water that would sit comfortably in the palm of the hand. These virtually mass-produced pilgrim flasks were made of terracotta, glass and even tin-lead, and were undoubtedly a significant part of the pilgrim economy in the holy city. The flasks were often stamped with representations of the sepulchre of Christ enclosed within the rotunda, or of Golgotha, the site of the cross. This image of Golgotha showed the cross erected on the rock by the Emperor Theodosius I.[62] The manufacture of these images, which were also imprinted on pilgrim badges, may well have continued even beyond the Islamic conquest of Jerusalem in the seventh century.[63]

The image of the cross and the sepulchre in Jerusalem impacted on the Christian imagination and influenced the ordering and the decoration of churches, particularly monastic churches. In later buildings the arrangement in Jerusalem influenced the positioning of the primary liturgical foci, and this is certainly the case in those churches constructed as a result of the monastic revival, first in the Carolingian period on the Continent and later as a result of the Benedictine revival in tenth-century England.[64]

The pattern of demarking the place of the cross and the resurrection, as in the church complex in Jerusalem, is evident in an early ninth-century plan of the buildings for a monastery, which is known as the St Gall, or St Gallan, Plan. From the dedicatory inscription it seems that this detailed plan, written and drawn in ink, had been requested by Abbot Gozbert (816–36) of St Gall, a monastery famous for its library and schools, situated some 50 kilometres south-east of Constance, in what is now Switzerland. The plan was made by scribes,

---

61 See Allan Doig, *Liturgy and Architecture: From the Early Church to the Middle Ages* (Aldershot: Ashgate 2008), pp. 37–8.
62 For illustrations, see Morris, *The Sepulchre of Christ and the Medieval West*, p. 75; Martin Biddle, *The Tomb of Christ* (Stroud: Sutton Publishing 1999), p. 23.
63 Morris, *The Sepulchre of Christ and the Medieval West*, p. 77.
64 See Elizabeth C. Parker, 'Architecture as Liturgical Setting' in Thomas J. Heffernan and E. Ann Matter (eds), *The Liturgy of the Medieval Church* (Kalamazoo, MI: Medieval Institute Publications, Western Michigan University 2001).

probably working under the direction of Abbot Haito, in the abbey of Reichenau, which was built on an island in Lake Constance. The plan has often puzzled historians because what resembles to all intents and purposes an architectural plan was never actually built. So what was it intended for, and how is it to be read? One suggestion is that the St Gall Plan is a plan of an ideal monastery,[65] and that it came to be regarded and read in monastic circles as a template, a cognitive model of the Christian temple. The most prominent and central space is the church and an adjacent cloister. The church itself, with two transepts, one north and one south, is deliberately cross shaped. In this way, the plan served to map the meaning of the monastic life. As Mary Carruthers has convincingly shown, the detailed St Gall Plan came to be regarded as a diagrammatic *pictura* or mental picture whereby monastics could recall and deepen their understanding of the monastic life[66] – a way of life that can be seen as a living out, in its most radical form, of the paschal mystery of Christ and the literal placing of oneself in the cross (cf. Galatians 6.14b).

Whether it was intended as an architectural plan or a mental map of the monastic life, attention paid to what is shown and described in the inscriptions of the St Gall Plan is instructive. A particular prominence is given to the entry into the monastic church, the *via* or 'way', and the different pathways of aisles and ambulatories through the church building are carefully mapped out. The delineation of the spaces within the building, and the connecting pathways through these spaces, indicate that the physical building itself was intended to articulate a kind of pilgrimage through the paschal mystery of Christ's cross and resurrection.

For on the plan a large cross is prominently marked in the centre of the nave, west of the monastic quire. This may represent either the position of a large free-standing cross, such as the one that stood on Golgotha in the Martyrium church or, more likely, an altar dedicated to the cross. The Carolingians had promoted the multiplication of altars, but there is evidence of prominent altars dedicated to the cross being placed centrally in the nave of abbey churches on the Continent during

---

65 Raw, *Anglo-Saxon Crucifixion Iconography*, p. 44.
66 Mary Carruthers, *The Craft of Thought: Meditation, Rhetoric, and the Making of Images, 400–1200* (Cambridge: Cambridge University Press 1998), pp. 228–31.

this time.[67] And we may assume that it was around this altar of the cross that the laity, locals, visitors and pilgrims would gather for worship. In the plan the nave altar is sited between a centrally placed ambo and the font, and is designated as the 'the altar of the holy Saviour at the Cross'. Written on either side of the cross on the plan is an inscription that speaks of the life, well-being and redemption that is brought to the sorrowful world by the holy cross. An elevated high altar, positioned further east of the choir, is dedicated to Mary and Gall, the patrons of the abbey church, but the inscription indicates its proximity to the tomb, presumably of St Gallan, which at least resonates with the site of the sepulchre in the rotunda church of the Anastasis in the original fourth-century Jerusalem complex. Finally, there is another feature in the plan that deserves attention, and that is an open semi-circular space that is designated *paradisi* or garden, located beyond the eastern apse of the church. This feature mirrors a similar space in front of the western apse and thereby suggests that the church was seen not only as prefiguring the heavenly city, the new Jerusalem, but also as representing the garden of paradise.

The longitudinal axis of an abbey basilican church heightened the sense of progression, of movement through the paschal mystery, as the pilgrim in Jerusalem physically moved from 'Golgotha' in the Martyrium to the 'sepulchre' in the Anastasis. Here indeed is the template for the location of an altar of the cross in the main body of the church, and for the high altar being associated with the resurrection. The high altar was often placed within an apsidal or semi-circular space and was often marked by columns. The foliate decoration of the capitals of these columns may well provide a reference to the garden, the site of encounter with the risen Christ. A late and impressive example is to be seen in the colonnaded space around the so-called 'morning altar' of the massive abbey church at Cluny.

The church, known as Cluny III, was the largest in western Europe between the eleventh and sixteenth centuries, and the abbey is well known as having led a major monastic reform on the Continent.[68] The

---

67 See Parker, 'Architecture as Liturgical Setting', pp. 286–95; Walter Horn and Ernest Born, *The Plan of St Gall: A Study of the Architecture and Economy of, and Life in a Paradigmatic Carolingian Monastery*, vol. 1 (Berkeley: University of California Press 1979), p. 134.
68 See Marcel Pacaut, *L'Ordre de Cluny (909–1789)* (Paris: Fayard Press 1986); Doig, *Liturgy and Architecture*, pp. 158–61.

chancel space is now reconstructed in the museum at Cluny, and there the visitor can see how the altar was surrounded by ten columns, each with elaborately carved capitals illustrating the different occupations and aspects of the monastic life and vocation. The carving on one of these capitals, known as 'the four rivers of paradise', links a paradisal motif with the altar and shows flowing waters, a fish and four different kinds of tree – apple, vine, fig and olive. Water and fish recall baptism, the fruiting trees and vine, paradise. And so the whole iconographical ensemble here registers the fruitfulness of Christ's sacrifice and how those who live out the baptismal life are invited to share in the marriage feast of the Lamb in paradise (Revelation 19.9).

What was mapped out in the St Gall Plan, and came to be seen in the monastic churches both on the Continent and in England, was an arrangement that ultimately took its inspiration from the proximity of the sites of the crucifixion and resurrection in the adjacent architectural spaces in the church complex at Jerusalem. And so it became customary to place a cross at the centre of the church. Examples of this arrangement are numerous, and some pre-Conquest English monastic churches – Ramsey built in 970 and Old Minster in Winchester – had centrally placed altars of the cross located in the nave.[69] It seems possible that the same arrangement was adopted in Lanfranc's church at Canterbury, with one centrally placed altar dedicated to the cross[70] and another eastern altar dedicated to the Saviour, the risen Christ. In this arrangement the cross and resurrection were spatially aligned, which illustrates both the paschal journey that worshippers commenced in baptism and the way in which the cross itself was regarded in the light of the resurrection.[71]

Attention has recently been drawn to how a cross set up in the church, or even erected outside of the building, as in the insular stone crosses of Britain and Ireland, became a stational point for liturgical processions in the celebration of daily prayer, probably at the end of Vespers.

---

69 Raw, *Anglo-Saxon Crucifixion Iconography*, p. 44.

70 According to Potts' plan of the Abbey Church of the Apostles Peter and Paul and Augustine of Canterbury, the altar just west of the rood was dedicated to the Holy Cross, but the high altar was dedicated in honour of the abbey's patrons. R. U. Potts, 'The Plan of St Austin's Abbey Canterbury', *Archeologia Cantiana*, vol. 46, 1934, pp. 179–94.

71 One might also consider the custom introduced in late Anglo-Saxon churches of the *depositio*, or the burial of the cross at the end of the Good Friday liturgy.

These short processional movements to the cross for a commemorative prayer may ultimately have originated from what happened in Jerusalem during the fourth century. George Guiver has suggested that this liturgical tradition can be understood as a ritual act of 'touching base' with the sign of that paschal mystery in which Christians die daily to sin and are raised as new creatures in the light of the resurrection.[72] However, it was in the development of the liturgy of Good Friday that the significance of the cross, its meaning, was most dramatically and definitively shown, and so it is to the development of that liturgy that we must specifically return.

The veneration of the cross during the Good Friday liturgy became elaborated with increasing drama. By the tenth century the cross, now a convenient cross, no bigger than a processional cross and no longer a relic, was veiled when it was brought into the church for the veneration. On the Continent it was gradually unveiled at three points or 'stations' as it was carried through the nave into the chancel, accompanied by appropriate chants and antiphons. At each station the veiled cross was raised so that it could be seen by the congregation, as the haunting acclamation *Ecce lignum crucis*, 'Behold the wood of the cross on which hung the Saviour of the world', was sung. This inevitably heightened the dramatic moment of the disclosure of the cross in the performance of the liturgy for Good Friday. The actual words of the *lignum crucis* acclamation were probably originally written earlier for the celebration of the veneration of the Cross in Rome, and are found in *Ordo* XXIV.

In England at this time, the liturgy for Good Friday had been embellished by the introduction of dramatic elements as a result of the Benedictine revival that had been spearheaded by Dunstan (910–88), alongside Aethelwold of Winchester and Oswald of Worcester. Dunstan, a scholar and musician, was a monk of Glastonbury, and was appointed Archbishop of Canterbury by King Edgar. The *Regularis Concordia*, a document issued in 970 by Aethelwold's gathering of abbots known as the Synod of Winchester, consolidated this monastic renewal and

---

72 George Guiver, *Vision Upon Vision: Processes of Change and Renewal in Christian Worship* (Norwich: Canterbury Press 2009), pp. 92–9. Note also the provision after Evening Prayer of 'prayers at the cross' on Fridays in *Celebrating Common Prayer* (London: Mowbray 1992), and now in the official Church of England's *Common Worship: Daily Prayer* (London: Church House Publishing 2005), 'Prayers at the Foot of the Cross', p. 317.

attempted to regularize the liturgical usages of monastic communities and also of some cathedrals.[73] The document made detailed provision for Good Friday, including the Veneration of the Cross that was to follow the Office of None. This source included the *Improperia* or Reproaches – words of lamentation and accusation – noted above, as well as additional chants and devotional prayers that had attached themselves to the Veneration. These additional texts undoubtedly heightened the dramatic element of the liturgy and introduced a sung response. The *Agios O Theos* and the *Sanctus Deus* were sung in both Greek and Latin respectively as the veiled cross was brought through the church to the chancel step for the adoration.[74] At that point the cross was unveiled, following the *lignum crucis*, 'Behold, the wood of the cross . . .', and the designated psalmody was the antiphon *Crucem tuam adoramus*.[75]

The wording of this antiphon indicates that the devotional adoration of the cross in monastic communities again focused on the suffering and death of Christ in the light of the resurrection.[76] So here we can see a line of continuity stretching back to earlier practice in Rome and ultimately to Jerusalem, confirming how the cross combined both the crucifixion and the resurrection: 'We adore thy *cross*, O Lord, and praise and glorify thy holy *resurrection*.'[77] The cross, in other words, represented the whole mystery of Christ. As such, and following the reference to the resurrection, the antiphon significantly concludes with a reference to creation as the recipient of God's saving work, and thereby relates the cross and the resurrection to the renewal of creation:

> We adore thy *cross*, O Lord, and praise and glorify thy holy *resurrection*; it is indeed because of the cross that joy of the world came for all *creation*.[78]

---

73 Pfaff, *The Liturgy in Medieval England*, p. 78.
74 M. Bradford Bedingfield, *The Dramatic Liturgy of Anglo-Saxon England* (Woodbridge: Boydell Press 2002), pp. 125–7.
75 The provenance and date of this antiphon is uncertain, but it was referred to by Amalarius of Metz and was known in northern France in the ninth century. See Keefer, 'The Veneration of the Cross in Anglo-Saxon England', pp. 147, 151.
76 Raw, *Anglo-Saxon Crucifixion Iconography*, p. 163.
77 *Regularis concordia anglicae nationis monachorum sanctimonialiumque*, iv. 44, trans. T. Symons (London: Nelson 1953).
78 Translation from Keefer, 'The Veneration of the Cross in Anglo-Saxon England', p. 147 (italics added).

The relating of the cross and the resurrection to God's work of re-creation proclaimed in this antiphon sung at the Veneration of the Cross was also expanded in a number of contemporary Anglo-Saxon homilies on the cross. An eloquent example is that of Aelfric (*c.* 955–*c.* 1020), a monk of Cerne who later became the first Abbot of Eynsham.[79] Aelfric, possibly a pupil of Aethelwold, was a prolific writer, and his sermons, preached in the vernacular, were arranged according to the liturgical calendar.[80] The extensive collection includes a sermon for the feasts of the Invention (discovery) of the Cross in which Aelfric recounts the story of Helena (see above).[81] In another sermon on the cross, Aelfric built on Augustine of Hippo's observation that the sixth day, when God created humankind, was also the day on which Christ was crucified (see Augustine's Commentary on John, *Tractate* XVII.15; cf. end of Chapter 5) and spoke eloquently of Good Friday as the day of God's re-creation, the day of God's making, and his making new through the paschal mystery of Christ.[82]

With what St Paul spoke of as the 'public portrayal of the cross' (Galatians 3.1b) in preaching and liturgical celebration, the mystery of God's purpose, or what we may call the divine secret, is out, and that is to restore creation. This we could call the long view of the cross, one that contrasts with the foreshortened view of the cross that focuses solely on Christ's human suffering and death. The longer view is suggested by the hints and intimations of God's intention to renew creation in both the liturgy and iconography of the cross that we have commented on in previous chapters. The present chapter has shown how the cross as a sign of victory and of resurrection, even on dark Good Friday, was regarded pre-eminently as a sign of Christ, incarnate, crucified and risen. It signifies the saving work of God in Christ, and its significance extends to, and is finally played out in, the remaking of creation. This linking of the cross and creation is concisely expressed in a modern eucharistic proper preface for the Passion telling how 'the tree

---

79 For further background and a selection of Aelfric's sermons, see Richard K. Emmerson, *Anglo-Saxon Spirituality: Selected Writings*, trans. Robert Boenig (New York: Paulist Press 2000).
80 *Anglo-Saxon Spirituality: Selected Writings*, p. 49.
81 See Malcolm Godden (ed.), *Aelfric's Catholic Homilies: The Second Series Texts*, Early English Text Society (Oxford: Oxford University Press 1979), pp. 174–6.
82 Cited by Raw, *Anglo-Saxon Crucifixion Iconography*, pp. 175–6.

of shame' has become 'the tree of glory', and 'where life was lost, there life has been restored'.[83] This articulation of the cross as a life-giving sign recalls the iconography of the living cross, to which we shall now turn.

83 Proper Preface for the Cross (10), first published in the Church of England's alternative provision, *The Alternative Service Book 1980*, Church of England, p. 155, and included as a shorter Preface for Palm Sunday in *Common Worship: Times and Seasons* (London: Church House Publishing 2006), p. 275.

Chapter 5

The living cross

The decoration around and immediately above the area of the sanctuary where the altar is located invariably provides the principal visual key to the meaning of what is enacted in the liturgical celebrations that occur in that designated holy space. One might consider the stunning apsidal mosaics that are seen, for example, in the Byzantine churches of the East and to particularly brilliant effect at Hosios Lukas, near Delphi and at St Apollinare in Classe, near Ravenna. But the apsidal mosaics I particularly wish the reader to reflect on are in two churches in the ancient city of Rome. Rome is the second centre of historic Christianity after Jerusalem, and in its church structures we can most fully trace how the practice and understanding of liturgy came to shape the architectural spaces in which Christians gathered together for worship. In both these churches, then, my focus will be on the apsidal mosaics, which are literally the visual backdrop to the offering of the Eucharist and whose composition provides a frame of reference for us to reconstruct an understanding of the saving death and resurrection of Christ that was commemorated and celebrated in the Eucharist.

The first church on my itinerary is the Papal Church of St John Lateran, so named because it was built in a quarter of Rome known in the fourth century as the Lateranus, a name derived from an influential first-century Roman family known as the Laterani.[1] The Basilica Salvatoris, as the church was originally known, was the first church to be built in Rome by the Emperor Constantine shortly after his conversion, and was completed in 318. Built for Pope Sylvester (314–35) to be the cathedral church of the Bishop of Rome, the claim was made that it

---

1 Matilda Webb, *The Churches and Catacombs of Early Christian Rome* (Brighton: Sussex Academic Press 2001), p. 41.

was the 'head and mother church of people everywhere', and for this reason it was decreed that its dedication festival on 9 November was to be celebrated throughout the churches of Rome and its environs.[2] The church followed the general plan of a basilica, literally a 'royal hall' designed for a public assembly. The basic architectural plan provided an arcaded nave, a gathering space lit by clerestory windows below the internal roof structure, allowing natural light to illuminate the frescoes or mosaics along its walls. The orientation of a basilica usually ran from west to east, with a semi-circular apse at the east end and in some cases an atrium or enclosed forecourt at the west end.[3]

The original Basilica Salvatoris was a monumental structure some 100 metres long and 53 metres wide. There were two twin colonnaded side-aisles leading to a semi-circular apse above the bishop's throne, which itself was covered by a highly decorated ciborium. It has been suggested that the object of building a church on this scale was not only to confer a magisterial dignity upon the Bishop of Rome but also to provide sufficient space for the considerable increase in numbers from this expanding cosmopolitan city in which Christianity was now the official cult.[4] The sizeable influx of new converts and catechumens – that is, those people being formed and instructed to receive the illumination of baptism – probably sat in the curtained side-aisles during the celebration of the liturgy. What they and the faithful saw as they entered the building is a fascinating question. The intention was undoubtedly to communicate something of the majesty of the God, of that light, into whose presence worshippers were drawn through the panoply of Christian worship.[5] We cannot say exactly how the first worshippers at the Lateran basilica perceived and read the visual symbols of its decorative scheme, but we can confidently aver that the interior of the church

2 Richard Kieckhefer, *Theology in Stone: Church Architecture from Byzantium to Berkeley* (Oxford: Oxford University Press 2004), p. 159.

3 Robert Milburn, *Early Christian Art and Architecture* (Aldershot: Scolar Press 1988), pp. 105–9.

4 Allan Doig, *Liturgy and Architecture: From the Early Church to the Middle Ages* (Aldershot: Ashgate 2008), pp. 24–6.

5 In a discussion of the early apse decoration, Robin Margaret Jensen cites a fourth-century baptismal homily of Gregory of Nazianzen that focuses on the element of baptism as illumination and speaks of the divine light 'contemplated in the Father and the Son and the Holy Spirit, whose wealth is their union of natures, and the one extension of their brightness'. See her *Understanding Early Christian Art* (London: Routledge 2000), p. 110.

would have made a considerable impact on those who gathered there for worship.

Constantine had donated lavish gifts for the dedication of this great church, including a number of large bronze candles, 10 crown lights and 12 bronze chandeliers, which when lit during services would have caused a most magnificent spectacle of light. The longitudinal axis of the structure would have led the eye along a visual path towards the focal point of the apse, for whose decoration Constantine had given a quantity of gold foil. Throughout its history the church has suffered pillage, from the Goths in the fifth century and fires and an earthquake. It was restored by Pope Leo I (440–61), who famously claimed in a sermon for the feast of the Ascension that what Christ offered and brought to people in his incarnate ministry had now passed over into the holy mysteries; that is, through the celebration of the sacraments. And if we apply this conviction to the liturgical space of the Lateran, we could say that the longitudinal axis of the basilica was not adapted to distance the laity deliberately or even to heighten a sense of mysterious otherness, but rather to provide a pathway – literally – that gave access to the holy mysteries. This sense of giving access to the mysteries celebrated at the altar came to be articulated in the assertion in a later collect for the annual feast of the Dedication of the Lateran that the basis for the celebration was that God had made it possible for his people to draw near to his holy mysteries.

A major restoration was undertaken during the pontificate of Hadrian (772–95), and the interior was radically remodelled in the seventeenth century to how it looks today. Despite the number of restorations and additions over the centuries, on entering this church the eye is still drawn to the primary focal point of the architectural space, the sanctuary. And above and around this space is the apsidal mosaic, made with countless small glass and stone tesserae. The mosaic bears the name of Toriti, a late thirteenth-century mosaicist,[6] but it is very likely that he followed the basic outline and decorative scheme of the original mosaic[7] dating back to the ninth century – or even earlier, if comparisons are drawn with a further baptistery mosaic that will be discussed in Chapter 7.

---

6 Walter Oakeshott, *The Mosaics of Rome: From the Third to the Fourteenth Centuries* (London: Thames & Hudson 1967), p. 70.
7 Oakeshott, *The Mosaics of Rome*, p. 94.

The medium of mosaic was deliberately deployed to catch and play with the light, and so when the building was in use the visual backdrop of the liturgy would have shimmered and drawn the eye of the worshipper as he or she looked towards the altar.

In terms of both composition and style, there are features that are reminiscent of some of the sixth-century mosaics in Ravenna. The top lunette contains a haloed bust of Christ surrounded by angels, and below, in a second band of decoration, is the jewelled cross, similar in effect to the apse mosaic at St Apollinare in Classe, as well as to the cupola decoration in the rotunda of the earlier titular church of St Stefano on the Caelian Hill in Rome. On either side of the cross stand Mary and John the Baptist, as in the Byzantine deesis icon (an icon of supplication), with two other Apostles. These figures of saints were a later Franciscan addition – they include, on a smaller scale, Francis of Assisi and his follower Anthony of Padua – and are set in a glittering background of gold tesserae. Within the overall decorative scheme, the oldest decorations are undoubtedly the bust of Christ and the cross, and between them is the figure of the dove, visually exfulging its influence in golden lines down through the cross. As a symbol of the Holy Spirit, the dove indicates that God himself was present and operative in the historic suffering and death of Jesus, and that the effect of that death was none other than the salvific work of God. Both artistically and theologically there is an important correspondence between the icon of Christ in the bust and the cross, and it has been said that both reveal to the viewer the reality of Christ, who was understood to be fully human and divine. The cross reveals the suffering humanity of Christ, while the bust, with its shimmering gold, represents the glorified humanity of the divine Christ, the eternal Son of God. The visual references in the decoration here are temporal and eschatological, in so far as the cross refers back to the historic event of the crucifixion while the bust looks forward to the final revelation of the Son of God in glory. This double reference finds a correspondence in the understanding of the Eucharist, which is both anamnetic – a commemoration of past events – and an anticipation or foretaste of the eschatological Supper of the Lamb (Revelation 19.9), looking both back and forward, as St Paul had said: 'For as often as you eat this bread and drink the cup, you proclaim the Lord's death until he comes' (1 Corinthians 11.26).

Below the cross is a complex of visual motifs recalling and resonating with a number of biblical images and liturgical practices. From the foot of the cross flow four rivers, and between them flourishes the verdant tree of life, with a bird at its centre. The immediate reference point of these four rivers is the four rivers that irrigated the paradisal garden of Eden (Genesis 2.10–14), but they also recall two other key biblical passages that speak of waters flowing from the temple, both earthly and heavenly, that cleanse and water the earth. These passages are Ezekiel 47.1–12 and Revelation 22.1–2. The first is the prophet's vision of the waters flowing from the restored temple, a passage that was probably read during the papal Easter Vigil at the Lateran, which was the primary occasion in Rome for the celebration of baptism.[8] The second text, again a visionary passage, speaks of the waters of the river of life flowing from the throne of God and the lamb in the midst of the heavenly Jerusalem, refreshing and sustaining the trees growing along the river bank, whose 'leaves . . . are for the healing of the nations' (Revelation 22.2; cf. Ezekiel 47.7). As the four named rivers divide, two on either side in the mosaic, there is a small architectural feature that probably represents the heavenly Jerusalem, guarded by an angel with a sword, which evokes the angel who guards paradise. Directly above is a palm tree with the bird of paradise perched on its top branches. With the combination of these decorative elements, what we can see here is the conflation of the images of the heavenly city and paradise restored.

Directly below the four rivers are three bands of decoration extending across the semi-circular width of the apsidal mosaic. The first, an almost bottle-green band, represents the fertile earth, sustaining a variety of forms of life. The second is the flowing River Jordan, decorated with playful classical putti figures – as also seen in the apse mosaic of St Maria Maggiore – being drawn over the water by swans. In the third, figures of sheep emerge left and right, from Bethlehem and Jerusalem respectively, and gather to adore the Lamb of God, the *Agnus Dei*, the Lamb who died and now lives and reigns for ever and ever.

The artistic articulation of the biblical imagery in this mosaic echoes an older tradition of iconography of the living cross that originates in Syria and is prevalent in Syriac Christianity. This tradition exploited the

---

8 The question of the choice and selection of readings for the Easter Vigil has long exercised the minds of liturgical scholars, and Patrick Regan has recently elucidated the criteria for selection in terms of Passion and passage, but to this we must also include those passages that would resonate with the celebration of Baptism. See Regan, 'Paschal Vigil: Passion and Passage' in *Worship*, vol. 79, no. 2, March 2005.

typology between the cross planted on the hill of Calvary and the tree of life that had been planted in the earthly paradise.[9] The patriarchate of Antioch was one of the key centres of the early Christian world, and although it was heavily influenced by Jerusalem because of its geographical proximity, the Antiochene church came to develop its own distinctive emphases, liturgical practices, art and architecture. The influence of the Syrian church was considerable, spreading north into Armenia, south as far as Ethiopia and east to the nascent church on the Malabar Coast in India. According to legend, Christianity had been brought to India by the Apostle Thomas.[10] A number of early Christian artefacts survive to this day, including some stone crosses. One stone cross of particular significance is the one that marks the tomb of St Thomas at Marlapore in Chennai (Madras). This alleged site of Thomas' martyrdom continues to be a major pilgrimage site for Christians to this day,[11] and the cross marking it shows strikingly similar features to the later Lateran apse mosaic.[12] On the relief-sculpted memorial stone, a cross with foliate ends at the top and at either end of the lateral bar grows out of budding leaves, and below these, waters flow as from a fountain. So in terms of its decorative motifs, the features of this cross correspond exactly to the composition of the mosaic at the Lateran. The significant addition in the case of the tombstone is a dove in flight, aligned with the vertical shaft of the cross so that its beak touches the tip of the cross. This additional iconographic feature is seen today in the altar crosses

---

9 See the study of Joseph Vazhuthanapally, *Archaeology of Mar Sliba* (Kottayam: Oriental Institute of Religious Studies 1988), pp. 86–100.

10 See Martin Stringer, *A Sociological History of Christian Worship* (Cambridge: Cambridge University Press 2005), pp. 154–5. The literary source for this legend of Thomas' founding of Christianity is the fifth-century apocryphal book composed in the Syrian city of Edessa, *The Acts of Thomas*, and features in the later influential medieval book, *The Golden Legend*. The *Acts of Thomas* was highly prized by Christians in Malabar as it told how Thomas was sold by Christ as a slave to India, and of his adventures there, including the story of how Thomas spent money that the king had allocated for the building of a palace on the poor and in building churches, as well as how he met a martyr's death having caused the destruction of idols and their shrines. See David R. Cartlidge and J. Keith Elliott, *Art and the Christian Apocrypha* (London and New York: Routledge 2001), pp. 219–22.

11 Christine Chaillot, 'The Ancient Oriental Churches' in Geoffrey Wainwright and Karen B. Westerfield Tucker (eds), *The Oxford History of Christian Worship* (Oxford and New York: Oxford University Press 2006), p. 159.

12 Illustration of this memorial cross, possibly dating back to the sixth century, is shown in Andrew Palmer, 'Paradise Restored', *Oriens Christianus*, vol. 87, 2003, p. 5.

and other liturgical objects of the Mar Thoma Church, literally the 'St Thomas Church' of Kerala, in south-west India.

The imagery may remind us of how in John's account of the crucifixion the Spirit was given, or more literally 'handed over', by Christ as he hung upon the cross (John 19.30b). But the combination here of a symbol of the Holy Spirit with the tree and the fountain of life evokes the vision of God's salvific purpose of renewing and remaking creation (see Psalm 104.30; Isaiah 32.15). To glimpse some sense of how the Christian may be drawn into this ongoing work of God, we can return again to the apsidal mosaic at the Lateran basilica.

Here, on either side of the cross we can see two thirsting stags bending to drink of the waters, evoking Psalm 42, a psalm that was closely associated with the liturgy of Christian initiation, and the approach to the waters of baptism by those who were 'thirsting after God'. Below the stags are the six sheep, representing the faithful who are led to the green pastures by the still waters described in Psalm 23. This Psalm was also appropriated for the celebration baptismal psalm, because of its reference not only to water but also to anointing and to the table prepared by the Lord. Reference has already been made to the River Jordan, which is actually named in the mosaic and runs directly below the sheep on either side of the base of the cross. The River Jordan, of course, has multiple biblical allusions, each of which points in its own way to the sacrament of baptism. This river is literally the 'living water' that flows into the Dead Sea; it represented the liminal point at which God's people crossed into the land of promise; and it was of course the site of Jesus' own baptism by John the Baptist. These biblical allusions reinforce the baptismal reference of the whole mosaic, which pictorially presents the vital connection between the cross and baptism, a theme that will be teased out in more detail in the final chapter.

Further baptismal images may be seen in other decorative motifs in the Lateran apse mosaic. They recall how the baptized are a new creation in Christ, and evoke particular themes in John's Gospel. Here, the new temple, the place of meeting between the human and divine, is Christ's body (John 2.19–21), and from this body crucified on the cross of Calvary flows blood and water (John 19.34). As we have seen, the water flowing from Christ's side evoked the prophetic vision of the life-giving water that was seen to flow from the new temple to sustain an abundance of fruitful life (see Ezekiel 47.8 and its related passage, Zechariah 14.8). It is this vision and its evident baptismal associations that are displayed in the rich decoration of the banks of the River Jordan in the apse mosaic with its portrayal of colourful birds, plants, animals and miniature human figures, now seen to be restored in a creation made new.

From the time of Pope Hilary (460–8), the Lateran basilica possessed a jewelled relic of the cross in the lavishly decorated Chapel of the Cross near the Baptistery; this, as noted in the previous chapter, was used for the veneration on Good Friday. The feast of the Exaltation of the Cross was gradually incorporated into the cycle of feasts in Rome, and propers, prayers, readings and chants for the Mass for this feast were included in both the *Gregorian* and the *Gelasian Sacramentaries*. Some of these texts may date back to the late sixth century and reflect earlier practice.[13] The profile of the feast in Rome was raised by Pope Sergius I (687–701), and the impetus for his doing so was probably the recovery of the true cross by Heraclius (as noted in the previous chapter). Despite a story recorded in the *Liber pontificalis* that the feast was instigated in Rome because a relic of the true cross was found in a dusty cupboard in the sacristy of St Peter's, the origin of the feast is traced back to Jerusalem and the dedication of the church complex there in 335. The pilgrim Egeria, who was introduced in the last chapter, records in her journal that the eight-day celebration of the dedication festival fell on the anniversary of the discovery of the cross.[14] The fifth-century Armenian Lectionary, a key source for the study of liturgical celebrations in Jerusalem, makes provision for this feast 'when the venerable and life-giving cross was displayed for the whole congregation' in the Martyrium on 14 September.[15]

The discovery of the cross was certainly marked by the fifth century, and at that time there was considerable popular demand for the wood of the cross to be seen by pilgrims and by the faithful, which gave rise to a separate commemoration known as the feast of the Invention of the Cross. This feast first spread to the East, where it was celebrated on

---

13 See Éamonn Ó Carragáin, *Ritual and the Rood: Liturgical Images and the Old English Poems of the Dream of the Rood Tradition* (London: British Library and University of Toronto Press 2005), p. 230; Louis van Tongeren, *Exaltation of the Cross: Towards the Origin of the Feast of the Cross and the Meaning of the Cross in Early Medieval Liturgy* (Leuven: Peeters 2000), pp. 82–98.

14 See *Egeria's Travels*, trans. John Wilkinson (Warminster: Aris & Phillips 1981, revised edn), pp. 237–9.

15 Cited by van Tongeren, *Exaltation of the Cross*, p. 17.

6 March during the reign of the Emperor Justinian (527–65), and then west to Rome, where it came to be celebrated on 3 May. It was certainly established in Rome by the middle of the seventh century.

It is impossible to reconstruct exactly how the feast was celebrated in Rome, but it is reasonable to infer that the ritual handling of the wood of the cross was influenced by what occurred in Jerusalem and Constantinople. The Persians had taken the wood of the cross when they invaded Jerusalem in 614, and its triumphal return by the Emperor Heraclius in 631 was recorded by a contemporary Armenian church historian. In his graphic description of the return of the true cross to Jerusalem, he tells how the crowds lining the streets were so overcome and choked with joy as the procession bearing the relic entered the city that they were unable to join in the singing of the hymns as it made its way to the basilica.[16] We can only assume that once inside the church, the wood of the cross was in some way shown to the people. From the time of Bishop Macarius of Jerusalem, it seems as though the wood of the true cross was at some point elevated by the bishop in the body of the main church on either 13 or 14 September, so that the people could see it. This ritual act was undoubtedly a response to popular piety and was literally an 'exaltation' or lifting up of the cross to make it visible to the crowd. A later Greek account of the origin of the feast records how the people responded spontaneously to the sight of the relic with repeated cries of *Kyrie eleison*, 'Lord, have mercy'.

Five years after the relic of the cross had been returned to Jerusalem, Heraclius, fearing the city of Jerusalem would be invaded again, as in fact it was by the Arabs in 637, removed the relic for safe keeping to Constantinople. There the feast was celebrated with great ceremony at Hagia Sophia by the Patriarch in the presence of the Emperor who, with some pageantry, processed through the city on the day of the feast. At Hagia Sophia the cross was shown to the people by being raised twice in the direction of the east, and then at each point of the compass as the people responded with a hundredfold *Kyrie eleison*.[17] A miniature in a late tenth-century Greek manuscript shows a saint standing at the top of a marble ambo, attended on either side by two

---

16 Cited by A. Stylianou and J. Stylianou in *By This Conquer*, Society of Cypriot Studies, no. 4 (Nicosia: Zavallis Press 1971), p. 15.
17 Van Tongeren, *Exaltation of the Cross*, p. 39.

deacons, and below them, standing on the lower step, are two other figures, one of whom is holding a large candle. It has been suggested that the ambo depicted here is similar to the ambo, with steps on either side, that originally stood in the middle of the nave at Hagia Sophia.[18] The displaying of the relic, which came to be called the *Hypsosis* of the Cross, was the core of the feast, and simply provided the people with a visual spectacle.[19]

Thus we know that the feast was well established in Constantinople before being brought to the local churches in Rome, probably around the middle of the seventh century. As a native of Antioch, Pope Sergius knew the East well, and given his other liturgical innovations at Rome, such as his embellishing of the feasts of Mary and introduction of the Mass antiphon, the *Agnus Dei*, we can reasonably infer that a similar ritual of the showing of the life-giving wood of the cross came to be practised in Rome on the feast of the Exaltation of the Cross on 14 September.

In Constantinople the faithful simply came to see and to pray before the relic, but in Rome a tactile veneration of the wood of the cross, similar to that practised on Good Friday, seems to have been introduced by Sergius. According to the record of the *Liber pontificalis*, the clergy and the laity would process in order to the entrance of the *presbyterium* of the Lateran where they would both see and kiss the wood of the cross. This was presented as the 'life-giving Cross', a symbol of the crucified and risen Christ, and may have been the relic of the true cross that had been sent to Pope Leo in the fifth century, and was 'venerated with a kiss by the whole Christian population, to the salvation of the human race, and is adored on the day of the Exaltation of the Holy Cross in the basilica of the Saviour'.[20] One scholar has imagined how those coming to venerate the cross at this feast in the Lateran would have seen the apsidal mosaic of the jewelled cross and the bust of Christ as they moved along the longitudinal space of the nave and approached the entrance of the sanctuary where the wood of the cross was presumably placed for veneration on both the feast of the Exaltation and on Good Friday.[21] The art, in other words, was an integral part of the intended experience of the liturgical celebration.

---

18 Stylianou and Stylianou, *By This Conquer*, p. 17.
19 Stylianou and Stylianou, *By This Conquer*, pp. 75, 119.
20 *Liber pontificalis* 1, 374.
21 Ó Carragáin, *Ritual and the Rood*, p. 223.

The observance of the feast of the Exaltation of the Cross eventually spread north of the Alps, and a key figure in the promotion of devotion to the cross and its liturgical expression was Alcuin of York (*c.* 733–804). Alcuin, born into a noble Northumbrian family and educated at York from an early age, became known for his devotion and for his liturgical expertise and was drawn into the scholarly circle of Charlemagne's court at Aachen. There the French monk Benedict of Aniane supplemented the late arriving and incomplete Sacramentary that Charlemagne had requested from Pope Hadrian I as a model of the Roman liturgy. It is unlikely that Alcuin directly assisted Benedict in this task, but what we do know is that during his time at Aachen, Alcuin compiled a *testimonia*, a set of citations to counter and correct a heterodox christological view that was being promoted by some of the bishops in Spain, namely that Christ merely 'adopted' rather than assumed human nature. The *testimonia* included some liturgical formulae, among which was an opening prayer or collect for the feast of the Exaltation.[22] From this we may adduce that Alcuin approved of the feast and sought to promote it in the kingdom of the Franks, and through his correspondence and travel in his native Britain he may well have influenced its observance here too. He was certainly noted for his devotion to the cross, and may have had a hand in the arrangement of weekday Masses in Benedict's *Supplementary*, in which the Mass for Friday focused on the cross. Whether or not Alcuin actually composed this liturgical material, it seems likely that he welcomed its use. Indeed, his biographer mentions how Alcuin attended a daily Mass at which the Propers assigned to each day of the week were used.[23]

On more certain ground we may consider the votive Masses that have been attributed to Alcuin and that he is believed to have compiled during the final years of his life when he was abbot of the prestigious monastery of St Martin at Tours (796–804).[24] The votive Mass of

---

22 D. A. Bullough, *Carolingian Renewal: Sources and Heritage* (Manchester: Manchester University Press 1991), p. 204.

23 A contrary view is presented by Ruth A. Meyers in 'The Wisdom of God and the Word of God: Alcuin's Mass "of Wisdom"', in Martin Dudley (ed.), *Like a Two-Edged Sword: The Word of God in Liturgy and History* (Norwich: Canterbury Press 1995), pp. 42–3.

24 For an analysis of the attribution of this Mass set to Alcuin of York, see J. Deshusses, 'A la Recherche du Missel d'Alcuin', *Ephemerides Liturgicae*, vol. 82, 1968.

particular interest in this set is a Mass for the Holy Cross. This consists of four prayers and a eucharistic Preface (the variable part of the Eucharistic Prayer). The opening prayer and the prayer over the people refer to the cross as a 'life-giving' sign. The Preface focuses on the material wood of the cross, and taking up the notion of recapitulation, first articulated by the second-century bishop Irenaeus of Lyons,[25] speaks of how the wood of the cross reversed the effect of the tree of knowledge through which mortality was brought to humankind: 'You have established that the salvation of the whole human race lies in the wood of the Cross, so that where death had its origin, from that point life should spring.'[26]

Alcuin is also credited with the composition of a devotional poem in praise of the cross, and this certainly demonstrates his literary dexterity. It was written in the form of an acrostic poem.[27] Its lines form the shape of the cross, and speak of the generations of people saved by the sign of the cross and of how the whole world is cleansed when the cross is raised above it. These references to the sign of the cross and to its raising may well echo the ritual action of the lifting of the cross during its veneration on the feast of the Exaltation. Indeed, some of the vocabulary of the poem seems to echo the theme of the Exaltation in its praise of the 'excellent' and 'exalted' cross. Overall then, the poem expresses the familiar Carolingian themes of the theology of the cross, and speaks of Christ's crucifixion as a 'victory', a triumphant freeing of humanity from the destroying powers of evil, and the restoring of humankind to the divine kingdom. In this perspective the cross is presented and understood to be a sign of salvation for the world,[28]

---

25 Irenaeus, *Against Heresies* 5.19.

26 Jean Deshusses, *Le Sacramentaire Grégorien* (Fribourg: Éditions Universitaire 1979), p. 44.

27 Peter Godman, *Poetry of the Carolingian Renaissance* (London: Duckworth 1985), p. 20.

28 One of Alcuin's pupils at the monastic school in Tours was Hrabanus Maurus, and his writings represent one of the most positive appraisals of the importance of art in the Church, and witness to the increasing popularity of the cult of the Cross. His major work, *In Honour of the Cross*, written between 810 and 814, contains a page where the image of the Christ figure is painted on to the text. Here Christ stands erect, his arms outstretched as if on the cross, and yet he is open-eyed and directly faces the reader. So here indeed is an image of the Word made flesh, the one who was crucified and was victorious over death; a figure to whom, as Hrabanus says, one may indeed kneel in adoration. For a full discussion, see Thomas F. X. Noble, *Images, Iconoclasm, and the Carolingians* (Philadelphia: University of Pennsylvania Press 2009), pp. 347–51.

a sign of resurrection, of victory over death, and the source of new life.

The liturgical scholar Joseph Jungmann correctly draws attention to the penitential character of much of Alcuin's devotional writings. He was acutely consciousness of human sin,[29] but this observation needs to be balanced by a wider appreciation of Alcuin's literary work. In the acrostic poem on the cross, the cross shape is contained within a perfect square, which at that time was taken to represent the whole created order.[30] In this way the cross is shown to have a wider cosmic significance. Further, although metaphors drawn from the natural world are not deployed in this particular poem, it should be noted that Alcuin was an accomplished poet of nature and that he evidently delighted in the natural environment around him.[31]

The conjunction of the themes and images of the cross and creation brings me to the second apsidal mosaic I have in mind. It is a stunning mosaic that can be seen in the twelfth-century church of St Clemente, situated just 300 metres from the Colosseum in Rome.[32] This church is one of the most fascinating structures in the city. Compared with the monumental building of St John Lateran, St Clemente is on a much smaller, one might almost say human, scale and the uncluttered space of the present church reveals the architectural lines and design of the basilica. As with a number of ancient sites, it is a multi-layered building. Below the present basilica church, approached through a colonnaded courtyard, is an earlier simple *aula* (hall) church dating back to the late fourth century. This was one of the many *tituli* churches in the city of Rome, and was constructed during the time when Siricius was Bishop of Rome (384–98), and who, according to his epitaph 'built up

---

29 Joseph A. Jungmann, *Christian Prayer through the Centuries* (London: SPCK 2007), p. 43.

30 Godman, *Poetry of the Carolingian Renaissance*, pp. 142–3.

31 See, for example, the opening lines of his elegiac poem written as he prepared to move to the monastery of St Martin, at Tours, from the royal court at Aachen, and the poem in celebration of the nightingale. In this poem, Alcuin not only sees the nightingale's song as calling us from our drowsy slumber to join in creation's praise, but audaciously suggests that the song itself inspires the very cherubim and seraphim in their endless praise in heaven. See Godman, *Poetry of the Carolingian Renaissance*, pp. 125, 145.

32 An inscription refers to a priest 'Anastasius who undertook this work and brought to completion', which it is thought would date the present church at around 1127. See Oakeshott, *The Mosaics of Rome*, p. 247.

anew the temples of the saints'.[33] The columns for this lower church were 'spoils' taken from earlier Roman monuments in the vicinity. The *aula* church, excavated in the middle of the nineteenth century, was itself built above another structure, possibly a warehouse dating back to the first century. And below *this*, excavated in 1867, is a *Mithraeum*, a temple to a Roman pagan god.[34] The first church on this site was associated with Clement, the Bishop of Rome at the end of the first century (88–97) who, if he is correctly identified as the author of a Letter to the Corinthians,[35] was concerned with the right ordering of the Christian assembly for worship, which he modelled on the Temple in Jerusalem. The older church on the site was considerably damaged by the invasion of the Normans in 1084, and the present one was built over it by Pope Paschal II in 1100.[36] Seeking to restore former architectural glories, marble columns and fittings, such as the striking twin ambos, were re-used from the earlier building below, but the decoration of the apse mosaic was, of course, new. Again, the basilican arrangement with its colonnaded longitudinal gathering space drew the eye towards the large apse mosaic of the cross as the tree of life. It is likely that tesserae from the mosaic decoration of the fourth-century church were re-used in the making of the apse mosaic, which was possibly made by Byzantine mosaicists. Attributing the work of Byzantine mosaicists would account for the pathos of the composition, of Christ with closed eyes on the cross flanked on either side by Mary and the beloved disciple John.

Originally, worship in a basilica was, as George Guiver characterizes it, vigorous and participatory,[37] but by the twelfth century the role and movement of the laity was reduced and restricted. The singing was now led by a *schola* in the clearly defined space of the chancel. At St Clemente, the chancel, raised above the level of the nave gathering-space for the people, is surrounded by *cancelli* or low walls, from which we derive the English word 'chancel'. But here we

---

33 Milburn, *Early Christian Art and Architecture*, p. 106.

34 Doig, *Liturgy and Architecture*, pp. 7–8, 89.

35 The date for this Letter, evidently elicited by a dispute regarding ministry in the house-churches at Corinth, is usually set around AD 96. See Paul F. Bradshaw, *The Search for the Origins of Christian Worship: Sources and Methods for the Study of Early Liturgy* (London: SPCK 2002, 2nd edn), p. 199.

36 Webb, *The Churches and Catacombs of Early Christian Rome*, p. 89.

37 George Guiver, *Vision Upon Vision: Processes of Change and Renewal in Christian Worship* (Norwich: Canterbury Press 2009), p. 23.

see a particularly striking feature of the church, namely a large marble ambo or pulpit with an imposing decorated paschal candle-stand. The ambo is reminiscent of the *bema* (a lectern platform) of earlier Syrian churches, which until the fourth century was built of wood and originally placed, as in a Jewish synagogue, in the centre of the nave to be the focal point for the readings from Scripture during the celebration of the liturgy.[38] Light would have been required for reading, and there is literary evidence from the sixth century to suggest that the *bema* in Syrian churches was lit with a cross-shape candle-stand. If this was the case, then the proclamation of the Word occurred in the light of the cross, the tree of life. It is interesting to note in relation to this sacred topography that the altar, which in the earliest centuries would have been made of wood, was called 'the tree of life' in the Syrian tradition.[39] Further, there is literary evidence in a liturgical commentary on the Anaphora of St James, of devotional prayers and sermons that speak of the eucharistic gifts as being the fruit of the cross,[40] which neatly locates the fruit of the cross in the Eucharist celebrated at the altar. The association of altar and the tree of life has inspired the design and making of some contemporary altars both in the United Kingdom and on the Continent. A striking example in Germany is the freestanding altar in the cathedral at Trier. A finely crafted example in England is to be seen on the nave altar in the Cathedral Church of Saints Mary and Chad, Lichfield. This wooden altar, designed jointly by the architect Martin Stancliffe and the artist Rod Kelley, was consecrated in 2004. The tree of life motif, facing into the nave, was carved in wood by Linford Bridgeman, and is decorated with silver fruits that were made by Rod Kelley (see Plate 3).

To catch the full resonance of this association of altar, ambo and the tree of life, we need to explore the Syrian tradition in a little more detail. It is evident from the ground plan of the church that the placing of the altar and the *bema* in the Syrian tradition was as much symbolic as it was utilitarian. And as the spatial relationship between ambo and altar was significant, so was the movement of the clergy and people

38 J. G. Davies, *The Origin and Development of Early Christian Architecture* (London: SCM Press 1952), pp. 83–4.
39 Baby Varghese, *West Syrian Liturgical Theology* (Aldershot: Ashgate 2004), pp. 163–5.
40 The evidence is marshalled by Vazhuthanapally in the *Archaeology of Mar Sliba*, pp. 87, 98.

during the celebration of the liturgy. The Gospel Book, symbolizing Christ, the eternal Word of the Father, was processed from the altar in the east end of the building to the *bema*, from where the Gospel was proclaimed. This liturgical movement and the orientation of the church are highly significant, and the Syrian Church Order known as the *Didascalia Apostolorum*, dated around 230,[41] validates the rule that Christians should pray facing east by citing the Old Testament text: 'Give glory to God, who rides upon the heaven of heavens toward the east.'[42] This eastward orientation of prayer, mirrored in both the positioning of the focal points of the liturgy in the church building and the processional movement of the clergy, was closely associated with an intense eschatological expectation, the fervent desire and hope for the final coming of Christ in glory at the end of human history. The Gospel text spoke about the appearing of the Son of Man with an inrush of glory at his second Advent, and says that his appearing would be heralded by the 'sign of the Son of Man' (Matthew 24.30). Early Christians took this sign to be the cross, a sign of victory, and so Ephrem the Syrian urged his listeners to be expectant and prepared for Christ's appearing, which he believed would occur on a Sunday, the day of resurrection that would dawn with the appearing of the sign of a luminous cross in the sky.[43]

The Gospel procession during the Sunday liturgy involved a literal descent of the steps on which the altar was placed into the midst of the people in the nave, and after the proclaiming of the Gospel, the book was processed back into the sanctuary and placed on the altar. It has been suggested that this dramatic movement deliberately mimicked the double movement of salvation – of Christ, the Word, being sent into the world by the Father, and of the incarnate Word's return to the Father in the Ascension. What we see here is a kinesic analogy of salvation, a physical, embodied movement through the deliberately zoned geography of the church building, showing the passage of the

---

41 Bradshaw, *The Search for the Origins of Christian Worship*, pp. 78–9.
42 *Didascalia* III.8 CSCO 402, p. 37.
43 '[L]et us also raise our eyes to the East to the highest heavens, in order to look for the sign of the cross every day and every night, for our Lord to be revealed', cited by Varghese, *West Syrian Liturgical Theology*, p. 124. As Christians faced east to pray in church, and the cross was a sign of Christ's presence, it was inevitable that a cross came to be placed or inscribed on the wall of the apse. See Cyril E. Pocknee, *Cross and Crucifix in Christian Worship and Devotion*, Alcuin Club Tract 32 (London: Mowbray 1962).

divine from the realm of the transcendent to the realm of our human social world, and of its return bearing our flesh and blood reality. But what is more (and this is the direct point that relates to our emerging theme of the cross as restoring paradise), in this Gospel processional route the eastern apse of the building represented heaven, the dwelling of the Father. In terms of biblical imagery, paradise was located in the East, and so the return of Christ to the Father was also the opening of the way for humankind to return to paradise.[44] No wonder then that an eastern apse mosaic directly above the altar, such as at St Clemente, should include paradisal motifs in its decoration. And it is in this light that we return to reflect further on this mosaic.

According to an inscription directly below the cross in the mosaic, a number of relics, including a fragment of the true cross, were embedded in the plaster wall directly behind the figure of the Crucified.[45] This makes the apsidal cross a kind of reliquary, and thereby adds to its register of symbolic meaning. So overall, what we can see here in this monumental backdrop to the liturgical action performed in the space below is not only a visual display of the cross but a revelation, literally an unveiling, of its meaning.

At the centre of the mosaic is a large cross with 12 doves, representing the Twelve Apostles, along the vertical shaft and the lateral bar. This figuring of the Apostles as doves is reminiscent of an earlier Syrian tradition, a hymn of the fourth-century poet-theologian Ephrem.[46] Other

---

44 Palmer, 'Paradise Restored', p. 37. Further, the association of different hours of prayer to aspects of the Passion was commonplace, and the West Syrian tradition came to associate the ninth hour of prayer, commemorating the death of Jesus on the cross, with the restoration of humankind to paradise. See Varghese, *West Syrian Liturgical Theology*, p. 131.

45 'A fragment of the true cross, a tooth of St James, and a tooth of St Ignatius rest in the body of Christ which is represented above this inscription.'

46 Ephrem the Syrian, born around 306, lived in the Roman garrison border town of Nisibis, and following a Persian invasion and period of fierce persecution, was exiled to Edessa, another significant Christian centre in what is now south-eastern Turkey. There he taught in a theological school and was ordained deacon. He died having ministered to victims of a plague in 373. The hymns of Ephrem, written in Syriac, a dialect of Aramaic, the language of Jesus and the first disciples, are sometimes polemical, always steeped in Scripture, and according to Brock show the author to have been an attentive observer of nature. See Sebastian Brock, *The Luminous Eye: The Spiritual World Vision of Saint Ephrem the Syrian*, Cistercian Studies Series 124 (Kalamazoo, MI: Cistercian Publications 1992, revised edn), pp. 164–8. Ephrem trained a women's choir to perform his hymns, which presumably would have been sung on the appropriate feast day, or season

significant correspondences can also be identified between the symbolic register of the St Clemente mosaic and the deep poetic strand of the Syrian tradition. Behind the condensed imagery of a poem in one of the series of Hymns on Virginity is the kernel of the literary tradition that identifies the wood of the cross with the tree of life in paradise. Here Ephrem speaks of how humanity is restored to paradise by the death of Christ, and suggestively conflates Christ's 'double gestation', first in the womb of Mary and then in the dark earth of the grave following his death and burial. Let me quote the relevant stanza in full:

> Very sad was the Tree of Life
> that saw Adam hidden from him.
> Into the virgin earth he sank and was buried,
> but he arose and shone forth from Golgotha.
> Humankind like a bird pursued,
> took refuge on it so it would arrive at its home.
> The persecutor is persecuted,
> and the persecuted doves rejoice in paradise. (16.10)[47]

We will see that the rich Syrian theology of the fecundity of the cross is visually represented in the apse mosaic at St Clemente, but first let us consider how the Crucified is figured here. The cross was a central and dominant theme in the apsidal mosaics in the late fourth-century churches, such as St Pudenziana and St John Lateran, but here at St Clemente the cross includes a figure of the Crucified, naked apart from a loin cloth. His head is slumped to the side with closed eyes. On either side of the cross, and below the cross-bar, stand the figures of Mary and John. Both figures incline their heads towards the cross. Mary has her hands open in a gesture of supplication, and John has his right hand raised pointing to the cross, thereby inviting the viewer to contemplate its meaning. Directly above the cross the hand of God appears through striated clouds, indicating that God the Father

---

of the Christian year. According to Varghese, his hymns were incorporated into both the East and West Syrian liturgical traditions by the sixth century – Varghese, *West Syrian Liturgical Theology*, p. 2.

47 *Ephrem the Syrian: Hymns*, trans. Kathleen E. McVey, Classics of Western Spirituality (New York: Paulist Press 1989), p. 332.

is at work in the death of Christ on the cross.[48] From the foot of the cross grows a large acanthus plant whose branches and twining tendrils unfurl through the whole surface area of the cap of the apse. Below this the four rivers, as in the earlier Lateran mosaic, flow from the roots of the acanthus plant, and two thirsting stags, again as in the Lateran mosaic, drink from the waters that issue from the cross. Dispersed throughout the swirling foliage of the acanthus are small human figures and antique *amorini*, figures of small winged cherubs, together with flowers, fruits, birds, including quails and peacocks, birds' nests with fledglings, and even dolphins, against a gleaming blue background.

The decorative scheme may well reproduce antique and pre-Christian decorative motifs. The *amorini* shown scrambling over the grapes or riding a dolphin are good examples of motifs found in earlier Roman floor mosaics, such as may be seen in the baths at Ostia.[49] But whatever borrowing there may have been from the classic repertoire of pictorial elements, many of the decorative motifs also have counterparts in Jewish and Christian scriptural imagery, particularly the multiple allusions to Israel, the covenanted people of God, as the vine of God's planting. Here we may specifically register Old Testament passages such as 2 Samuel 7.10, Jeremiah 2.21 and especially Psalm 80 and Isaiah 5.1–2. These two passages lie behind the multiply attested parable of the vineyard through which Jesus disclosed his own destiny of suffering and death (Mark 12.1–11 and parallels), and the Johannine passage in which Christ and the Church are presented in the organic imagery of the vine and the branches (John 15.1–5).

Refracted through these multiple references in Christian literature, we can see the unfurling vine growing out of the fronds of the acanthus plant in the mosaic as an image of the Church, the New Israel.

---

48 For a discussion of this anthropomorphic representation of God the Father as a disembodied hand, its Jewish prototype in the synagogue in Dura Europa and its appearance in the fourth-century dome mosaic in the baptistery of San Giovanni Fonte in Naples, see Robin Margaret Jensen, *Face to Face: Portraits of the Divine in Early Christianity* (Minneapolis, MN: Fortress Press 2005), pp. 120–1.

49 The curious feature of the single deer with its head to the ground at the centre of the acanthus plant could originally have been an illustration of the classical myth in the *Physiologus*, which tells how the deer renews its youth by eating a snake and shedding its antlers and growing new ones. See Oakeshott, *The Mosaics of Rome*, p. 248.

This reading is confirmed not only by the inclusion of small individual figures (probably representing the Fathers of the Church) and the small groups of people (possibly representing the baptized people of God) seen to inhabit the vine, but also by an inscription, notoriously difficult to translate, whose first and final lines have been paraphrased as saying: 'We liken the Church of Christ to this vine, Under the Law it withered, but the Cross of Christ makes it flourish again with green.'[50]

The multiple allusions and references in the mosaic are given a coherence in the overall composition, whose intended purpose, I would suggest, was to present a Christian understanding of the cross as the renewal of creation through the death of Christ on the cross. As we have seen, the Christ figure of the cross in the apsidal mosaic at St Clemente is no longer the open-eyed victorious Christ of earlier liturgical art but the Christ who died on the cross. But this death is not the extinction of a life but its release. A death that, given the paradisal background of the cross, seems to lead to the burgeoning of new and vigorous life, and is none other than God's redeeming work. Here both humanity and the whole natural order are seen to be caught up in this divine work of redemption, the setting free and flourishing of creation from its devastating exploitation, death and decay. As St Paul wrote:

> For the creation waits with eager longing for the revealing of the children of God; for the creation was subjected to futility, not of its own will but by the will of the one who subjected it, in hope that the creation itself will be set free from its bondage to decay and obtain the freedom of the glory of the children of God. We know that the whole creation has been groaning in labour pains until now. (Romans 8.19–22)

As the backdrop to the altar, the imagery of cross and the renewal of creation is brought into play with the Eucharist. Here the dominant image is that of the vine, and the association of the vine, the altar and the Eucharist, melded in the Christian imagination of early Syrian Christianity, has persisted through the Christian centuries in different cultural contexts and through different artistic media.

---

50 Oakeshott, *The Mosaics of Rome*, p. 250.

In Luke's account of the Last Supper, Jesus is recorded as saying, as he took the first of the two cups in this narrative, that he would not drink of the fruit of the vine again until it was fulfilled in the kingdom of God (Luke 22.16). Given the promise made to the penitent thief, also recorded in Luke, it seems that the entry into the kingdom, the paradise of God, was through his suffering and death on the cross. It is as though the fruit of Christ's body, the new wine of the kingdom, was released and offered on and through the cross. Examples of this image of the fruitfulness of the cross can be seen in the iconography of the cross in the twelfth-century painted glass of Western churches. The verticality of Gothic architecture allowed for far larger areas of the walls of the building to be given to windows, and the result of this is brilliantly seen in the stunning glass of the cathedrals at Chartres and in Notre Dame in Paris.

An example of twelfth-century glass, designed some 40 years later than the glass at St Denys (the abbey church just north of Paris, enlarged and beautified by Abbot Suger, who placed jewel-like glass into the windows to simulate the illuminating *lux* of God), is to be seen in the Corona at Canterbury Cathedral. The heavily restored glass is in the centrally placed 'Redemption Window' in the Corona, completed in 1184 to house a fragment of Thomas Becket's skull (see Plate 4). This central window arrangement, placed alongside a Jesse tree window, has three central square panels, showing the three pivotal aspects of the story of salvation – the cross, the resurrection and the giving of the Spirit at Pentecost – each connected by ornamental foliage. Each of these three square panels is surrounded by quadrilobe windows showing Old Testament figures or events that prefigure the subject depicted in the central panels. The whole scheme was evidently designed by someone who was conversant with the typological method of reading Scripture,[51] and was intended to be read in an ascending way, from the bottom upwards. The lowest authentic quadrilobe image placed directly below the restored square panel of the crucifixion is a representation of the story of the two men who were sent by Moses to spy out Canaan,

---

51 This patristic typological reading had been defended by John of Salisbury in the 1160s when he saw that it was likely to be superseded by the scholasticism of the emerging universities. On this particular example of typologically designed glass, see Madeline Harrison Caviness, *The Early Stained Glass of Canterbury Cathedral, circa 1175–1220*, (Princeton, NJ: Princeton University Press), 1977.

the land of promise. In this jewel coloured glass the two men are shown returning from the Valley of Eshcol with a huge bunch of grapes carried on a pole (Numbers 13.17–23).[52]

So how are we to read this arrangement of images? The text of the inscription echoes a recurrent twelfth-century theme of the rejection of Christ by the Jews, but the visual language of the image contributes to the whole picture of the crucifixion like a single piece of a jigsaw puzzle. In this instance the death of Christ on the cross is seen as being fruitful. The primary reference of this fruitfulness was the Eucharist, as the grapes symbolized the vintage of the eucharistic wine. And further, as the bunch of bulging grapes was brought back from the land of promise, so the eucharistic cup in the new dispensation could be seen as offering a foretaste of that promised kingdom, the paradise that Jesus had promised to the repentant thief who was crucified with him: 'Truly I tell you, today you will be with me in Paradise' (Luke 23.43).

What then are we to make of what we have seen so far in this exploration of the life-giving cross? The first tentative conclusion is that the examples of the apse mosaics and stained glass that I have described so far lead me to suggest that the artwork was not intended simply as a backdrop against which the Mass was celebrated but as an interpretative visual register, and one that presents the eucharistic gifts as being the fruit of the cross. The imagery of the vine holds together the cross and the Eucharist, and is presented in a way that suggests that it is the Passion and death of Christ that yield the vintage of Communion. Again, there is a deep echo with the Syrian tradition of Ephrem. His poetry speaks of the incarnate Jesus, born of Mary, as the vine-shoot whose body on the cross, like a cluster of grapes, was pressed to provide the eucharistic cup of salvation:[53]

---

52 The two heads of the figures and parts of the drapery are also modern restorations. See 'The Crucifixion, Stained Glass Medallion in the Corona, Canterbury Cathedral', *Annual Report of the Friends of Canterbury Cathedral, 1948.* Canterbury Cathedral Archive, CCA-U167/P/E36/10.

53 Robert Murray, *Symbols of Church and Kingdom: A Study in Early Syriac Tradition* (Cambridge: Cambridge University Press 1975). The first two citations, from 'Nativity' and 'Crucifixion' respectively, are from *Ephrem the Syrian: Hymns,* and the third from 'Virginity' is a translation of Brock from his study *The Luminous Eye,* p. 99. The reference to the Eucharist as 'the medicine of immortality' was a metaphor forged by Ignatius of Antioch that he used in his *Epistle to the Ephesians* 20.3.

the 'Nine Saints', who have been traditionally identified with a group of Syrian monks who in 500 extended Christianity beyond the area of Axum and the higher echelons of society, and promoted the development of monasticism in the Miaphysite, or non-Chalcedonian, Church in Ethiopia.

The stories of the origins of Christianity in Ethiopia testify to the close connections between the country and Syria, that ancient cradle of Christianity with its proximity and affinity to its Jewish roots.[60] We know too that strong pilgrimage links were established with Jerusalem, and yet even with these strong connections to Syria and Palestine it is also clear that Aksumite Christianity came in time to develop its own distinctive architectural and liturgical traditions.

Ethiopian Christianity is particularly famous for its churches. Many of these follow the basic basilican rectangular ground plan, but others are round and some are cross shape within a square. A particular Aksumite feature in some of these buildings is the carved crosses above doorways or more commonly in windows. Most famous of all are the later twelfth- or early thirteenth-century cruciform churches in the Tigray and Lalibela regions, which are literally carved out of the pink volcanic rock of cliff faces or on elevated planes.[61] The most stunning example of a cross-shape church hypogean or rock-hewn church is the twelfth-century Beta Giyorgis in the mountainous region of Lalibela.[62] The cross shape, repeated in relief carving on the roof, corresponds to the shape of a Greek cross, and according to Phillipson stands in a vertical-sided court measuring 22 by 16 metres and 11 metres at its deepest point. The church evidently served the needs of pilgrims, and what we would describe as a pilgrims' hostel was carved into the tuff rock adjacent to the church. One particular decorative feature is relevant to our theme, and that is the relief carving around and above the upper windows. This carving above the incised point of the window is of vine leaves and tendrils growing out on either side from the base of the cross. The composition is remarkably similar to the pattern of the vine-cross

---

60 For a summary of scholarly discussion of the close relationship between early Syrian Christianity and Judaism, see A. Gelston, *The Eucharistic Prayer of Addai and Mari* (Oxford: Oxford University Press 1991), p. 23.
61 David W. Phillipson argues that these rock-hewn churches, technically known as hypogean, were built over a span of time from as early as the seventh to the tenth century. See Phillipson, *Ancient Churches of Ethiopia*, pp. 87–150.
62 Phillipson, *Ancient Churches of Ethiopia*, pp. 148–52.

mosaic on the floor of the Syrian basilica mentioned above which, as a symbol of the fecundity of the cross, is found in a variety of media in a number of geographical locations.[63]

The Ethiopian Orthodox Church, the largest of the Oriental Orthodox Churches, has had and continues to have a particular devotion to the cross, and from the time of the revered King Lalibala, Christians in Ethiopia were known as 'the servants of the cross'. The liturgical feasts celebrating Helena's discovery of the cross and the *Masqal* or Exaltation of the Holy Cross celebrated on 27 September are major communal events, and involve the building of bonfires decorated with green branches and flowers on the top. After the burning of the wood the faithful take the ash and mark their foreheads with the sign of the cross.[64]

In Ethiopia the cross is ubiquitous, and crosses are found in many forms and made from a variety of materials, from wood to precious metals. A recently published cultural history of the cross is reticent in assigning symbolic meanings to the different decorative features of Ethiopian crosses. However, its author, Stanislaw Chojnacki, cites with apparent approval the observation that a range of biomorphic forms, including fish, dolphins, birds and foliate patterns, decorate the crosses used for a variety of liturgical purposes.[65] These crosses fall into three basic categories. The first is the hand-held blessing cross always carried by a priest and used when giving a blessing, for example when the reader of the epistle is blessed by the principal celebrant. The second category of cross, similar in size and shape to the first, is the liturgical cross held by the deacon when he censes the congregation, the altar (the *manbara tabot*, which is like a cabinet with drawers)[66] in the sanctuary and other designated holy objects. The third type of Ethiopian cross is the famous processional cross mounted on a pole and held up during the reading of the Gospel and during the final blessing of the people at the end of the celebration of the liturgy.

---

63 The 'vine-cross' juxtaposing the motifs of the cross and the vine are found in relief-carved capitals, panels on chancel barriers, and sarcophagi. See plates 13, 15, 22 in Guntram Koch, *Early Christian Art and Architecture: An Introduction*, trans. John Bowden (London: SCM Press 1996).

64 Stanislaw Chojnacki, *Ethiopian Crosses: A Cultural History and Chronology* (Milan: Skira 2006), p. 45.

65 Chojnacki, *Ethiopian Crosses*, pp. 30, 31, 81.

66 Chojnacki, *Ethiopian Crosses*, p. 44.

Etchmiadzin, the centre of the Apostolic Catholic Church of Armenia, I was told that although the cross stones – found inside and outside their architecturally unique stone-built churches[75] – have a common style, each is allegedly different in the detail of its design and patterning. Some of these stone crosses date back to the end of the seventh century, but the *khachkar* did not reach its standard form until the turn of the ninth century. It is likely that they originally replaced earlier wooden crosses that literally marked the advance of the Christian mission on Armenian soil.[76] In time, however, they came to be used as commemorative memorials for both people and significant historic events, and were fixed onto the facades of churches, shrines and monasteries. This latter group, although having no direct liturgical function, came to be regarded as being visual memorials of Christ's death and resurrection. Many of these cross stones depict the cross as the tree of life. One of the most dominant cultural influences in Armenia was from its neighbour, Iran, the ancient biblical land of Persia, and particularly from the dualistic religion of Zoroastrianism that competed with Christianity in Armenia during the period of Sassanidic rule in the third century, when Christians were brutally persecuted. The motif of the tree of life would have had clear resonances with the Zoroastrian myth of the cosmic tree, which linked the centre of heaven and the centre of the earth.[77] An early

---

75 Armenian and Georgian churches are designed as a central plan domed space, and each has a distinctive conical spire.

76 The Christianization of the Armenian people is significantly depicted as a 'planting' in an acrostic hymn (sharakan) attributed to the thirteenth-century monk musician, Hovhannes of Erznka: 'A garden of renewed joy was planted in the land of Armenia by the many efforts and suffering of St Gregory; watered by the flowing streams of the truly proclaimed Word, and filled with beautiful blossoming plants.' See *Hymns and Odes in Honor of St. Gregory the Illuminator* (New York: St Nersess Armenian Seminary 2001).

77 See Katharina van Loo, 'Zur Ikonographie des armenischen Kreuzsteins', in Museum Bochum/Stiftung für Armenische Studien, *Armenien: 5000 Jahre Kunst und Kultur* (Tübingen: Wasmuth 1995), pp. 115–16. For a detailed study of the cosmic tree of life from a study of religious perspective, see E. O. James, *The Tree of Life: An Archaeological Study* (Leiden: Brill 1966). A Syrian legend in *The Book of Cave Treasures*, probably a sixth-century compilation of stories that possibly circulated around the fourth century, claimed that Golgotha was the centre, or navel, of the created world, and identified the place as the site in which Adam, the first man, was buried. The correspondence of the burial site of the first Adam, and the place of Christ's crucifixion at 'the place of the skull', played on the medieval Christian imagination, and the placing of a skull at the base of the cross, first seen in the Byzantine icons of the crucifixion, became commonplace in Western paintings of the crucifixion.

variant of this myth surfaced in the Jewish writing of the exilic period. The prophet Ezekiel, for instance, in pronouncing ʏʜᴡʜ's judgement against the pretensions of Egypt, describes the nation as a mighty tree with its top piercing the heavens, its roots reaching down to the deepest waters and its branches giving shelter to all living things (Ezekiel 17.22–24). This image is echoed in the later account of a dream of the Babylonian king Nebuchadnezzar in the apocalyptic book of Daniel:

> there was a tree at the centre of the earth,
> and its height was great.
> The tree grew great and strong,
> its top reached to heaven,
> and it was visible to the ends of the whole earth.
> Its foliage was beautiful,
> its fruit abundant,
> and it provided food for all.
> The animals of the field found shade under it,
> the birds of the air nested in its branches,
> and from it all living beings were fed.
>   (Daniel 4.10–12)

Readers will no doubt recognize that this image of the tree of life, used in a negative sense in these two Old Testament passages, was appropriated and given a positive application as an image of the coming Reign of God in a familiar parabolic saying of Jesus:

> [The kingdom of God] is like a mustard seed, which, when sown upon the ground, is the smallest of all the seeds on earth; yet when it is sown it grows up and becomes the greatest of all shrubs, and puts forth large branches, so that the birds of the air can make nests in its shade.   (Mark 4.31–32 and parallels)

The Armenian cross stone transposes the primordial tree of life motif into a figure of the life-giving tree, the cross. To give a particular example of this, let me describe the cross stone found in the mausoleum chapel of the monastery of St Davit, in an area of the country that is now part of modern Turkey. Here the cross is identified as the tree of life,[78]

---

78 This particular *khachkar* is discussed and illustrated by van Loo, 'Zur Ikonographie

and two paradisal peacocks, symbols of immortality, face each other below it. Above that tree, on a plinth, stands the cross, with flared ends sculpted as unfurling leaves. The whole compositional arrangement and the detail evoke that 'the leaves of the tree are for the healing of the nations' (Revelation 22.2), and recall both the tree of life that was planted at the centre of paradise (Genesis 2.9) and the vision of the trees planted by the waters that flow from the new heavenly temple (Revelation 22.1; cf. Ezekiel 47.1–2).

More generally, the symmetrical decoration of Armenian cross stones, which are usually between one and two metres high, is comparatively sparse and simple, with unfurling vine leaves, grapes and palm fronds carved on the flat surface of the stone. The cross is generally set on a stepped or rosette-like base, and the whole surrounding surface is formed of finely chiselled interweaving lacework decoration.[79] From the thirteenth century it became common for the cross to depict the figure of the Crucified, but the surrounding organic foliage decoration persisted. It is this decorative feature that invites us to read the cross stone as a sign of the resurrection, of that new life that grows from the sacrificial death of Christ. Medieval Armenian liturgical and devotional texts deliberately speak of the 'wood' of the cross, and this naming of the organic material relates the cross directly to the root metaphor of a fruiting tree. For the Apostolic Armenian Christian, the wood of the cross is fruitful and it alone bears the paradisal fruit of Christ's resurrection.[80]

What I have attempted to do in this chapter is indicate the ubiquity of images that present the cross in relation to the divine purpose of renewing creation. Such a figuring of the cross in Christian liturgy and iconography of the cross developed from a root metaphor in Christian discourse that speaks of the setting up of Christ's cross on Calvary as a kind of planting. A telling phrase occurs in the writing of the Venerable Bede about the cross being planted at the centre of the world, an idea that, as we have seen, surfaces in various forms in the complex literary

---

des armenischen Kreuzsteins', p. 116.
79 Levon Asarin, 'Die Kunst der armenischen Kreuzsteins', in *Armenien: 5000 Jahre Kunst und Kultur*, p. 110.
80 Vrej Nersessian, *Treasures from the Ark: 1700 Years of Armenian Christian Art* (London: British Library 2001), pp. 110–12.

tradition of the *Legend of the True Cross*. The metaphor of Christ's death as a planting is melded from the imagery in a short passage in John's Gospel. The passage in question is actually the only parabolic passage in the whole of John's Gospel narrative, and it is placed on the lips of Jesus. Having arrived in the holy city of Jerusalem, Jesus alludes to his impending death, already identified in the narrative as the hour of Christ's glorification, and says: 'Very truly, I tell you, unless a grain of wheat falls into the earth and dies, it remains just a single grain; but if it dies, it bears much fruit.' (John 12.24). The new reality that this parable opens up is that the death and burial of Jesus was, and is, fruitful. Something new can grow and blossom on the earth because, as the earliest Christian proclamation says, the one who 'hung upon the tree' was none other than 'the Author of life' (Acts 3.15).

So in the telling of the story of Christian origins, it could be said that the cross was planted so that something new could grow on the earth, and this theological conviction, I believe, is articulated by the art and liturgy of the living cross. The images of the living cross – in mosaics, stone relief carving and liturgical poetry – that we have discussed above, hint at a renewal of life figuratively sprouting from the base of the cross, the very source and fount of Christian life. In showing the issuing of new life from the cross, the iconography discloses that something new is possible and that it can grow, burgeon and flourish on the earth. And this new thing is nothing less than the maturing of the fruit of the Spirit in human lives (see Galatians 5.22; Matthew 7.16–20) and the renewal of nature – nothing less than the divine making of creation anew. This linking of the cross with a new creation is, as illustrated towards the end of Chapter 3, at least implicit in the thought of St Paul. In a passage towards the end of his epistle to the Galatians, which came to be selected as the epistle for the Mass on the feast of the Exaltation of the Cross, the Apostle speaks of how he glories in the cross of Christ (6.14). In the following verse – one could almost say in the same breath – Paul speaks of what really counts, and this, he says, is 'a new creation' (6.15). So on the basis of the vocabulary he uses and the underlying logic of what he wrote in the final chapter of this epistle, we can infer a theological premiss in Paul's thought that the death, burial and resurrection of Christ inaugurated a new creation.

The image of the cross and the death of Christ as a kind of planting was vibrantly expressed in the work of the distinguished English artist Norman Adams (1927–2005), particularly in his brilliantly coloured oil paintings of the 1990s. Although Adams was not in any sense a conventional churchgoer, he knew the Christian story and was evidently a person of considerable religious sensibility. Whether in his early expressive landscape watercolours or his later large oil canvases, colour was at the centre of his art. On one occasion he wrote of how his art was fired by the discovery of colour, and that through the use of significant colour he felt able to reach even intangible things.[81] This, I suppose, is why his paintings seem to have such a charged spiritual field. Indeed, because of the vibrant colour tones of his canvases, we could place Norman Adams in the English visionary tradition of William Blake and Samuel Palmer, although Adams generally painted on a larger scale and in a more abstract expressive form. He is on record as saying that in his view the Christian religion was essentially about life,[82] and it is probably this conviction that made his religious paintings such potent visual statements of the power of life even in and through death. The theme of life through death is theologically richly nuanced and is deeply embedded in the narrative of John's Gospel. There we find in the juxtaposition of the theme of glory and the cross, the paradoxical holding together of both life and death. It was this same theme that is presented visually in the apse mosaic of the Lateran basilica, as it reveals the cross to be the source and fount of Christian life.

A similar effect was produced in the contemporary art of Norman Adams, exemplified in *The Golden Crucifixion* (1993), an oil painting that simultaneously holds within a singular pictorial space images of suffering, lamentation and loss, and symbols of transformation and new life. The canvas shows the women shielding their faces from the horror of the cross, but above the cross of Jesus is the blazing disc of the sun, which in the pictorial language of an earlier vivid colourist, Vincent van Gogh, was a natural symbol of divinity. In Adams' painting a further natural symbol, the abstracted pattern of the peacock butterfly – a symbol of transformation – is painted with open wings directly behind each of the three crosses of Calvary.

Opportunities to rework the classic subject of Christ's Passion, death and burial came to Adams in commissions to paint the Stations of the Cross. The Stations, more a corporate devotional act than a liturgical

---

81 Norman Adams, 'Painting and Poetry', *English in Education*, vol. 3, no. 2, June 1969, p. 19; cited in Nicholas Usherwood et al., *Norman Adams* (Harrogate: 108 Fine Art 2007), p. 85.
82 Usherwood et al., *Norman Adams*, p. 89.

celebration, provides the opportunity for Christians to enter imaginatively into the Passion of Christ and to journey with him, through prayers, readings, song and visual art, along the Way of the Cross.[83] In 1975 Adams was commissioned to make a series of ceramic Stations of the Cross for the Roman Catholic church in what was then the new city of Milton Keynes. This gave him the opportunity to work on a 'big subject', but a later commission, a set of large panel Stations installed in 1995 in St Mary's Roman Catholic church (known as the 'Hidden Gem') in Manchester, gave him the opportunity to deploy the full range of painterly and stylistic vocabulary. Here we see colours as vibrant as a Van Gogh, geometric patterns and, more significant for our purposes, an expansive rendering of his developed organic forms, reminiscent of the earlier liturgical art we have surveyed in this chapter.

In the large canvases that were painted for the Manchester Stations of the Cross, Adams takes a close-focus approach, and each Station panel is painted with visceral energy and a vibrancy of colour. In painting these large canvases that virtually cover the surfaces of the wall-space along both aisles of the church, Adams said that he wanted to be close to the experience of Christ, and so he focused on the most expressive parts of the body – the hands, the face and particularly the eyes[84] – and produced these imposing mask shape images. And so in the Stations showing Christ's suffering, we see Adams' use of violent red colours, his jagged shapes and close facial depiction. In the Station depicting the final fall of Jesus under the weight of the cross, the crown of thorns looks like shards of broken glass, and in this panel the artist cannot be accused of avoiding the stark and bloody reality of the Way of the Cross. Various artistic influences on Adams' work have been identified, and the most recognizable are African face-masks and the large figural carving of Fenwick Lawson. But what released the creative energy of the artist in painting this set of Stations of the Cross was the Christian story of Christ's suffering and death, and the resonances that it had with the then breaking news stories of violence and brutality in the contemporary world.[85]

---

83 Benjamin Gordon-Taylor and Simon Jones, *Celebrating Christ's Victory: Ash Wednesday to Trinity* (London: SPCK 2007), pp. 17–24.
84 Cited in *The Stations of the Cross by Norman Adams RA*, published by St Mary's Church, Manchester, 1995.
85 Anna Adams, 'A Catalogue of Commissions', in Usherwood et al., *Norman Adams*, pp. 70–1.

The final Station, the Fourteenth, beautifully captures in a single canvas two aspects of the paschal story: the burial and the resurrection. In the Christian story of Christ's Passion, the burial represents the finality of death. John's extended account of the Passion gives the additional detail that in the place where Jesus was crucified, 'there was a garden'(John 19.41). Far from being an incidental piece of topographical information, the evangelist signals to the reader in these words that we need to look beyond the starkness of the cross to its hinterland.[86] For after the death comes the burial in the garden, and even there and then, when Jesus is dead and buried, something stirs, something is present there in the very absence of life in the dark cavern of death. For this death was a recapitulation – we could say a rewinding – of the creation story back to the beginning. The creation hymn in Genesis 1 tells of God drawing beauty, life and form from the primeval chaos in six days, and the narrative of Christ's death and resurrection seems to recapitulate this same cycle. According to the Genesis story, humankind was formed of the earth on the sixth day (a Friday), and it was on a Friday (the sixth day, as Augustine of Hippo observed) that Jesus was crucified and buried in the tomb.[87]

The coincidence of the days between the day of the making of humankind and the day on that Christ suffered, died and was buried caught the minds and imaginations of some of the greatest of early Christian thinkers and writers. And these numerical sequences and coincidences evidently fascinated Augustine of Hippo. In the opening paragraph of his exposition of Psalm 92 (93), Augustine states that humankind was first made in the image of God on the sixth day, and then proceeds to express how we need to be formed anew. Elsewhere, the significance of the sixth day becomes even more complex in his thinking. He made great play on the coincidence of God's work in shaping the body of Christ, first in the womb of Mary and then in the depths of the earth, and speculated on the numerical sequence of days between Christ's conception in the womb of Mary and his being laid in the tomb.[88] Although the emphasis on womb and tomb is different in terms of the

---

86 I am indebted to Anthony Moore for first drawing my attention to the theological import of these words. His own, yet unpublished, research maps the structure of John's Gospel against the first creation story of Genesis.
87 See Augustine's Commentary on John, *Tractate* XVII.15.
88 See Augustine, *Quaest. In Heptateuchum* II.90; *De Trinitate* IV.5.

point we want to make, it does lend some support to the correspondence between birth and death, death and rebirth. God's work on the sixth day covers our human making and the beginning of our human remaking. When it is put in these terms we can see a perfect symmetry, one that conveys the theological conviction that as humankind was formed from the earth, so in Christ's burial in the earth humankind is re-formed or made anew.[89] The meta-narrative, in other words, returns us to the sixth day, and so the 'plot' of the Christian story of salvation moves from the making to the remaking of creation, with the crucified and risen Christ as the harbinger of a new creation.[90]

These rich strands of theological thinking come to luminous expression in Adams' Fourteenth Station. Although there is no figural representation, the final Station, 'Jesus is buried . . .', alludes to how the crucified Christ was placed in the dark tomb. But through the use of colour and form in this canvas, the burial is presented here as the sowing of the seed of re-creation. Looking at the canvas we see that tender shoots gradually begin to unfurl, and at the top we can see the breaking golden light of Sunday, the day of resurrection, when God's remaking begins. And so a light slowly rises from the dark hues of the knotted roots at the bottom of the canvas. Resurrection, we could say, is already taking place in the very bowels of the earth as the flowers and petal shapes begin to form.

These same organic forms of twining tendrils, bordered by the dark root-knotted earth, unfurling upward into an apple-green light, occur in another painting of Norman Adams', *And Lazarus Saw the Light* (1996). This painting, with its brightly coloured geometric patterns, is again a brilliant painterly depiction of 'life through death', and again a portrayal of death as a sowing or planting, reminiscent of the imagery of pullulating forms of life that we noted in the apse mosaic of St Clemente in Rome.

What I have attempted to show in drawing parallels between the apse mosaics in Rome and the paintings of Norman Adams is that part

---

89 A similar pattern of thinking touching on creation and re-creation is evident in Paul's use of an Adam typology and his designation of Christ as the New Adam.

90 The point is vividly shown in the most successful painting of the resurrection, Piero della Francesca's *Resurrection* (1463) in his home town, Sansepolcro, named after the sepulchre in Jerusalem. Set in a Tuscan landscape, the risen Christ, marked with the wounds of his Passion, stands with his left foot on the tomb, and one side the trees are bare, on the other they are in full leaf.

of the visual language of the meaning of the story celebrated in Christian worship speaks powerfully of Christ's death and burial as a kind of planting, or the making possible of a new life on the earth. The theme is deeply nuanced theologically, and one is struck by the coincidence of meaning when one attempts to attend carefully to what an artist is saying in his or her work, as well as to the Christian story told and enacted in the liturgical space of a church. In the case of Norman Adams, although he would not have claimed to be a Christian artist in any direct sense, he was biblically literate and an artist who appreciated that some of the greatest art in Europe was inspired by and sought to articulate something of the Christian story. This later belief was impressed upon him when he visited the basilica of St Francis in Assisi. Adams admitted that the art in that Franciscan church was a considerable influence on him. He had been particularly struck by the narrative frescoes of Giotto and Cimabue, and so it is to the art of the Franciscan movement, which began in the Umbrian city of Assisi, that we now turn to explore further the cross as the icon of God's loving regard for creation, and the developing theme of the crucified and risen Christ as the tree of life.

Chapter 6

The tree of life

The story of the cross as a sign of Christ's death and resurrection takes a new turn with St Francis (1181–1226), the son of Pietro Bernardone, a merchant of the city of Assisi in Umbria, and the nascent Franciscan movement from 1205–39. The earliest sources of the life of Francis witness, with some variation, to how his sense of being called by God occurred in the context of a sacred space, in the near derelict church of San Damiano. This comparatively small church was originally a simple structure – consisting of a nave and apse, with a small crypt beneath the presbytery – that was typical of the chapels of small Benedictine houses resulting from the Benedictine reforms of the tenth and eleventh centuries. We know that Francis had a great love of church buildings, and that when passing one he would enter the space in order to pray. In one text, probably an authentic piece written by Francis himself, he weaves a liturgical formula used at the Veneration of the Cross on Good Friday and at the feast of the Exaltation of the Cross into a phrase that celebrates sacred space: 'And the Lord gave me such faith in churches that I would pray with simplicity in this way and say: "We adore you, Lord Jesus Christ, in all your churches throughout the whole world and we bless you because by your holy cross you have redeemed the world."'[1] Implicit in this exuberant expression of praise addressed to Christ is a strong conviction that such sacred places are the loci in which Christ's name is invoked and in which he is present with, and meets, his people in prayer. The church building, in other words, is affirmed as a place of encounter with the living, crucified Lord. The particular church of San Damiano, with its prominent painted cross, has pride of place in the

---

1 *Testament of Saint Francis*, 4–5 in Regis J. Armstrong, J. A. Wayne Hellmann, William J. Short (eds), *Francis of Assisi: Early Documents* (FAED), vol. 1, *The Saint* (New York and London: New City Press 1999), pp. 124–5.

foundational story of Francis' call, and it is this episode with which we begin this exploration of the iconography of the cross as the tree of life in Franciscan art and liturgical sources.

According to Thomas of Celano, who wrote the earliest life of Francis in Franciscan hagiography, the call and conversion of Francis was closely associated with a little dilapidated rural church, dedicated to San Damiano, which is outside the city of Assisi on the lower slope of Mount Subasio.[2] The *First Life*, written around 1229, tells how Francis offered money towards the restoration of the church, but later sources, such as Celano's *Second Life*, written nearly 20 years later, focus on an experience Francis had while he was praying before the cross of San Damiano.[3] This lateral cross, painted on walnut wood in the twelfth century, has received considerable scholarly attention and attracted much debate on the artistic influences on the style of this particular Umbrian cross.[4] Some art historians have detected similarities in style with Italian-Byzantine work familiar in Ravenna and Venice; others have noted similarities with Carolingian and Romanesque art, but this is not sufficient to postulate direct influence. The provenance of the artefact is Umbrian, and the Franciscan art historian Leone Bracaloni has drawn attention to the similarities between the San Damiano cross and crosses that were painted in the region of Spoleto in Umbria. It seems likely that the Eastern style of this cross was influenced by Syrian iconography as a number of Syrian monks had settled in the area following the second wave of iconoclasm in the Byzantine world. Indeed, a monastic settlement of exiled monks from Palestine and Syria was established on Mount Luco overlooking the stable city of Spoleto, and this settlement apparently drew comparisons at the time with Mount Athos.[5] It is most likely that these Eastern monastic communities were centres of icon writing, as it is traditionally termed, and their influence may well have extended along the valleys from Spoleto, up to Assisi and beyond to Perugia. This Syrian association, of course, returns us again to the cultural seedbed of early Christianity in which the motif of the

---

2 FAED, vol. 1, *The Saint*, 1C8, pp. 188–9, 196.

3 FAED, vol. 2, *The Founder* (New York and London: New City Press 2000), C5, p. 249.

4 For a summary following the major restoration work on the cross in the summer of 1939, see Leone Bracaloni, 'Il prodigioso Crocifisso che parlò a San Francesco', *Studi Francescani* 36, pp. 185–212.

5 Bracaloni, 'Il prodigioso Crocifisso che parlò a San Francesco', pp. 195, 197, 210.

living cross was conceived and frequently expressed, as we have seen, in both liturgical art and poetry.

The cross itself, with its red background, as is characteristic of crosses from Spoleto, is framed with a deep yellow palm-leaf decoration, a decorative feature that specifically evokes the Syrian motif of the tree of life. The tradition, as it has been transmitted through literary and artistic sources, tells that it was from this cross, which was probably suspended above the altar, that Christ addressed Francis directly, saying: 'My house is in ruins. Go, then, and rebuild it for me.'[6] There are variations in the sources that tell of this incident. Celano's *Second Life*, for instance, tells us that the lips of the Crucified actually moved as the figure spoke,[7] and another, the *Major Life of Saint Francis*, written at an even later date by St Bonaventure (1221–74), tells us that the divine command was spoken three times. But however the incident was experienced by Francis, it does seem as though he took the command to rebuild the church at face value, and set to restoring San Damiano to be a model of a small monastic church. It has been suggested that in the restoration of the building, Francis was constructing what he considered a church building ought to be, namely a single space in which a community could gather together with the clergy around the Word, in prayer and reading, and in communion with each other and the Lord.[8] However the space was configured and understood, the cross retained a prominent position. But what exactly was this image, and how may it be understood?

Looking at the cross we can see that the dominant figure is that of Christ, with figures painted on either side. A series of locally revered saints are painted below, and a number of surrounding angels. It is impossible to say exactly where and how this cross was sited in the small church, but later artistic representations offer some plausible clues. One of the frescoes in the cycle of paintings, often attributed to Giotto and his assistants, depicting the life of St Francis in the Upper Church of the basilica of Francis, shows Francis at prayer before the cross in the dilapidated church. It is just possible that the artist himself knew the

---

6 The earliest source of this episode is in *The Legend of the Three Companions* (1241–7), FAED, vol. 2, *The Founder*, p. 76.

7 Thomas of Celano, *The Second Life of Saint Francis*, FAED, vol. 2, *The Founder*, C5, p. 249.

8 M. Bigaroni, 'San Damiano – Assisi: The First Church of St. Francis', *Franciscan Studies*, 47, 1987, pp. 78–9.

painted cross and had seen it in situ in San Damiano, but it is a stylized picture, and the dilapidated church is so painted that the viewer can conveniently see into its interior. Part of the south wall has evidently collapsed, and roof tiles are missing above the presbytery area, revealing the saint kneeling in the chancel in the centre of the composition. His hands are raised in a posture of prayer and his eyes look intently at the face of the Crucified on the painted cross. The cross dominates the space and appears to be fixed directly behind a square stone pedestal altar below a blue-painted domed apse. The dimensions of the cross fill the wall space, with the vertical shaft reaching from the base of the altar to the rim of the dome and the horizontal bar extending across the width of the apse wall.[9]

Once the building had been repaired, Francis installed St Clare and the Poor Ladies at San Damiano, which led Thomas of Celano to refer to the church as Clare's 'little nest'.[10] Clare venerated the cross with an ardent fervour, and it was taken by her community of sisters to their new monastic church within the city walls of Assisi around 1260, and placed in the enclosed choir of the new monastery church. The San Damiano cross, now heavily restored, can be seen in a side chapel of this church dedicated to Santa Clara in Assisi, and has become one of the most reproduced and familiar images of the cross in the Western Christian world.

The figure of Christ on this cross is flanked on either side by the figures of Mary and John, showing a particular dependence on the narrative of Christ's crucifixion in the Gospel of John. In addition there is a unique medallion showing the ascended Christ holding the resurrection cross in his right hand, surrounded by angels and triumphantly striding through heaven towards the hand of God that is painted at the top of the lateral bar of the cross.

---

9 Two other frescoes in this Francis cycle show a different arrangement for the siting of a painted cross in a church setting. The fresco depicting the crib at Greccio shows a painted cross fixed directly above the arch of a tall chancel wall. Another fresco, the Recognition of the Stigmata, is fixed to an architrave and flanked on either side by icons of the Madonna and Child and Michael the Archangel. In both of these paintings the painted cross faces the nave.

10 *The Legend of St Clare Virgin*, Part 1, 9, a hagiographical source, attributed to Thomas of Celano, but probably multi-authored, applies the scriptural imagery (Jeremiah 48.28) to Clare and her household at San Damiano. See *Clare of Assisi: Early Documents* (CAED), revised and expanded by Regis J. Armstrong, Franciscan Institution Publications (New York: St Bonaventure University 1993), p. 262.

This feature is reminiscent of the large Umbrian painted crosses referred to as 'historiated crosses' by art historians.[11] These crosses were suspended above the entrance to the chancel or in the apse directly above the high altar at the east end of a church, and thereby provided a key focal point for the worshipper. They were a typical form of liturgical art, particularly in Umbria and Tuscany. Some imposing examples of these crosses survive, but as Hans Belting has observed, those that do survive could represent a mere fraction of those painted at the time.[12] It is extremely likely that Francis and his first group of followers would have been familiar with these crosses and would have seen examples of them as they visited churches during their travels. If this is the case, then the historiated crosses would have been part of the spiritual culture they inhabited.

A historiated cross is basically a painted cross with a series of six or eight painted panels that form an apron on either side of the vertical bar of the cross. From extant examples we can see that although there was some variation in the exact choice of subject, each panel invariably depicted a particular scene from the Gospel stories of Christ's Passion and resurrection. In this way they functioned as a visual anamnesis (memorial of Christ), and set the figure of the crucified Lord in the wider narrative frame of Christ's physical suffering, death and post-resurrection appearances. One late twelfth-century example, painted for the church of San Sepolcro in Pisa and now to be seen in the Museum of San Matteo there, portrays the crucified Lord as he is depicted in the San Damiano cross, with open eyes and arms outstretched. The six panel paintings, three each side of the crucified figure, pictorially cover the whole paschal story, from the Last Supper to Pentecost. The inclusion of two resurrection scenes provides a balanced view of the Passion and the resurrection.[13] In this way, the whole paschal mystery of Christ's Passion and resurrection would have been made present for the viewer

---

11 See Anne Derbes, *Picturing the Passion in Late Medieval Italy: Narrative Painting, Franciscan Ideologies, and the Levant* (Cambridge: Cambridge University Press 1996), pp. 3–7, 20, 170.

12 Hans Belting, *Likeness and Presence: A History of the Image before the Era of Art*, trans. Edmund Jephcott (Chicago: University of Chicago Press 1996), p. 349.

13 Another example of this type of historiated cross, the work of a Florentine painter and dated the last quarter of the twelfth century, is to be seen in the Uffizi Museum in Florence (Inv. 1890 no. 432). The panels include: the foot-washing at the Last Supper, the betrayal in Gethsemane, the flagellation, the deposition, the entombment and, finally, Easter morning.

as worshipper as he or she encountered such a cross. Such an encounter is profoundly liturgical, and was in all likelihood an experience known by St Francis, and one that profoundly informed his understanding of the saving significance of the cross.

Rather like the image of the Byzantine-style cross, the cross of San Damiano includes, on a much smaller scale and on either side of the figure of the Crucified, the figures of Longinus, who pierced Christ's side with his lance, and Stephanatus, who raised the sponge soaked in vinegar to the lips of the dying Jesus. These two figures conventionally feature in the Eastern iconography of the cross. In the cross of San Damiano the painted figure of Christ is depicted with arms outstretched, as in a gesture of welcome, and although blood visibly trickles from his pierced hands, feet and side, the figure faces the viewer without any signs of pain, with large open almond shape eyes and slightly smiling lips. So far from being an artistic representation of the death of the Son of God or of the physical human suffering of the God-man contemplated by Bernard of Clairvaux and Anselm,[14] what is presented here is an icon of the incarnate Lord, who suffered, died and was raised and now ever lives in the glory of the Father. This is not to deny a devotional focus on the human suffering of the Christ who, according to the *locus classicus* of Franciscan devotion, emptied himself in love and obedience to the very point of death (see Philippians 2.1–11). Indeed, Thomas of Celano, in his account of the life of Francis written some 20 years after Francis' death, places the saint's *Lamentations on the Passion of Christ* soon after his account of the call of the saint.

Nevertheless, the figure of the Crucified on the cross of San Damiano certainly belongs to the type of *Christus triumphans*, the victorious Christ.[15] And as such, what we see here is a depiction of the God who 'reigns from the wood', the *regnavit a ligno Deus* of the old Latin text of Psalm 96.10 which was echoed in the hymn *Pange Lingua* of Fortunatus. Further, the very physical construction of the wooden painted cross serves its iconic purpose, which was to mediate the living

---

14 This is not to deny that both Francis and Clare were deeply moved and affected by images of the Crucified Christ. The Lamentation of the Cross, possibly composed by Francis soon after his experience at San Damiano, eloquently testifies to Francis' affective devotion.

15 Rosalind B. Brooke, *The Image of St Francis: Responses to Sainthood in the Thirteenth Century* (Cambridge: Cambridge University Press 2006), p. 166.

Christ. The face of the figure on the cross is painted on tilted board, producing a deliberate angle so that the face actually looks down upon those who pray in the sacred space of the church. So what we see in the cross of San Damiano is the glorified Christ who looks upon his people from the throne of the cross. The viewer is not so much invited to look *into* the painting and there to contemplate a scene of physical human suffering, as to return the attention, the actual gaze, of the Crucified, who faces the viewer directly. The question that occurs when one stands before this image is: Who is looking at whom? The painted figure of the Crucified on this cross functions in the same way as a typical Eastern icon, with its inverse perspective, its large face and exaggerated eyes.[16] This feature, common in all early icons of the Christian East, recalls the Hebrew word *panim* (literally 'faces'), usually translated as 'face'. The term denotes God's loving regard and carries the deeper sense of 'presence'. It frequently occurs in the poetry of the Psalms.[17]

The imagery of God's face in the Hebrew poetry of the Psalms functions as a metaphor for the human experience of God. It holds together in tension the mystery of God's essential unknowability with the human apprehension of his presence and absence, his anger and his favour. The language is not to be dismissed as crudely anthropomorphic but understood as a metaphor that amplifies the meaning and discloses the relation of God to the created order, and particularly YHWH's attentive and loving gaze towards Israel, his covenanted people (see Psalm 33.18,19). For when they 'look to the LORD', the people recognize God as the creator and the very source of life, but when God 'hides his face' the people are banished from his presence, condemned to their own devices (Isaiah 64.7) and suffer all kinds of vicissitudes (Ezekiel 39.21–29).

Life itself flourishes under YHWH's gaze, but when God looks away all

---

16 As described by Besançon, 'the line of force extends from within the icon toward the beholder's eye', in Alain Besançon, *The Forbidden Image: An Intellectual History of Iconoclasm*, trans J. M. Todd (Chicago and London: University of Chicago Press 2000). For an Eastern Orthodox account of this convention, see Leonid Ouspensky, 'The Meaning and Language of Icons' in Leonid Ouspensky and Vladimir Lossky, *The Meaning of Icons* (Crestwood, NY: St Vladimir's Seminary Press 1982, 2nd edn), pp. 25–49.

17 The way the word is deployed in the Psalms figures the life-giving and transfiguring presence of God. For a discussion of this theme in relation to the death and resurrection of Jesus, see David F. Ford, *Self and Salvation: Being Transformed* (Cambridge: Cambridge University Press 1999), ch. 8, pp. 192–214.

life shrivels and decays: 'When you hide your face, they are dismayed; when you take away their breath, they die and return to their dust' (Psalm 104.29). And what happens at the cosmic and corporate level applies equally at the individual personal level. For before this God, our hidden motives become transparent and the things we would rather hide are brought into the light (Psalm 90.8; cf. Ezra 9). But those who are called by the gracious God into a covenant relationship are invited to 'seek his face' (Psalm 27.8), and when that loving attention is reciprocated, those who stand before the Lord are enlightened. For the gaze of YHWH's face is both a graced and a gracing countenance. 'Happy are the people . . . who walk, O LORD, in the light of your countenance' (Psalm 89.15). 'Who is like the LORD our God, who is seated on high, who looks far down on the heavens and the earth? He raises the poor from the dust, and lifts the needy from the ash heap . . . He gives the barren woman a home, making her the joyous mother of children' (Psalm 113.5–9).

Thus for the people of God, YHWH's countenance is the source of their saving help and his searching gaze their very judgement (Psalm 89.46; Psalm 139). The aspect of God's gracing countenance is condensed in the so-called Aaronic blessing (Numbers 6.24–26), a text that Francis deftly wove into the blessing he composed for his companion and secretary Brother Leo during a time of intense prayer at his cell on Mount La Verna:[18] 'May the Lord bless you and keep you. May he show his face to you and have mercy on you. May he turn his countenance to you and give you peace.'[19]

As in this form of blessing, the nexus of biblical imagery of 'the face of God' finds potent and evocative expression in the liturgical poetry of the Church's repertoire of daily prayer. A couple of examples will suffice to illustrate this. First, a stanza of an early Vespers Office hymn possibly dating back to the sixth century, *Immense caeli Conditor* (O boundless wisdom, God most high), asks the creator God to 'pour on us, who seek your face, / the waters of your quickening grace; renew the source of life within, / wash from our souls the stain of sin'.[20] Second, a couple of

---

18 The autographed parchment containing this blessing, collaborated by Thomas of Celano (2 Cel. 2.18), is revered as a primary relic of the saint, and is preserved in the Basilica of San Francesco in Assisi.

19 See FAED, vol. 1, *The Saint*, p. 112.

20 Text of hymn 247 from John Harper (ed.), *Hymns for Prayer and Praise* (Norwich: Canterbury Press 1996).

psalm antiphons: one associated with Psalm 89 that reads 'Your loving mercy and your righteous truth shine out before your face, O Lord our God'; and in similar vein one set for a commemoration of Apostles and evangelists that speaks of how the saints in glory radiate the splendour of God, 'The righteous shall shine bright as the sun before the face of God.'[21]

From infancy most of us learn the very rudiments of language from the expressive face of our mother, and as we grow up we learn that others can read how we really feel and think by the expressions on our faces. Indeed, as Rowan Williams has argued, all true forms of personal knowing and mutual honouring occur in a 'face to face' relationship between persons, and that it is precisely by being lovingly faced by another that the individual self can become a soul.[22] And as the face is so vital in our relating to others, it should not surprise us that the term 'face' came to be regarded as able to bear a freight of theological meaning, even in the arena of theological controversy and in the definition of key theological doctrine. At the Council of Chalcedon in 451, for example, as the bishops of the early Church wrangled over the vocabulary with which to articulate the truth of Christ's humanity and divinity, it is interesting to see that they finally seized upon the Greek term *prosopon* – literally the human face – as a key term in the Council's finally agreed definition of the person of Christ as being perfect God and perfect man.

As well as being appropriated as a technical theological term in the Chalcedonian understanding of the person of Christ, the imagery of the face can also be used in telling the Christian story of salvation. After all, when the unfolding narrative of Luke's Gospel reaches its crucial turning point, we are told that Jesus set his face towards Jerusalem and that he was resolved to enter the arena of hostility, rejection, brutality and death. But this was not an inexorable step towards annihilation, because his entering into the darkness of his Passion and death on the cross of Calvary occurred before the very face of God. And because this death occurred before God's face, so Jesus' face, which had been disfigured and distorted by physical pain, was transfigured into the transforming

---

21 The examples are drawn from Evensong in the Office Book of the Community of the Resurrection, Mirfield, 2000, pp. 31, 42, 220.
22 See Rowan Williams, *Lost Icons: Reflections on Cultural Bereavement* (London: T. & T. Clark 2000), ch. 4.

countenance of the risen Christ, a countenance that, when pondered by others, led them to be changed and transformed. For those who ponder that radiant face find themselves enlightened and changed, as St Paul testified, from one degree of glory to another, until they finally came to reflect the very likeness of God (2 Corinthians 3.18; 4.6).[23]

The image of being faced by God in Christ returns us to the scene of Francis at prayer before the cross at San Damiano. The scene depicted in the fresco panel in the lower band of decoration on the north side of the nave of the basilica of St Francis in Assisi does not simply show Francis contemplating the Crucified, but Francis himself being engaged by the crucified and risen Christ himself.[24] So what this cross represents is not a single historical scene as such but a painted medium that pictorially displays – one might almost say unveils – the Christ who suffered and died before the face of the Father and who was raised by the power and glory of the Spirit. In other words, what we see in the cross of San Damiano is an icon of the mystery of Christ's death and resurrection that meets the gaze of the viewer as he or she attentively focuses in prayer upon the image of the cross.

We know from the earliest historical sources of the life of St Francis that he adopted the sign of the Tau (the letter 'T') as his personal signature, and sketched the sign on the walls of his cell wherever he stayed on his travels. The hagiographical sources of the saint's life record how Brother Pacificus saw the sign of the Tau emblazoned on the saint's forehead.[25] But what did the sign signify? Tau functioned as a condensed and resonant sign of the biblical story of salvation. It evoked earlier Hebrew stories of deliverance and divine protection, as in the exodus when the divine displeasure passed over the homes of the children of Israel that had been marked with the blood of the sacrificed Passover lamb (Exodus 12.13); and of how God's faithful ones enduring suffering

---

23 For a more detailed systematic treatment of the theological significance of the figure of the face of God in the drama of Christian salvation, see Hans Urs von Balthasar, *The Glory of the Lord* (Edinburgh: T. & T. Clark 1982), vol. 1, pp. 328f. and vol. 6 (Edinburgh: T. & T. Clark 1991), pp. 66–73.

24 The pictorial convention of signalling both the death and resurrection of Christ is also found in twelfth- and thirteenth-century Umbrian and Tuscan panel crosses. For further discussion, see Derbes, *Picturing the Passion in Late Medieval Italy*, pp. 3–7, 170.

25 See Thomas of Celano, *Second Life*, pt. 2, ch. 72; Thomas of Celano, *The Treatise of Miracles* ch. II, 3, ch. XVII, 159; and St Bonaventure of Bagnoregio, *Major Life*, ch. IV, 9.

and tribulation were marked with a sign on their foreheads (Ezekiel 9.4; cf. Revelation 7.2). But why did Francis adopt this particular sign as his personal signature?

We know that the sign of the Tau featured in the sermon that Pope Innocent III preached at the opening service of the Fourth Lateran Council in November 1215, at which Francis may well have been present.[26] The Pope saw the Tau as an acrostic or abbreviation that condensed the various aims he wanted the Council to endorse and promote. One of these aims was a further crusade to recapture the Church of the Holy Sepulchre in Jerusalem, the site of Christ's death and resurrection. Another aim was the insistence that the Eucharist should be revered and celebrated with dignity and care, as he articulated in the opening sermon of the Council. Francis certainly had sympathy with these two aims, as both his own travels and devotion to the Eucharist testify.[27]

The reason why Francis adopted the Tau sign may finally reside in its evocative power as a multivalent symbol. The resemblance of the shape of the letter Tau to the cross is central to the sign's power to communicate the mystery of God's work, but it is the completeness of that work, the fullness of Christ's *parousia*, embraced by the arms of the Tau, that gives the sign its symbolic potency. I deliberately use the rich Greek word of the New Testament – *parousia* – as it denotes Christ's presence in the flesh, his suffering, glorification and final appearing at the end of time. Further, the semiotic function of the Tau becomes apparent when we recognize that it is the last letter of the Hebrew alphabet, as the omega is the final letter of the Greek. In the book of Revelation, Christ is claimed as being the alpha and the omega, the beginning and the end, a phrase that is echoed in the annual celebration of the Christian *Pasch* in the blessing of the Easter candle at the Vigil of Holy Saturday. Correspondingly, the symbolic function of the Tau in holding together the whole saving mystery of God in Christ again speaks of the completeness of God's saving work in Christ, his incarnate life, death, glorification and second coming. So what we see in this favoured emblem of Francis is an apt sign of such significant symbolic power that it conveyed not only Christ's victory on the cross but the very fullness of God's salvation.

---

26 See 'The Tau: The Meaning of the Cross for Francis of Assisi', in Michael F. Cusato (ed.), *The Early Franciscan Movement (1205–1239): History, Sources and Hermeneutics* (Spoleto: Fondazione Centro Italiano di Studi Sull'alto Medioevo 2009).
27 *Testament*, FAED, vol. 1, *The Saint*, p. 125.

The holding together of cross and resurrection, suffering and life through death, returns us yet again to the use of the word *glorification* in the Gospel of John, and particularly to his account of the cross and Passion as the revealing of the glory that the eternal Son shares with the Father.[28] Francis' appropriation and use of the Johannine term 'glory' is evidenced in his own writing, and in all likelihood was a frequent theme in his preaching as well. We are particularly interested here in what came to be known as Francis' 'Office of the Passion'. This Office may well have begun to take shape around the year 1215. Hagiographical sources claim that Clare of Assisi frequently used it, as Francis had taught her, in her own pattern of daily prayer,[29] and it is reasonable to suppose that this Little Office was central to the round of daily prayer of Francis and his closest companions. Nevertheless, it would seem that it fell into disuse soon after his death in 1226, its demise probably hastened by the 'Office of the Passion of the Lord' compiled by Bonaventure, generally considered the second founder of the Franciscan Order.[30] So how may we account for the Little Office of St Francis and its relation to the Liturgy of the Hours, the services of daily prayer marking the periods of day and night? Various explanations have been offered. A comparison has been drawn, for example, between this Office and the votive Offices, such as the Office of the Dead and the Office of Our Lady, which were widely used in monastic households by the thirteenth century. But the emerging scholarly consensus on Francis' Office is that it is 'a unique work that does not follow any previous pattern'.[31]

The Office of St Francis, the 'lover of the cross', was not intended to be an additional Office to the seven- or eightfold Office that was customary in monastic houses during the time of St Francis. What is more likely is that it was intended as a preparatory form of prayer, a unit of prayer and praise to be prayed before each of the canonical Hours, or forms for daily prayer. As such it could be regarded as a stand-alone composition,

---

28 See, for instance, John 3.14, 8.28, 12.32.

29 *The Legend of St. Clare Virgin*, in CAED, p. 284.

30 Bonaventure, born at Bagnoregio, near Orvieto, was a sickly child and his mother vowed that if he survived she would give him to God as a friar. He was intellectually gifted, studied under Alexander of Hales, and taught in Paris for some 21 years before his election as the seventh Minister General of the Friars Minor.

31 Edward Foley, 'Franciscan Liturgical Prayer' in Timothy J. Johnson (ed.), *Franciscans at Prayer* (Leiden: Brill 2007), p. 405.

bearing some similarity to the so-called minor Offices or Hours of the Old Roman and Benedictine tradition, Prime, Terce, Sext and None. Although there is no direct linkage or thematic connection between the choice of the fixed hymnody, psalms and short Scripture readings for these essentially monastic Offices and the story of Christ's suffering and death on the cross, from the third century these Hours of prayer were associated with particular moments in the unfolding drama of Christ's Passion. The basis of the association simply rested on the time of day these minor Offices were prayed. The first, at the beginning of the day, corresponded to the time of Jesus' trial, the second, at 9 a.m., to the time he was mocked and tortured, the third, at noon, to when he was nailed to the cross, and the fourth, at 3 p.m., to the time he died on the cross. This association between the Hours of prayer and the story of Christ's Passion and death was commended and commented upon by the third-century North African bishop, Cyprian of Carthage (d. 258), and found its fullest and most explicit expression in *The Apostolic Tradition*, a document that tells us of the faith and practice of at least one section of the Church in Rome during the second decade of the third century.[32]

The story of the Passion of Christ, from the arrest in Gethsemane to the cross of Calvary, is certainly in the background of Francis' Office, but this is not the sole or exclusive focus of its content. The text of the Office suggests that some provision was made to fit it to the liturgical seasons, particularly the triduum, Easter, Advent and Christmas. But basically, both the form and content of the Office are shaped to provide a form of prayer to supplement the seven Offices or Hours of prayer. As such, Francis' Office adds something more to the conventional Offices and, moreover, it is broadly consistent with the strand of the theology of the Liturgy of the Hours that sees the evening Office of Vespers as a celebration of the paschal victory of Christ, and the morning Office as the greeting of the sun's rising as a symbol of the resurrection.[33]

---

32 For the text and analysis, see Paul F. Bradshaw, *Daily Prayer in the Early Church: A Study of the Origin and Early Development of the Divine Office* (London: SPCK 1981), pp. 53–5.

33 The first unit of the Little Office is associated with Vespers and so draws verses from Psalm 96 into the 'psalm', and the unit of prayer to be used in association with the Office of Prime draws on Psalm 57. For a comprehensive and analytical account of this movement from night to morning, death to resurrection, in the Liturgy of the Hours, see Gregory W. Woolfenden, *Daily Liturgical Prayer: Origins and Theology* (Aldershot: Ashgate 2004).

Joseph Jungmann provided a concise summary of the construction of each of the seven units of prayer and praise that constitute Francis' Office, and said that it was 'structured mainly on a free selection of verses from different psalms, concluding with a *Gloria Patri* and framed by a Marian antiphon'.[34] Commenting on the content of the Office, Jungmann went on to assert that the psalmody had been deliberately structured to give expression to the voice of the suffering redeemer. But I would suggest that this stress on the suffering redeemer rather narrows the focus and does not do justice to the scope of the material contained within the Office. For the sheer thematic range and the combinations made in the Office suggest a far longer trajectory from pre-existence to final glorification. Indeed, a theological line can be traced through the material, from references to, first, the glory of the pre-existent Word, second, the vulnerable flesh of the babe at Bethlehem, third, the cross, and on to life through death, ending with the reference to the return of the Son in glory to the right hand of the Father. So here again, in these repeated references to glory it seems as though we can detect how Francis followed, or was guided by, the theological logic of John's Gospel story of salvation.

A growing appreciation of the broad theological sweep represented by the material of this Office has recently led to a reconsideration of its nomenclature, and what had been known as the 'Office of the Passion' is now more generally referred to as *The Geste of the Great King*.[35] The very title indicates that these seven liturgical forms encompass the whole mystery of Christ and are written in a celebratory as much as in a commemorative mood. A recent commentator on this Office simply describes how each of these 'bolt-on' liturgical forms of prayer and praise weaves a clear line, as we have already intimated, from glory to suffering and then onwards from death to glory.[36]

Having established the general tenor and scope of this liturgical provision, let us look in a little more detail at the structure and the content

---

34 Joseph A. Jungmann, *Christian Prayer through the Centuries* (London: SPCK 2007), p. 74.

35 Laurant Gallant OFM and André Cirino OFM, *The Geste of the Great King: Office of the Passion of Francis of Assisi* (St Bonaventure, NY: Franciscan Institute 2001). Gallant and Cirino see the Office as a medieval *geste* in which Jesus, cast in the role of a hero, is in dialogue with his heavenly Father as he fulfils his divine mission in working the world's salvation.

36 Gallant and Cirino, *The Geste of the Great King*, p. 25.

of each of these liturgical units of prayer. The shape of each unit within the Office is simply structured and consists of:

1 the Lord's Prayer
2 a Canticle of Praise (opening with 'Holy, holy, holy' from Isaiah 6.3 and a weaving of praises from Revelation around the text of Daniel 3.57)
3 an antiphon honouring Mary the mother of the Lord
4 the Psalm (a composite single compilation)
5 a doxology (an ascription of praise).

The 'Psalm' in each unit is composed from lines drawn from the Latin Psalter, into which Francis inserted other lines either from Scripture or of his own composition. Each psalm, in other words, is a composite structure. But what can be said of its content? It is likely that some of Francis' psalms, such as Psalms 9 and 15, predate the compilation of the Office, and may have originated as Praises for the Nativity. Francis' Psalm 15 includes the verse 'the Most Holy Father of Heaven . . . sent His beloved Son from on High, and was born of the Blessed Virgin Mary', which artfully incorporates words from 1 John 4.9 ('God's love was revealed among us in this way: God sent his only Son into the world so that we might live through him.') into his own composition praising the mystery of the Incarnation.

Again, the full sweep of salvation is clearly celebrated in Psalm 7. Here Francis alludes to the sending of the pre-existent Word, and voices how the Father 'sent the beloved Son from on high'. Images of psalmody are appropriated as figures of the incarnate, crucified and glorified Christ. In using the Latin text of Psalm 96.10 as the final line of the ninth verse of this psalm,[37] Francis portrays the incarnate Christ reigning triumphant from the cross, the cross that was planted at the 'centre of the earth' as the tree of life had been planted at the

---

37 The origin of this expression is simply stated by Anthony Gelston where he explains how the Christocentric interpretation of the Hebrew Psalmody in this instance takes a further step: 'Devout meditation suggested the further thought, in line with the Fourth Gospel (see especially John 19.19), that the focus of Christ's kingly reign is the Cross. So it came about that in some very early Greek and Latin texts of the Psalm the words "from the tree" were added as a gloss on "is king" or "reigns"' – *The Psalms in Christian Worship: Patristic Precedent and Anglican Practice*, Joint Liturgical Studies 66 (Norwich: Canterbury Press 2008), p. 10.

centre of Eden. Indeed, the whole figurative language of this psalm suggests that it is the whole of creation that looks to Christ for its redemption and flourishing and acclaims Christ who reigns from the tree of the cross:

> Let the whole earth tremble before his face:
> tell among the nations that
> the Lord has reigned from a tree. (v. 4)[38]

And so far from presenting a restricted anthropocentric view of salvation focusing on human anguish and physical suffering, Francis seems to place the emphasis on how the whole of creation benefits from and is enjoined to acclaim Christ's redeeming work. And this he does by inserting further words from Psalm 96 (vv. 11–12a) into his composition:

> Let heavens rejoice and earth exult,
> let the sea and all that is in it be moved;
> let the fields and all that is in them be glad. (v. 9)[39]

This rich liturgical material goes beyond a preoccupation with the human suffering of Jesus on the cross and opens up a further horizon of meaning. And yet the liturgical art of the cross that was commissioned and inspired by the Franciscan movement is often credited with being the catalyst, if not the cause, of a significant shift in the way the figure of the crucified was depicted in thirteenth-century liturgical art.[40] The typical Romanesque portrayal of a priestly Christ, victorious over death, the so-called *Christus victor* style, moved to a more naturalistic portrayal of the suffering Christ, now shown dead on the cross, known as the *Christus patiens* style. It is undeniable that there was a shift in the way the figure of Christ was portrayed on the cross in the thirteenth century, but the fact is that both styles persisted in Italy for some considerable

---

38 See FAED, vol. 1, *The Saint*, p. 147.
39 FAED, vol. 1, *The Saint*, p. 147.
40 See, for example, Belting, *Likeness and Presence*, p. 358; Timothy Verdon, 'Environments of Experience and Imagination' in Timothy Verdon and John Henderson (eds), *Christianity and the Renaissance: Image and Religious Imagination in the Quattrocento* (New York: Syracuse University Press 1990), pp. 12–13; Nigel Spivey, *Enduring Creation: Art, Pain and Fortitude* (London: Thames & Hudson 2001), p. 58.

time. This is convincingly demonstrated by Richard Viladesau who, in his discussion of a thirteenth-century processional cross, draws attention to how the *Christus triumphans* – the style of the figure of the *Christus victor* – was on one side of the cross and a *Christus patiens* figure on the other.[41] The causes for this shift in the portrayal of Christ on the cross, from an open-eyed figure with extended arms in the *orans* position to a more slumped body with an inclined head resting on the right shoulder, were numerous and complex. First, as it emphasized the humanity of Christ it appealed more directly to the affective type of prayer. Second, the image asserted the reality of Christ's death and thereby countered some contemporary heretical views, such as the one advanced by the Cathars, who taught that Christ, as the Son of God, could not have physically suffered. Finally, it is generally thought that the *Christus patiens* style was probably influenced by what had become, again for doctrinal reasons, the conventional way of depicting Christ in the Good Friday Byzantine icon of the Cross.[42] We know that the sack of Constantinople in 1204 had caused a further wave of immigration into Italy, and the style of writing icons would again have become familiar. But as we shall see, this influence was more than a change in artistic style or simply a movement in the renaissance direction towards a more naturalistic and expressive portrayal of the human form.

The commissioning of liturgical art in this new style and sensibility returns us again to Assisi and to the monumental church that was built as a shrine to St Francis. The building work was begun just two years after his death in 1228, and its cost was underwritten by Pope Gregory IX. The basilica, built in the warm pink stone of Monte Subasio, towers above the olive groves – which to this day run down to the expansive plain below – and proudly dominates the landscape. We know that Elias of Cortona, a key figure in the earliest group of Franciscans, commissioned a large painted crucifix from Giunta Pisano (*c.* 1180–1250)

---

41 For an illustration, see Richard Viladesau, *The Beauty of the Cross: The Passion of Christ in Theology and the Arts – from the Catacombs to the Eve of the Reformation* (Oxford: Oxford University Press 2006), p. 112.

42 A frequently cited Byzantine Icon of the Cross is the mosaic of the crucifixion in Hosios Lukas, which was painted in the narthex of the monastic church around 1000. The painted panel Icon of the Incarnation had a prominent liturgical function on Good Friday and the feast of the Exaltation (and at other times might be displayed in the nave), and typically has the title, *The Lord of Glory*. See Constantine Cavarnos, *Guide to Byzantine Iconography*, vol. 1 (Boston: Holy Transfiguration Monastery 1993), pp. 169–76.

to hang in the newly constructed basilica, and that this crucifix reflected the shift in sensibility and artistic style. The ground plan of the new church followed the shape of the Tau, and its focal point was this large painted cross suspended above the high altar, beneath which Francis' body was buried.

Pisano's crucifix, believed to have been painted around 1236, is no longer extant, but its type and style can reasonably be deduced by considering an earlier painted cross by the artist that is now to be seen in the Museo della Porziuncola attached to the basilica of Santa Maria degli Angeli, on the plain below Assisi. In addition there is an imposing cross, signed by the painter, that was commissioned by the Dominicans sometime in the 1240s to hang in the transept of the basilica of St Dominic in Bologna, and now in a museum in Pisa. These two crosses are similar to the monumental painted cross suspended above the high altar in the church of San Francesco at Arezzo, on which Francis himself is depicted as kneeling and embracing the foot of the Crucified. It has been suggested that this motif may well have been included by Pisano in his cross for the basilica in Assisi, the mother church of the Order of Friars Minor. The gesture of embracing the foot of the cross has often been read as emblematic of Franciscan spirituality because of its apparent emphasis on the human response of empathy and contrite sorrow before the image of the crucified Christ.

However, it would be misguided simply to infer that the artist Pisano was requested to paint a cross with the single purpose of eliciting feelings of sympathy and contrition from those who saw it. The cross, simply by its dimensions, its colour and its prominent placing above the high altar, would certainly have had an impact on those who gathered in that space for worship. But as a piece of liturgical art as distinct from art produced for private reflection and devotion, the meaning of Pisano's cross would extend beyond the affective subjective responses of the viewer and would convey a wider range of theological meanings. Some of these can be recovered by taking a more detailed look at the extant crosses painted by Pisano.

In Pisano's crosses in Assisi (that is, in the Museo della Porziuncola) and in Bologna, the figure of the Crucified is stripped naked, apart from an opaque loin cloth. His head hangs forward and the body is collapsed under its dead weight to produce the gently curved 'z' shape of the dead Christ. The shape of the corpus resembles the Byzantine crucifixion icon that began to emerge in the eleventh century and that showed the figure not twisted by pain but in the peaceful repose of the Son of God.[43] The semiotics of this rendering of the figure of the crucified is not without its theological significance, for the letter 'z' is the first letter of the Greek word *zoe*, which means 'life', and this makes the image an icon of death defeated by death and of life through death.[44] Pisano's cross in Assisi has a painted panel at each end of the transverse bar of the cross, showing Mary and the evangelist John respectively, both painted in a pose of contemplative witness. These two figures invite the viewer to ponder the mystery of the dawning of a new horizon of life through the humility and obedience of the Son of God. The crucified figure is not shown to be contorted by physical pain, but as the eyes of the figure are closed we may infer an intention to portray the dead Christ. Above the cross is a roundel on which is painted an image of the risen Christ, with his right hand raised in blessing. The whole painted surface, in other words, is an icon of the whole saving work of the Christ.

Looking again recently at the cross of Pisano in the Museum of the Porziuncola, I was struck by the serenity of the painted figure of Christ. On this occasion the cross struck me as an image of the 'sleep-ing Lord', and so I was reminded of the story of how the 'mother of all living' was taken by God from the side of the sleeping Adam in Eden. The suggestion I am making here is that the painted cross, like its prototype, the Byzantine icon of the crucifixion, was not intended to evoke in the viewer a feeling of sad remorse but to reveal the full extent of God's solidarity with the human predicament and to see this death, the death of Christ, as generative and as opening into a fuller life. So Pisano's cross may be seen as an icon of the death of Christ that paradoxically shows the realization of the promise of abundant life (John 10.10).

The divine gift of eternal life was understood to have been fully incarnate, enfleshed in Christ, and it is this key theological conviction that brings us to recognize another feature of the Franciscan cross. This

---

43 Late eleventh- and early twelfth-century examples of Byzantine Passion and cruci-fixion icons are treasured possessions in the monastery of St Catherine on Mount Sinai.
44 Following F. P. Pickering, Richard Viladesau suggests that this figuring of Christ on the cross derived from the patristic reading of the story of Moses lifting up the serpent in the wilderness (Numbers 21.8–9) as a type of the crucifixion (Viladesau, *The Beauty of the Cross*, p. 116). This prefiguring of the cross is certainly alluded to in John's Gospel, (specifically in John 3.14), in which 'life through death' is such a prominent theme.

is the near naked body of the figure of the Crucified. The display of flesh is accentuated by an opaque loin cloth, which in Cimabue's imposing cross, painted around 1280 for the Franciscan church of Santa Croce in Florence, is famously diaphanous.[45] At one level the cross could be said to reveal to the viewer the vulnerability of Jesus, but this would be to miss a deeper theological concern, which was to show the incarnate Christ, the very Son of God, as being flesh of our flesh and bone of our bone. Anne Derbes has convincingly argued that following the election of Bonaventure as the Minister General of the Order of Friars Minor in 1257, the motif of the naked Christ as depicted in the art of the Passion was appropriated to validate the Franciscan ideal of poverty.[46] This may well be the case in the narrative paintings of the Passion, but in the case of the cross itself I would argue that the primary reference of the nakedness of Christ is to the theological doctrine of the Incarnation. This, I believe, is the perspective in which we should view the cross of Pisano in the Museum of the Porziuncola, and when we see it in this doctrinal register, it is seen to be as much an icon of the Incarnation as of the Passion, and as such perfectly reflects the reported preoccupations of Francis' heart and mind. For as Thomas of Celano testified in his *First Life of Saint Francis*, the humility of the Incarnation and the charity of the Passion so preoccupied Francis that he scarcely ever wanted to think of anything else.

The mystery of the Incarnation, principally celebrated on the feast of the Nativity of Christ, was undoubtedly the second pole of Francis' spirituality, and the story of how Francis, unable to return to Assisi because of bad weather in 1223, celebrated the feast of Christmas at the manger in Greccio is well documented and illustrated in the church art commissioned by the Franciscans.[47] The sumptuous fresco decoration covering the surfaces of the Upper Church in Assisi includes the scene of Francis at the crib in Greccio. This fresco, part of a whole cycle showing the saint's life, transposes the scene into a church interior. The occasion is the midnight Mass, and here Francis, vested in a deacon's dalmatic, is shown gently holding the Christ child above the crib placed

---

45 See Derbes, *Picturing the Passion in Late Medieval Italy*, pp. 28–30.
46 Derbes, *Picturing the Passion in Late Medieval Italy*, p. 32.
47 Thomas of Celano, *First Life of Saint Francis*, Bk 2, ch. 3; Bonaventure, *Legend Major*, 10.7. As well as in the Assisi fresco, the scene of the crib at Greccio is also shown on the Bardi altar-panel in the Franciscan Church of Santa Croce in Florence.

before the altar, while his habited companions, open-mouthed, sing the praise of 'the King, the Babe of Bethlehem' as the good burghers of the town stand around and their womenfolk peer through the chancel arch looking somewhat bemused by the spectacle.

The equal weighting of Incarnation and Passion is particularly striking in the nave of the Lower Church, where frescoes of the life of Francis are interspersed with frescoes of the life of Christ. The purpose of this decorative scheme alternating the figures of Francis and of Christ is undoubtedly to portray Francis as an *alter Christus*, literally as another Christ. The identity of Blessed Francis as an *alter Christus* was taken as being vindicated through the dramatic gift of the stigmata, the wounds of the crucifixion that Francis received towards the end of his life in 1224, while he was alone at prayer on Mount La Verna. In his account of this incident, Bonaventure repeatedly claimed that the stigmata had been a *unique* gift conferred upon Francis. It was certainly seen as a gift that both confirmed his status as a saint and seemed to highlight the suffering figure of Christ on the cross as a prominent image and theme in Franciscan devotion. There is an undeniable emphasis on *compassio* (literally fellow-suffering) in Franciscan spirituality, reinforced and graphically portrayed in the large painted cross in the church of San Francesco at Arezzo. Mention has already been made of the habited figure of Francis in this painted cross, who kneels before the figure of the Crucified, his head inclined towards the cross as he caresses the bloodied right foot of the Lord with his hands.

However, such an image and the affective devotion that it elicited should not foreclose the discussion by saying that the relationship between Christ and Francis centred upon a solidarity of physical bodily suffering. For we may recall that, in John's Gospel, although the risen Christ is not immediately recognizable when he mysteriously appears to his disciples, he continues to bear on his risen body the marks of suffering, and so even the wounds inflicted by the spear in his side and the nails through his hands and feet, the very marks replicated in the stigmata, are of a body that has passed through death. So to focus on the wounds of the cross is to see the whole Christ, crucified and risen. Further, this wider perspective is at least implicit in the way the episode is reported in the sources. Bonaventure, for instance, recounts the story of the gift of the stigmata in the context of a discussion of love and desire, and so this transforming gift is spoken of in terms of the marvel and joy elicited by manifestations of the incarnate love of God.[48] Finally, there is another significant element in the circumstances in which Francis received the stigmata, and that is the day on which he received them. According to the sources, that day was 14 September, on which the feast of the Exaltation of the Cross was celebrated.[49] And as we have seen, this day in the liturgical calendar is first and foremost a celebration of the victory of the cross, again as life through death.

So although the identity of Francis with Christ entailed solidarity with Christ's suffering, this solidarity was predicated upon the Incarnation and manifest in a life characterized by the joy that issues from being met by the Risen Christ. The fact of the Incarnation and the revealing of the resurrection body both validate the depiction of a fleshly Christ on the cross, for both together speak of the Word made flesh and of human nature being taken into God. The semiotics of a near naked figure of Christ on the cross in Franciscan art and devotion call us back to the flesh, to the physical human nature taken by Christ in the womb of Mary. George Steiner considers the emergence of the image of the crucified incarnate Christ an epochal shift in world view and a cultural turning point in how the flesh was viewed.[50] The world view to which he refers is certainly reflected in the decorative scheme of the Lower Church of St Francis in Assisi. Indeed, the point has been made that equal attention is given to the Christmas cycle of events as to those of the Passion[51] in these frescoes.

Indeed, a consistent pattern seems to emerge in this survey of early Franciscan liturgical art. For, as in the twelfth-century panel crosses, the focus is on the whole Christ and the *whole* saving mystery[52] rather than exclusively on any single aspect or episode in the drama of salvation. And this drama is not only grounded in creation but returns to creation in its final scene. It is to this axis, namely the cross and creation, that

---

48 See FAED, vol. 2, *The Founder*, pp. 632–3.

49 The account of the stigmata being received on this feast day is multiply attested by both Thomas of Celano and Bonaventure.

50 George Steiner, *Grammars of Creation* (London: Faber & Faber 2001), p. 61.

51 What is seen in the frescoes in the Lower Church is 'perhaps the largest sequence of its kind in Western art devoted to the Nativity and Jesus' early years' – Gianfranco Malafarina (ed.), *The Basilica of St Francis in Assisi* (Modena: F. C. Panini 2005), p. 11.

52 This sense of 'mystery' was first articulated by Paul in words that may well echo the earliest Christian hymnody: '[Christ] was revealed in flesh, vindicated in spirit, seen by angels, proclaimed among Gentiles, believed in throughout the world, taken up in glory' (1 Timothy 3.16).

we shall turn as we consider further the Franciscan image of Christ. Again we will draw on two sources, one literary, the other artistic, and see in both an important connection being drawn between the cross and creation, between Christ's physical suffering and the renewal of the natural world.

Let us look at the literary evidence first. In the first written account of Francis receiving the stigmata, the marks of Christ's crucifixion on his own body, Thomas of Celano writes with considerable rhetorical flourish, setting out the event as a key episode in his story of the saint. But before taking up the narrative of Francis' life, he inserts what Rosalind Brooke has aptly described as a panegyric of Francis.[53] In this passage, redolent with the imagery and scriptural allusions that link the cross with paradise and salvation with creation being new-made, Francis is presented as the new evangelist, a fruitful vine planted in the desert of the world who, like one of the rivers of paradise, carries the gospel over the whole earth and renews the whole earth.[54]

The figurative language of this exuberant praise of Francis suggests a double correspondence, first between the figure of Francis and the Crucified Christ, and second between the cross of Calvary and the natural world of creation. Here both Christ and the cross elide as the tree of life, the tree of life that was planted at the centre of creation.

The second source of evidence is iconographic and relates to the work of the thirteenth-century anonymous Umbrian artist who, with his associates, was responsible for the painting of the cycle of frescoes in the Lower Church of St Francis in Assisi. This artist, known as the Master of St Francis because of the fine panel of the saint that he painted, also made a number of painted crosses. An example may be seen in the National Gallery in London, and in all probability was originally a double-sided processional cross like its contemporary in the Perkins Collection in Assisi known as the 'Blue Cross'. A recently painted and enlarged copy of the blue processional cross, painted in 2007 by Jennifer Holmes, now hangs on the east wall behind the altar of the Lower Church of the Community of the Resurrection's church at Mirfield (see Plate 5). By comparing the cross of the Master of St Francis in the National Gallery with the few other surviving crosses attributed to

---

53 Rosalind B. Brooke, *The Image of St Francis*, p. 46.
54 Thomas of Celano, *First Life*; see FAED, vol. 1, *The Saint*, 1C, pp. 88–90.

him, this is thought to be a late work, even as late as the 1280s.[55] On this cross the figure of the Crucified is of the *Christus patiens* type (see above), and on either side are two apron panels. The first shows the two Marys supporting Mary the Mother of the Lord as she collapses at the sight of her dead son. The other panel shows two figures, John the evangelist, painted in characteristic pose with his right hand raised to his cheek, and the figure of the Centurion, who in Mark's narrative of the crucifixion acclaimed Christ as the Son of God.

Although the figure on both the cross of the Master of St Francis and the 'Blue Cross' is that of the dead Christ, both crosses have the letters REX GLE (*Rex Gloriae*, King of Glory) inscribed in gold on the blue-painted lateral bar of the cross. This inscription resonates strongly with the Apostle Paul's sentiment of 'glorying in the cross' (see Galatians 6.14) but may also allude to the paschal psalm, Psalm 24, with its reference to the King of Glory. The association would relate these crosses back to the earlier Romanesque cross and the figure of the *Christus victor*, and to the iconography of the cross as a sign of Christ's paschal victory. Further lettering inscribed on the top terminal of the National Gallery cross is also significant. What is written there is reminiscent of the words that were sung at the unveiling of the cross in the Veneration of the Cross on Good Friday, and explicitly designate the cross as the tree of life: 'Behold, this is Jesus Christ, King of Jews, Saviour of the World, and our Salvation, who for us hung upon the Tree of Life.'

The motif of the cross as the tree of life gained currency through the Franciscan movement as both a literary trope and as a visual image. A large corpus of literary work has been attributed to Bonaventure, and the image of the tree of life figures in some of the major works considered the most authentic. Among these is a large poem of some 39 stanzas known as *The Praise of the Holy Cross*, which reads like a litany of praise to the cross, described in the seventh stanza as the 'salvation-bearing tree'. The reference to Eden becomes explicit in a further stanza that speaks of the cross of Calvary as a 'garden of true delectation / where the fairest blooms are found' (stanza 18). Although the poet appropriates earlier imagery, such as we saw expressed in earlier Passion poetry, and speaks of the cross being bejewelled with the blood of Christ, a

---

55 David Bomford, Jill Dunkerton, Dillian Gordon and Ashok Roy, *Italian Painting before 1400*, Art in the Making (London: National Gallery 1989), p. 57.

preponderance of metaphors depicts the work of Christ on the cross as bringing forth the fruits of redemption. What these fruits are, and their relationship to the cross, is spelt out further in another work of Bonaventure, *The Mystical Vine: A Treatise on the Passion of the Lord*. This treatise, dense with biblical allusions, combines the Johannine imagery of Christ as the Vine (John 15.1) with that of the tree of life that is set in the midst of paradise (Genesis 2.9). In this treatise the cross itself is likened to the trellis upon which the vine grows and spreads its branches. The analogy is extended by drawing a parallel between Christ being bound and the vine being tied to the trellis, and is developed by spelling out the fate of Jesus in terms of vine-growing (ch. 3).

Again, the motif of Christ's blood emerges as a dominant metaphor. In this treatise some seven chapters are devoted to its shedding, first at his circumcision and through to his Passion. The sacrificial blood of Christ is understood to fructify the soil around the vine/tree, so that it produces leaves for healing and the fruit of eternal life (Revelation 22.2; cf. Ezekiel 47.12). These benefits of the cross are ultimately predicated on the Incarnation, and here Bonaventure echoes the patristic conviction that Christ was united to our humanity so that he might unite us to his divinity. In this treatise, the cross becomes the means whereby Christians are united with Christ, enter the garden of paradise and find themselves refashioned and formed anew in Christ's image and by his virtue. This is poetically presented by Bonaventure as a scene from Eden, of Christians being like flowers that bloom around the red and ardent rose of Christ.[56]

In a way that is entirely consistent with earlier Franciscan sources, Bonaventure presents the cross within the context of the whole economy of salvation, and in his well-known treatise *Lignum Vitae* (*The Tree of Life*), he relates the image of the tree of life to each aspect of the story of salvation. This treatise, intended to be read aloud, is full of figural language to engage the imaginations of those who listened to it, and it combines the Incarnation, Passion and resurrection of Christ as a eucharistic anamnesis is intended to do. In the following conflated passage of Bonaventure, the rather florid expression of the aspects of the saving mystery of Christ contrasts sharply with the more familiar compressed

---

56 'The Mystical Vine: A Treatise of the Passion of the Lord' in *The Works of Bonaventure*, vol. 1, *Mystical Opuscula*, trans. José de Vinck (Princeton, NJ: St Anthony Guild Press 1960), p. 186.

language of a typical Preface in a Western Eucharistic Prayer, which rehearses the saving work of Christ:

> This is the fruit that took its origin from the Virgin's womb and reached its savoury maturity on the tree of the cross under the midday heat of the Eternal Sun, that is, the love of Christ (sec. 3) . . . This most beautiful 'flower of the root of Jesse' (Isaiah 11.1) which has blossomed in the incarnation and withered in the Passion, thus blossomed again in the resurrection so as to become the beauty of all. (sec. 35)[57]

Through his appreciation of the full sweep of salvation, Bonaventure is able to refer to both the cross and to Christ himself as being 'the tree of life', and thereby coin what was to become the key descriptive Franciscan phrase for the saving work of God in Christ. The metaphor of Christ as the tree of life has literary antecedents in some of the earliest Christian writing, and one might cite such second-century sources as Justin Martyr (1 *Apology* XL, 7–9; *Dialogue with Trypho* LXXXVI.1,4), Ignatius of Antioch (*Ep. to the Trallians* 11), and among the Alexandrian writers, Clement (*Stromata* III.17, 103, 4; V.11, 72, 2) and Origen (*Comm. Jhn.* xx.36). We have seen in Chapter 5 how this rich and varied store of writing inspired the iconography of the living cross, but Bonaventure's achievement was the seamless elision of the two images of the cross and of Christ as the tree of life, and it was this combined figuration that provided the inspiration for the art that was commissioned for the churches and convents of the Franciscan movement of the fourteenth century.[58]

Pictorially, the image of the cross as the tree of life was developed and became a distinctive motif in that art. Around 1310, Pacino di Bonaguida painted a large and elaborate panel for the oldest Poor Clare convent in Florence, the Convento delle Monache di Monticello, that shows the figure of Christ crucified against a twelve-branched tree. A major achievement in this painting is the matching of word with image,

---

57 *Bonaventure: The Tree of Life*, trans. Ewert Cousins (London: SPCK 1978), sec. 3, p. 121, sec. 35, p. 160.
58 See Louise Bourdua, *The Franciscans and Art Patronage in Late Medieval Italy* (Cambridge: Cambridge University Press 2004).

as the 48 headings of Bonaventure's *Lignum Vitae*[59] are inscribed along the branches. These headings announce the benefit, or fruit, that issues from each episode and aspect of the story of salvation, from Christ's divine origins to his glorification in the heavenly places. This highly decorative piece, which can now be seen in the Academia in Florence, was commissioned by the Poor Clares to aid them in their contemplation and internalization of the story of Christ, so that they might attain that stage in Christian life described by Paul as being crucified with Christ. This Pauline passage is quoted by Bonaventure in the Prologue of his treatise: 'I have been crucified with Christ; and it is no longer I who live, but it is Christ who lives in me' (Galatians 2.20). In Pacino's painting of the tree of life, each of the 12 green and red branches against which Christ is crucified contains four gold medallions, hanging like the ripe fruits on a tree, depicting a particular Gospel scene or incident and resembling, perhaps more than coincidentally, the shape of a eucharistic host.

The whole complex pictorial scene can be read in two directions, both vertically and horizontally from the bottom upwards. Along the bottom of the painting, rather as if it were a frieze, we see the tiny figures of Adam and Eve, picturing the creation, fall and expulsion from the Garden. Four rivers, as in the biblical Eden, here flow from the base of the tree of life to 'water the garden of the entire Church' as Bonaventure puts it the prologue of the treatise.[60] Directly above the figures representing the story of the creation and fall, and below the lowest branches of the tree, are the figures of Moses and Francis, and on the opposite side of the trunk, Clare and John the evangelist. In the apex of the painting, above the tree and its *titulas* (the title fixed to the cross), are painted the figures of the glorified Christ and the Virgin Mary, and below them are ranks of heavenly saints in festal gathering. Perched at the very top of the tree is a pelican in her nest, a bird that according to legend pecked her breast in order to feed her young with her own blood. This legend had been appropriated as an image of the Eucharist, and famously occurs in the Vespers Office hymn for the feast of Corpus Christi, *Adoro te devote* (Godhead hidden, whom I adore), attributed to Thomas Aquinas, which honours the sacramental presence of Christ. So although the vertical

---

59 Hayden B. J. Maginnis, *Painting in the Age of Giotto: A Historical Reevaluation* (University Park, PA: Pennsylvania State University Press 1997), p. 158.
60 *Bonaventure, The Tree of Life*, Prologue 3, p. 120.

reading, from bottom to the top, takes us from Eden to the heavenly Jerusalem, the whole pictorial schema is topped by a eucharistic motif. This explicit eucharistic reference may well confirm the suggestion that this work of Pacino di Bonaguida was originally commissioned as an altarpiece for the high altar of the convent church. Another stunning fourteenth-century example of a painted tree of life, which was again commissioned by the Poor Clares, is to be seen in Milan.[61]

A large tree-of-life fresco, with 12 fruit-bearing branches, was painted in the mid fourteenth century by Taddeo Gaddi, who had been trained by Giotto. This fresco, painted for the refectory (which is now the museum) of the Franciscan church of Santa Croce in Florence, was intended as a visual representation of Bonaventure's treatise, the *Tree of Life*. The heading from each chapter is inscribed on each of the fruits hanging from the branches, and a fine portrait of a prophet, holding a scroll upon which is inscribed further texts, is painted on the tip of each of the unfurling branches. In Gaddi's fresco a cross bearing the figure of the crucified Lord is superimposed upon the tree. Below, the figure of Francis embraces the cross-tree, as a seated Bonaventure, contemplating the scene above, is shown composing the opening line of his treatise. Written on the scroll upon which he writes are the opening words of a hymn that he incorporated into the text of his treatise: *O crux, frutex salvificus*, 'O cross, tree bearing the fruit of salvation / Refreshed by a living stream / Your blossom so sweetly scented / Your fruit so worthy of desire.'[62] A further stanza of this devotional poem, possibly composed by Bonaventure himself, occurs later in the text and begins with the request: 'Feed us with these fruits'.

One commentator has drawn attention to the ways in which Gaddi's composition of the tree of life is related to the activity of eating.[63] The Last Supper, a common theme in refectory decoration, is painted directly below the tree of life. In addition, three of the four panels on either side of the tree depict scenes of eating, namely St Louis of Tours

61 For further details, see Bourdua, *The Franciscans and Art Patronage in Late Medieval Italy*, pp. 51–9; Jeryldene Wood, *Women, Art, and Spirituality: The Poor Clares of Early Modern Italy* (Cambridge: Cambridge University Press 1996), p. 74.
62 *The Works of Bonaventure*, vol. 1, *Mystical Opuscula*, p. 90.
63 Rab Hatfield, 'The Tree of Life and the Holy Cross: Franciscan Spirituality in the Trecento and Quattrocento' in Verdon and Henderson (eds), *Christianity and the Renaissance*, p. 142.

offering a meal to the poor, the priest who while eating his Easter meal heard of St Benedict's hunger, and the New Testament story of Jesus dining at the house of Simon the Pharisee when a woman, traditionally identified as Mary Magdalene, arrived uninvited and washed the feet of Christ. The fourth panel shows Francis receiving the stigmata, the supreme image of identification of a follower of Christ with his crucified and risen Lord. The choice of these subjects provides another resonance, as the refectory in Religious houses was often regarded as mirroring or at least extending what happened in church. A household of faith gathers to be nourished by God. So given the context of this fresco and the combination of the pictorial scenes surrounding Gaddi's tree of life, we may infer that the fruit of the tree was also identified with the gift of the Eucharist. Indeed, although allegorical meanings may be multiplied, it was the Eucharist that was seen as the primary fruit of Christ's Passion, and this was understood to be made available and received by Christians at the table of the Lord. The Eucharist was heavenly food, understood to appeal to every taste and to nourish all who received it for eternal life in the paradise of God.

In this chapter we have recovered the sense of the cross as the sign of the whole mystery of God's saving work in Christ, and have seen how the prominence of the motif of the cross as the tree of life found its fullest literary and artistic expression through Franciscan writing and patronage of ecclesial art. The image of the cross as the tree of life gathers to itself all that we have said about the living cross, and the pictorial message it communicates is of God's purpose of salvation extending to the whole of creation. Some of the finest artistic expressions of this theological conviction are to be seen in the frescoes depicting the story of the holy cross recorded in the *Golden Legend*. We have already noted, in Chapter 1, the holy cross frescoes painted towards the end of the fourteenth century by Agnolo Taddeo in the Franciscan church of Santa Croce in Florence. A later example is the celebrated holy cross frescoes by Piero della Francesca in the church of San Francesco at Arezzo that were painted in the mid fifteenth century. This narrative sequence effectively links the material wood of the cross of Calvary to the tree in the garden of Eden.

Piero's fifteenth-century fresco cycle in the Cappella Maggiore (chancel) decorates the friars' choir, and because of its exquisite forms and colouring is an undisputed masterpiece. Stephen Bann refers to it as the most celebrated cycle of paintings representing the legend of the true cross.[64] As in Agnolo's frescoes in Florence, Piero's subject is the complex story of the *Legend of the True Cross*. This legend tells the story of how Helena discovered the material cross of Jesus and of how it came to be returned to Jerusalem by the Emperor Heraclius. However, Piero is selective and somewhat creative in his use of scenes suggested by the *Legend*, and extends Agnolo's earlier pictorial schema by including a representation of the Hebrew legend, the *Quest of Seth*. This story tells how the dying Adam asked his son Seth to return to Eden to obtain the oil of mercy, and how he returned with a branch of the tree from Eden, which was planted in the mouth of the dead Adam. The frescoes in Arezzo are painted in three registers, with the presentation of two battles facing each other on the lowest register. The composition suggests an intentional pairing of scenes on the north and south walls of the choir,[65] and the two battle scenes reflect the contemporary exploits of seeking to secure the holy sites in Jerusalem and its environs as places of Christian pilgrimage.[66] The complex pattern of the frescoes on the surrounding wall space and ceiling tells the story, but dominating the view is the painting of the magnificent tree in the central lunette.[67] Painted in the opposite lunette is the fresco representing the exaltation of the cross, and so the two images, the tree and the cross, are presented as visual counterparts in that architectural space. This deliberate arrangement of these images not only links the cross to creation but also evokes the earlier patristic typological reading of Mary and Christ reversing the consequences of Eve's and Adam's transgression. The reading I have proposed here presents Christ as the new Adam, the one through whom the fruits of the tree of life are now freely given to humankind, and in whom paradise comes to be restored.

---

64 For an artistic appraisal of Piero's frescoes in Arezzo, see Stephen Bann, *The True Vine: On Visual Representation and the Western Tradition* (Cambridge: Cambridge University Press 1989), pp. 227–36.

65 The pairing of images and the sequence in which they were intended to be read is contested by art historians, such as John Pope-Hennessy, but an alternate reading of the pictures certainly provides a plausible reading.

66 Unfortunately, a great deal of detail and colour of the frescoes has been lost through water damage and earthquakes. For a fuller account, see Jeryldene M. Wood 'Piero's *Legend of the True Cross* and the Friars of San Francesco' in Jeryldene M. Wood (ed.), *The Cambridge Companion to Piero della Francesca* (Cambridge: Cambridge University Press 2002), pp. 51–65.

67 Unfortunately only traces of the painted foliage of this tree remain to be seen by the viewer today.

Given the predominant imagery of the tree, it is unsurprising that even the late medieval Franciscan schoolmen included a sense of the renewal of creation in their accounts of the atonement.[68] And given our contemporary preoccupations, in particular the increasing awareness of our disconnection from the world of nature, perhaps we should not be surprised to see how the figure of the tree has reoccurred as a resonant image in some of the contemporary art that has been placed within liturgical spaces and places of worship. A number of examples deserve note. Among them is Mark Cazalet's *Tree of Life* (2003) in the Anglican Cathedral at Chelmsford. This painting is fully integrated into its architectural setting and depicts a large English oak tree. The central image of the tree contains other balanced motifs, such as the tragedy of Judas and intimations of the resurrection harvest. An earlier and equally rich composition is to be seen in John Piper's tree of life window in St Peter's Church at Firle in East Sussex. This glass was commissioned as a memorial to Henry Rainald Gage and was installed in 1982. Inspiration for its composition is thought to have been drawn from the eighteenth-century English visionary artist William Blake, who used the motif of the tree of life as the backdrop for Job in his illustrations of the book of Job.[69] At Firle the tree is colourfully rendered through Piper's rich tonal palette. It shows a mature tree bearing a range of different fruits, including the greengage, and around the trunk are a variety of musical instruments. On either side of the gnarled trunk are the sun and the moon, traditional emblems used in some of the earliest depictions of the crucifixion in Christian art – such as in the eighth-century painting in a niche behind the altar in the Theodotus chapel at Santa Maria Antiqua in Rome – to show the cosmic catastrophe of the crucifixion.[70] In Piper's window, the various elements of the tree, the rich variety of fruits and the musical instruments all combine to form a complex picture that evokes the paschal mystery of Christ's death and

---

68 See Richard Viladesau, *The Triumph of the Cross: The Passion of Christ in Theology and the Arts, from the Renaissance to the Counter-Reformation* (Oxford: Oxford University Press 2008), ch. 1.
69 Frances Spalding, *John Piper, Myfanwy Piper: Lives in Art* (Oxford: Oxford University Press 2009), p. 418.
70 See Hans Belting, *Likeness and Presence*, pp. 120–3. The imagery of a darkened sun and moon occurs in a passage in Isaiah (24.23) that speaks of the appearing of God's reign.

resurrection and expresses nature's praise of its creator. And at this point we may return again to the figure of Francis.

Throughout this chapter we have repeatedly returned to the depiction of the whole mystery of Christ in Franciscan sources, and hinted at the place of nature in the story of Francis. The popular image of Francis is that of the lover of nature, but he is probably more accurately seen in relation to creation, and by way of a conclusion it is to this theme of creation to which we must turn.

The French Reformer, Jean Calvin, spoke of the world as the theatre of God's glory. This is a suggestive phrase, but within Calvin's theological scheme it would not have included even the potential of the natural world to reflect the impress and brilliance of its divine making. By contrast, and some three centuries earlier, what we see in the Franciscan tradition is a sense that the curse of creation had been definitively, if not completely, lifted by the Incarnation, death and resurrection of Christ, and that the physical creation itself joyously proclaimed its divine making. Again the evidence for this conviction is both artistic and literary. Returning to the decorative scheme of the Upper Church of St Francis in Assisi with its three registers of scenes from the Old and New Testaments and scenes from the life of Francis, we see an illustration of this in relation to the panel that depicts the incident of Francis exhorting the birds to praise their creator.[71] This panel concludes the series on the west wall, and is placed directly below the New Testament scene of Pentecost. The placing of these two images is not coincidental, as it provides a significant theological resonance. The feast of Pentecost is the climax of the Easter season, the culmination of the Easter mystery, and celebrates the giving of the promised Spirit to Mary and the disciples in the Upper Room. It is, of course, that same Spirit that, according to the Psalmist, 'renew[s] the face of the earth' (Psalm 104.30 NIV; Isaiah 32.15). And so the sequence and placing of the scenes draws a theological point, namely that the fullness of God's saving work overflows and reaches into the whole created world of nature through the Spirit-filled proclamation of the gospel. Hence the image of the fresco cycle of Francis exhorting the birds to praise their creator.

---

71 The incident is recorded by Thomas of Celano, *First Life*, ch. 21, in FAED, vol. 1, *The Saint*, p. 234.

This brings us to the final piece of literary evidence, which as we will see is deeply indebted to liturgical texts and their uses in the practice of daily prayer. Francis is often imagined as being an unlettered, simple person who followed the words of Jesus in their most literal sense. But such a characterization does not really do him justice. His literary achievements should certainly not be overlooked, and when examined they provide further confirmation of the view that the natural world of creation is not simply a backdrop to the divine drama of salvation but is implicated and involved in it. This conviction is brought to poetic expression in what is popularly known as Francis' *Canticle of the Sun*, a composition probably most familiar to readers in the versified form of the hymn by William Draper (1855–1933), 'All creatures of our God and King'. The original canticle, more accurately designated the *Canticle of Creation*, was written by Francis after a particularly troubled and tormented night towards the end of his life, some point in the spring of 1225, when he was recuperating with the Sisters at San Damiano after a serious illness. In those circumstances Francis' writing was far from being a spontaneous and sentimental rhapsody on nature. It was hammered out on the anvil of suffering, as he was all too aware of physical pain and human frailty. And so in all probability Francis laboured hard over it, refining the phrasing and finely tuning the musicality of the language in which he wrote. The *Canticle* was written in the vernacular, and it shows that Francis was not only familiar with conventional poetic forms but was something of an accomplished wordsmith himself. The musicality of the language is driven by the rhythmic repetition of the phrase *Laudate si*, 'Praised be you', as each element of nature finds its voice in a world redeemed and being made anew. The vocabulary Francis used was significantly drawn from liturgical texts. This enabled him to transpose his experience of human frailty and mortality into the higher key of creation's praise, fulfilling the petition in the model of Christian prayer, 'on earth, as in heaven'.[72]

A recent study has outlined the complex construction of the *Canticle* and highlighted the artful use of assonance and alliteration and the verbal dexterity of these verses.[73] The content has evident similarities with Psalm

72 Jay M. Hammond, 'Saint Francis' Doxological Mysticism in Light of his Prayers' in Jay M. Hammond (ed.), *Francis of Assisi: History, Hagiography and Hermeneutics in the Early Documents* (Hyde Park, NY: New City Press 2004), p. 143.
73 Edoardo Fumagalli, 'Saint Francis, the Canticle, the Our Father', trans. Edward Hagman, *Greyfriars Review*, vol. 19, Supplement, 2005.

148, particularly in its references to the praise of the sun and the moon, and in its wider reference to the created world: 'Praise the Lord from the heavens: praise him in the height' (v. 1); 'Praise him sun and moon: praise him all you stars of light' (v. 3); 'Mountains and all hills: fruit trees and all cedars' (v. 9). The structure of this psalm follows the pattern of the creation hymn in Genesis 1, and ranges from the cosmic elements of the heavenly bodies down to the earth and humankind, as the whole created order is enjoined to voice its praise to the Creator God.[74]

Thematic and tonal correspondences can also be drawn between Francis' *Canticle of Creation* and the *Benedicite*, a canticle whose verses expand those of Psalm 148 and that, like the *Canticle*, speaks of the natural element of the waters and the wind. The *Benedicite* suggests a carnival procession of praise in which the invisible and the visible elements of creation, the green things of the earth, the creatures of the seas and rivers, the birds and finally humankind, are repeatedly exhorted to bless and praise the Lord. The canticle, sometimes known as 'A Song of Creation',[75] is drawn from chapter 3 of the book of Daniel. Further verses (36–65), the so-called 'Song of the three', ascribed to the three figures Shadrach, Meshach and Abednego, who were cast into Nebuchadnezzar's fiery furnace in Babylon, were added to the Septuagint, the Greek translation of the Hebrew Scriptures. It is thought that a form of the *Benedicite* was appropriated to supplement the psalmody of the morning Office from earliest times, and may quite possibly have been one of the 'morning hymns' referred to in the pilgrim Egeria's description of daily prayer in fourth-century Jerusalem.[76] The purpose of the morning Office in its ancient form was conceived as the voicing of praise for Christ's resurrection at the dawn of the day, and so had a close association with Easter. This account may well explain its use as a canticle for the morning Office on Sundays.

The historical evidence of the use of this canticle certainly suggests a link between the renewal of creation and the celebration of the resurrection. In the churches of the East, the *Benedicite* was associated with the Paschal Vigil and with vigils of the resurrection, and in the Western

---

74 Robert Alter, *The Book of Psalms: A Translation with Commentary* (New York: W. W. Norton 2007), p. 509.
75 See the Church of England's provision, *Daily Prayer* (London: Church House Publishing 2005), p. 602.
76 See George Guiver CR, *The Company of Voices: Daily Prayer and the People of God* (London: SPCK 1988), pp. 60, 156.

Roman Benedictine tradition the canticle was sung during the Office of Lauds on Sundays.[77] What this liturgical use of the *Benedicite* achieves is the evocation of the natural created world within the context of the Christian celebrating the dawning light of the risen Christ. Thereby it juxtaposes the theme of creation with that of resurrection in a way that inextricably links the two themes together. And it is this viewpoint, generated by a life's habitual practice of sharing the Church's prayer, that ultimately inspired Francis' *Canticle of Creation* and provided him with the vocabulary to express the praise of creation.

In terms of composition, Francis was undoubtedly influenced by Psalm 148 and the *Benedicite*, but a striking and significant difference between these two similar liturgical texts and the *Canticle of Creation* is that the physical elements of the created world, the wind, fire, water and earth, are not simply being exhorted or enjoined to praise their Creator but are recognized as actually doing so. By its very being the mute creation is declared to voice its praise to the 'Most High, all-powerful, good Lord'. The phrase 'praised by you (*per*) through . . .' recurs throughout the central stanzas of the poem: 'through Sister Moon and the stars', 'through Brother Wind', 'through Sister Water', 'through Brother Fire', 'through our Sister Mother Earth'.

Whether the repeated word 'through' in this context is read in an instrumental sense or in terms of the subject being an acting agent, the sense is that creation itself has found a voice to praise its Creator. Creation is jubilant, and 'the trees of the field shall clap their hands' (Isaiah 55.12b)[78] as they celebrate the final purposes of God unfolding in the renewal and restoration of the natural world through the saving mystery of Christ. That is, the mystery of Christ's death and resurrection and the ongoing revealing of the Father's sons and daughters. It is these same sons and daughters of God who, as God's planting in Christ, are called to delight in creation and to act as good stewards and caretakers of the earth. And it is this process of being grafted into Christ, the eschatological tree of life, to which we now turn as we look, in the final chapter, to the place of baptism.

---

77 See Gregory W. Woolfenden, *Daily Liturgical Prayer: Origins and Theology* (Aldershot: Ashgate 2004), pp. 65, 118, 276; and the primary source, *The Rule of St. Benedict*, ch. 12.
78 Other passages suggest the animation of creation as God's saving work and deliverance is made manifest. Isaiah 44.23 speaks of every mountain, forest and tree breaking forth into song, and likewise Psalm 96.12 tells how each tree of the wood will joyfully sing in response to the God who comes in judgement to reorder the world.

Chapter 7

Restoring paradise

The image of the crucifixion as a kind of planting that brought the possibility of a new way of living in the world has its antecedents in the Hebrew biblical literature that speaks of God *planting* his people Israel. Having been delivered through the waters of the Red Sea, the pilgrim people of Israel are led to Horeb, the mount of the Lord: 'You will bring them, and plant them on your holy mountain'(cf. Exodus 15.17). The metaphor of planting was taken up and deployed by the prophets as they declared the reassuring message of hope that God intended to restore the people to the land of promise: 'I will plant them upon their land, and they shall never again be plucked up' (Amos 9.15; cf. Isaiah 27.2–6).[1] This way of figuring the hope, corporate identity and destiny of God's people persisted and was reiterated by the later prophet who declared to God's people at the time of their exile in Babylon that in the messianic age when all would be restored, the people themselves would be called 'oaks of righteousness, the planting of the LORD' (Isaiah 61.3c).

The immediate, though not exclusive, image of this metaphor of God's planting was that of the vine and the vineyard. In Psalm 80, Israel is the vine of God's planting[2] but, as the prophets announced, God looked to Israel, a 'luxuriant vine' (Hosea 10.1), to bear fruit, but it yielded only wild grapes (Isaiah 5.2b). The prophet Jeremiah lamented how the vine of God's planting had become a wild vine because of their repeated acts of unfaithfulness (Jeremiah 2.21; 11.17), and again, the

---

1 Compare this text with Hosea 9.10a, 16a; 2 Samuel 7.10 and Isaiah 27.2–6, which announces God's future care for his vine.
2 The metaphor of the vine/vineyard for the people of Israel is prefigured in the enigmatic text in Genesis recording Jacob's blessing of Judah; see Genesis 49.10.

visionary prophet Ezekiel saw the wilful turning away from God as the reason why Jerusalem would face the full fury of divine judgement (Ezekiel 15.6). The historic fate of Israel is presented as the ravaging of the vineyard in Psalm 80 and again in the story of God's vineyard in Isaiah 5.1–7.[3] This particular Hebrew narrative of the vineyard was appropriated by Jesus and retold by him as a parable to express the fate that awaited him (Mark 12.1–12).[4] Here, as in Psalm 80 and Isaiah's parable, the primary reference was to Israel, the people of God, and through the early centuries of Christianity the image of the vine became a dominant metaphor in Christian writing, art and worship. As the primary metaphor for the people of God, it is not surprising that the design of an unfurling vine-scroll inhabited by animals, birds and people became a ubiquitous design for floor mosaics in both fifth- and seventh-century synagogues and churches in the Levant, especially in the regions of Palestine, Syria and Jordan.[5]

Zeno, Bishop of Verona (*c.* 362–*c.* 370),[6] included a number of sermons on the parable of the vineyard in Isaiah 5.1–7 in his extensive series of baptismal homilies addressed to those preparing for baptism at Easter. This same passage was listed, either as a reading or as a chant text, for the Easter Vigil in the Luxeuil, Gregorian, Gelasian and Mozarabic Lectionaries.[7] Today the parable of the vineyard in Isaiah is listed in the lectionaries of liturgical churches as the Old Testament reading for the second service (Evensong or Vespers) on Palm Sunday, as it focuses on Christ's rejection, suffering and death. The image of the people of God as God's vineyard recurs in the Reproaches which,

3 The complex history of the modern interpretation of this passage is set out by Kirsten Nielsen in her Old Testament study, *There is Hope for a Tree: The Tree as Metaphor in Isaiah* (Sheffield: JSOT Press 1989), pp. 87–123.
4 The parable is multiply attested in the Gospel tradition; see Matthew 21.33–41; Luke 20.9–17.
5 See Rachel Hachlili, *Ancient Mosaic Pavements: Themes, Issues, and Trends* (Leiden and Boston: Brill 2009).
6 Dates drawn from Bryan D. Spinks, *Early and Medieval Rituals and Theologies of Baptism: From the New Testament to the Council of Trent* (Aldershot: Ashgate 2006), p. 57.
7 As tabulated by Gordon Jeanes in *The Day has Come! Easter and Baptism in Zeno of Verona* (Collegeville, MN: Liturgical Press 1995), p. 202. On the basis of his study of the sermons, and by drawing comparisons with how other readings entered the Vigil service, Gordon Jeanes ventures to say that Isaiah 5.1–7 may have first been used as a chant text before it was adopted as a reading; see p. 203.

as we have seen in Chapter 4, may be sung at the Veneration of the Cross during the liturgy of Good Friday: 'O vineyard, my chosen one. I planted you. How is your sweetness turned into bitterness, to crucify me and take Barabbas in my place.'[8]

The appropriation of this image of the vine illustrates how the Gospel writers saw the fate of Israel as being personified and embodied in Jesus himself, and this is explicit in the discourse in John's Gospel where the vine is presented as Christ's self-designation and his followers are described as the branches (John 15.1–7). Christ is the new vine, the Father is the vine-grower and Christians are the branches (John 15.5). From here it is only a small step to think of the growth of the Christian in relation to baptism as being God's work, an implication drawn by Paul in his first letter to the Church in Corinth (1 Corinthians 3.6–9). Thus the second-century apologist, Justin Martyr, explains in his polemical account of Christianity to the Jew, Trypho, that the vine planted by Christ is his people. The image is prevalent in a range of early Christian writings, such as those of Clement of Alexandria and the *Shepherd of Hermas* and the *Didascalia Apostolorum*, which opens with the description of the Church catholic as God's 'holy vineyard'.[9] For Clement, the moral life of the Christian is the cultivation of virtue, the continual caring of what God in Christ has planted: 'Now the lusts and other sins have been called briars and thorns. The gnostic therefore toils in the Lord's vineyard . . . planting, pruning, watering, being indeed a divine husbandman for those who have been planted in the faith.'[10]

The opening psalm in the book of Psalms depicts those who live by the wisdom of God as 'trees planted by streams of water, which yield their fruit in its season', and whose 'leaves do not wither' (Psalm 1.3).[11] This image of the tree growing by living water took hold of the Christian imagination, and the compressed imagery of foliage, flowers, fruit and water was applied analogically, in the instruction given to those preparing for baptism, to the effects of being taken to the water of

---

8 *Vinea mea electa.*
9 See *Strom.* VII, 12, 74.1; *Hermas* V, 5, 2; *Didascalia* 1.1.
10 Clement of Alexandria, *Strom.* VII, 12, 74, 1 from *The Library of Christian Classics*, vol. 2, *Alexandrian Christianity* (London: SCM Press 1954).
11 See also Jeremiah 17.7–8 and Isaiah 44.3–5.

baptism. A similar trope to that of the fruitful tree planted by water in Psalm 1 recurs in Psalm 92.12–14. Here we read that:

> The righteous shall flourish like the palm tree, and grow like a cedar in Lebanon.
>
> They are planted in the house of the LORD; they flourish in the courts of our God.
>
> In old age they still produce fruit; they are always green and full of sap.

Again, these words would have informed the imagination of early Christian teachers and writers. In his catechetical instruction, Ambrose of Milan (*c.* 339–97), for instance, drew an analogy between the flowering of Aaron's rod in the Jewish temple (Numbers 17) and the neophyte who had entered into the abundant waters of the font.[12]

The rich analogy between being planted by water and baptism produced the metaphor of fruitfulness in life, which informed Christian reflection and writing about how the baptized were expected to grow in wisdom in order that the fruit of the Spirit might mature in their Christian lives.[13] The image of a tree with luscious leaves and laden with fruit was used by a late Anglo-Saxon monastic scribe at St Augustine's Abbey in Canterbury to give a rather literal illustration of this verse of the psalm in the famous Harley Psalter,[14] which around the mid eleventh century became something of a model for the brightly coloured and patterned decoration of medieval liturgical books. The juxtaposition of the image of a tree and water recalls the iconography of the living cross, as in the twelfth-century mosaic at St Clemente in Rome in which, as we have observed in Chapter 5, the paradisal waters flow from the base of the cross. The tree of life

---

12 Ambrose, *De Sacramentis*, IV.1 and 2; see Edward Yarnold SJ, *The Awe-Inspiring Rites of Initiation: The Origins of the RCIA* (Edinburgh: T. & T. Clark 1994, 2nd edn), p. 128.

13 Examples of how this idea, implicit in Colossians 1, was worked can be seen in the writings of Eusebius, *Com. Psalm* 1.3 PG 23,77b–c, Gregory of Nyssa, *In bapt.*; PG,46, 593d–96a, and Cyril of Jerusalem, who exhorts those seeking baptism to be fruitful: 'As then it is [God's] part to plant and to water, so it is yours to bear fruit' – *Catechesis* 1.4.

14 See Richard Gameson, *The Role of Art in the Late Anglo-Saxon Church* (Oxford: Clarendon Press 1995), p. 48. The Harley Psalter is now in the British Library (MS Harley 603).

and the fountain of life coincide, as Christ crucified is both the occasion and the inexhaustible source of that divine life that alone can cleanse, restore and renew creation. An intriguing passage in an early piece of Jewish-Christian writing known as Pseudo-Barnabas makes enquires about what the Lord has taught about water and the cross,[15] and this juxtaposition of themes emerges again in the later fourth-century poetic tradition of Syrian Christianity, as is well illustrated by Ephrem: 'From the wood on Golgotha', he writes, 'a fountain of life flowed for the Gentiles' (Armenian Hymn 49.8). The allusion here to the piercing of Christ's side in John's Passion narrative (19.34), a familiar trope for the origin of the sacraments of baptism and Eucharist, is made explicit by Ephrem in a line that pinpoints a theology of baptism that directly links the water-washing to paradise: 'There came forth from Christ water / Adam washed, revived, and returned to paradise' (Nisibis 39.7).[16]

The richly textured language of poetic texts cannot be ironed out into straightforward doctrinal propositions, but what is suggested in these lines of Ephrem is a theology of baptism that is related to the cross and the resurrection in equal measure. It is precisely this later resurrection motif that I intend to tease out further in considering the design and decoration of baptismal fonts and baptisteries. But before dipping a toe in paradise, let us first uncover more of the roots of this language and its earliest appropriation in Christian iconography.

The roots of paradisal imagery in relation to baptism are to be found in the metaphors deployed by the writers of the New Testament, particularly John and Paul. Reference has already been made to the discourse in John's Gospel following the assertion that Christ is the vine and his disciples the branches. The analogy is considerably elaborated in the mid third century by Hippolytus of Rome,[17] who asserted that Christ is the spiritual vine and the shoots and branches are his saints and all who believe in him. The implication is that those who have made the profession of faith in baptism are grafted into Christ, the

---

15 Cited by Jean Daniélou in *Primitive Christian Symbols*, trans. Donald Attwater (London: Burns & Oates 1964), p. 33.

16 These citations are taken from Sebastian Brock, *The Luminous Eye: The Spiritual World Vision of Saint Ephrem the Syrian*, Cistercian Studies Series 124 (Kalamazoo, MI: Cistercian Publications 1992, revised edn), p. 82.

17 Hippolytus, *De bene. Iacob 25*, cited by Robin Margaret Jensen in *Understanding Early Christian Art* (London: Routledge 2000), p. 61.

spiritual vine, which points to the Eucharist, the sacramental means of continuing to 'abide' in Christ, and underscores the point rehearsed in John 15 that a fruitful Christian life can only be drawn from Christ. The horticultural metaphor of grafting is explicitly used by St Paul in the Letter to the Romans where he argues how the Gentiles are incorporated into Israel and become the people of God and inheritors of the promise of life:

> if some of the branches were broken off, and you, a wild olive shoot, were grafted in their place to share the rich root of the olive tree, do not vaunt yourselves over the branches. If you do vaunt yourselves, remember that it is not you that support the root, but the root that supports you. (Romans 11.17–18)

The context of this passage is a discussion of the relationship between the old and the new Israel, a topic resolved in the Letter to the Galatians in a rhetorically charged affirmation of baptism:

> As many of you as were baptized into Christ have clothed yourselves with Christ. There is no longer Jew or Greek . . . for all of you are one in Christ Jesus. And if you belong to Christ, then you are Abraham's offspring, heirs according to the promise.' (Galatians 3.27–29)

The metaphorical language of planting in relation to the making of God's people is refined by Paul in his account of baptism in the Letter to the Romans. Here those who are baptized are literally 'planted together' with Christ in his death and his resurrection: 'if we have been united with him in a death like his, we will certainly be united with him in a resurrection like his' (Romans 6.5). The Greek word *sumphutoi*, translated here as 'united', literally means being 'planted or grown together with', a sense that is not distant from the language of grafting deployed by Paul in a later chapter of Romans. Attention is often drawn to the change in tense in Paul's account of baptism between the present sense of the Christian being identified with Christ's death in baptism, and the future reference to sharing his resurrection. But grammatical structure alone does not fix the multiple meanings of baptism, and elsewhere Paul has no hesitation in suggesting that through baptism, the Christian shares the whole paschal mystery of Christ, his death *and* his resurrection[18] (see Romans 6.5–11).[19]

Although it is unlikely that Paul saw baptism as a *mimesis*, a ritual acting out of Christ's death and resurrection, he did regard it as the means whereby the believer was joined to the risen and crucified Lord as the gardener grafts a new shoot on to the trunk of another living tree. The image in Romans 11 of being grafted into the tree of God elides with that of being 'planted together' with Christ in a wider Pauline understanding of baptism, an understanding that, according to Bryan Spinks, was not far from the mind of the Bishop of Jerusalem when he addressed the newly baptized during Easter Week in late fourth-century Jerusalem.[20] Scholarly opinion is divided on the question of whether the *Mystagogical Catecheses* were delivered by Cyril of Jerusalem or his successor John. Edward Yarnold, followed by John Baldovin, argued for Cyril, but more recently Juliette Day has marshalled convincing arguments that the post-baptismal instructions were delivered by John. But as our synchronic reading is concerned more with thematic content than strict chronology, we shall refer to the mystagogue as Cyril. As the mystagogue draws out the significance of baptism, he casts himself in the role of a guide who will lead the newly baptized to the fragrant meadows of paradise.[21]

In speaking of how the candidates were anointed with the exorcized olive oil before being led to the water bath, Cyril refers to Jesus Christ as the good olive tree and explains that the baptized were 'transplanted from the wild olive tree, and grafted into the good one, and were made to share the richness of the true olive tree'.[22] Here, as in Paul, the language of participation is grounded in organic and horticultural metaphors, suggesting that the sap of life drawn by the Christian is drawn from none other than Christ himself. New life, in other words, can only be drawn from the plenitude of the risen Christ, and in this assertion we can detect a distinct echo of John's true vine discourse and the emphatic claim of Christ that: 'apart from me you can do nothing' (15.5b).

18 See Tor Vegge, 'Baptismal Phrases in the Deuteropauline Epistles' in David Hellholm et al. (eds), *Ablution, Initiation, and Baptism: Late Antiquity, Early Judaism, and Early Christianity*, vol. 1 (Berlin and New York: De Gruyter 2011); Christopher Irvine, *The Art of God: The Making of Christians and the Meaning of Worship* (London: SPCK 2005), pp. 26–32.
19 See also Philippians 3.21; Ephesians 2.4–6; Colossians 2.12, 3.1–4.
20 Bryan Spinks, *Early and Medieval Rituals and Theologies of Baptism*, p. 41.
21 *Mystagogical Catechesis* 1.1, from Yarnold, *The Awe-Inspiring Rites of Initiation*, p. 71.
22 *Mystagogical Catechesis* 2.3, from Yarnold, *The Awe-Inspiring Rites of Initiation*, p. 77.

The language of 'planting' was carried over and used in early Christian writing to depict the Church. The prophet had foretold that God's restored people would be seen as God's planting, the work of his hand (Isaiah 60.21), and some early Christian writers read that forward-looking passage as being fulfilled by the Church, the community of the baptized. The Syrian bishop Ignatius of Antioch (martyred in 107) spoke in a number of his Letters to the churches of Asia Minor of the newly baptized and the ecclesial community itself as the 'Father's planting'. In the *Letter to the Trallians*, Ignatius warns his readers to shun the wild offshoots, and designates the Father's planting as being branches of the cross, a reference that brings us back to the congruence of baptismal imagery with that of the tree of life, implanting itself again within the Christian imagination.

There are few extant examples of tree of life decoration in baptisteries, the space for the celebration of baptism. A fine example, discussed by Jennifer O'Reilly, a scholar who has undertaken the most thorough exploration of the tree of life motif over a considerable period of time, is an eighth-century relief carving that survives from the baptistery of the cathedral at Cividale del Friuli in north-eastern Italy.[23] The baptistery was demolished in the seventeenth century but the surviving stone relief carving, considered to be typical of the area, is rectangular in shape and highly symmetrical in its design, and thought to have been prominently placed on the wall directly above the baptismal font. Four creatures representing the four evangelists are set in roundels in the four corners of the stone. The centre is divided into two registers with an inscribed band referring to John the Baptist. Below the central band of inscription is the unfurling tree of life with fantastical animals – possibly griffins – and two birds, one each side of the tree, pecking the top of a bunch of grapes. Directly above the tree of life is the cross, with a cypress tree on either side below the cross bar and two flowers above, one each side of the vertical bar. In her discussion of this Lombardic relief, O'Reilly states that the iconography is integral to the liturgical context in which it is set, and that it is bound up with the meaning of what was actually celebrated there. In her reading, the central carving

---

23 See Jennifer O'Reilly, 'The Tree of Life in Medieval Iconography' in Paul Morris and Deborah Sawyer (eds), *A Walk in the Garden: Biblical, Iconographical and Literary Images of Eden* (Sheffield: Sheffield Academic Press 1992), p. 176 and illustration on p. 177. The octagonal font, bearing eight elegant pillars, survives and is to be seen in the cathedral.

represents the tree of life in paradise (the bottom half of the relief), while the top represents the heavenly tree of life, which according to the vision of Revelation 22.2 is planted on either side of the river of life, hence the tree being positioned each side of the decorated cross. However the relief carving is read, the combination of setting and the range of iconographical motifs deployed by the artist suggest a liturgical reading of baptism in relation to paradise and the river of life.

The image of the cross, the tree of life and baptism are juxtaposed in the fresco decoration of the late fifth- or sixth-century Catacomb of Pontianus on the Via Portuensis in Rome. Here a square basin fed from a natural spring of water is sunk into the floor adjacent to the tombs of the martyrs Abdon and Sennon. Whether baptism was actually celebrated in this site is a matter of conjecture, but it has been traditionally referred to as a baptistery,[24] and to my mind certainly functions as a place for remembering our baptism, a space in which we may see the meaning of Christian baptism. The decorative scheme of the chamber, painted on plaster some time between the sixth and the eighth centuries, is patently on a baptismal theme. On the facing wall, under the recessed arch beyond the square basin of water, is painted a jewelled cross whose foot stands in the water that apparently falls and rises with the River Tiber. The lower part of the cross consists of sprouting leaves and flowers in full bloom. The blooms look like roses, a flower that in the natural symbolism of the time was apparently considered to be a flower of paradise.[25] On either side of the transverse bar of the cross are two candles, and on the wall directly above the recessed arch is a fresco of the baptism of Christ in the River Jordan, reminiscent in compositional terms of the dome mosaics of the famous fifth- and sixth-century baptisteries in Ravenna. But the most striking feature here is undoubtedly the cross from which new life blossoms and grows. It is a living tree.

In modern times the biblical images of the tree of life and the river of life featured particularly in the stained-glass work of Marc Chagall[26]

---

24 W. Henry was of the opinion that this was a site for the celebration of baptism. See *Dictionnaire d'Archéologie Chrétienne et Liturgie* (Paris: Letouzey et Ané 1926), p. 407.

25 S. Anita Stauffer, 'Fonts: Baptism, Pascha and Paradise', *Studia Liturgica*, vol. 24, no. 1, 1994, p. 64.

26 A stunning example is to be seen in the central panel of Chagall's east window Jesse tree in the Fraumünster in Zurich, which shows the figure of Christ towards the top of the window set in an explosion of glorious green.

and the English artist John Piper.[27] More recently a window by Roger Wagner, who works in the English visionary tradition associated with Samuel Palmer, has been installed in St Mary's Church at Iffley in Oxford (see Plate 7).[28] The composition of the window is site specific and is located at the westernmost end of this Norman church, directly opposite Piper's nativity window with its green-tree motif. In Wagner's flowering tree window, the river of life winds its way down the green hill of Calvary from the base of the tree in the direction of the font sited immediately below in the centre of the nave aisle. The figure of the Crucified is set against an iridescent tree in full bloom. The pink and white flowers against a dark blue and green background produce a dappled light in the church. The two windows complement each other, and Wagner's tree of life window particularly resonates with the ritual action of baptism performed at the font below. Here the combination of glass and font constitutes a wondrous ensemble of liturgical art and strikingly illuminates the meaning of baptism as the regeneration of creation.

Once the baptismal water is seen as the water of life, then images of life and growth suggest themselves. In the fourth-century mystagogical teaching delivered to the newly baptized by Cyril of Jerusalem, John Chrysostom, Theodore of Mopsuestia and Ambrose of Milan, the newly baptized are routinely referred to as 'neophytes', a Greek word that may be rendered as 'new growth'. The new life and growth of the baptized was understood in some sense to be an anticipation of resurrection, and a proleptic manifestation of God's ultimate, or eschatological, purpose to renew the face of the earth and restore paradise.

This line of thinking is common in early Eastern sources, such as Origen of Alexandria, and in the lyrical Syriac text, *The Odes of Solomon*. In his commentary on Genesis, Origen asserts that those who are born in the waters of baptism are placed in paradise which, he explains, is a type – or as we may say, a template – of the visible Church. The *Odes*

---

27 See Frances Spalding, *John Piper, Myfanwy Piper: Lives in Art* (Oxford University Press 2009), pp. 417–18.

28 *The Flowering Tree*, commissioned by the parish, is Roger Wagner's first work in stained glass. The artist, in conversation with the author, spoke of his long fascination with trees as a subject, and of how two years previously he had been struck by the imagery of the apse mosaic at San Clemente in Rome. Wagner learnt the painterly way of making stained glass from the renowned stained glassmaker Tom Denny.

of Solomon, a composite text consisting of some 42 liturgical hymns, is variously dated between the first and third centuries and is thought to have been composed in East Syria, most probably in Edessa.[29] The poems treating baptism in this collection are rich in paradisal typology, suggesting that the waters of baptism return the baptized to paradise as the penitent thief was restored by Jesus on the cross. It is as though the death of Christ released the waters of paradise and becomes the cleansing flood that carries the baptized into the 'garden of delights':

> And [the Most High, my God] took me to his Paradise
> Wherein is the wealth of the Lord's pleasure.
> (I contemplated blossoming and fruit-bearing trees . . .)
> And I said, blessed, O Lord, are they
> who are planted in your land,
> And who grow in the growth of your trees.
>
> (*Ode* II)[30]

The implicit correspondence between the place of baptism and re-entry into paradise persisted in Eastern thought and occurs in the baptismal teaching of the fourth-century theologian and bishop, Gregory of Nyssa. In a sermon preached on the feast of the Epiphany, which included a commemoration of the baptism of Christ, Gregory alludes to Christian baptism and boldly declares: 'Paradise, yes, heaven itself may be trodden by man; and the creation in the world and above the world that was once at variance is knit together in friendship.'[31] As in the writings of Ephrem the Syrian, the biblical trope of paradise became the destiny and call of those who entered into the baptismal waters and were drawn up into the fellowship of the resurrected Christ. In his mystical treatise, the *Life of Moses*, Gregory sets in parallel the exodus of the Hebrews from Egypt celebrated at the Passover and the Christian's passage into paradise through the waters of baptism.[32]

29 Thomas M. Finn, *Early Christian Baptism and the Catechumenate: West and East Syria* (Collegeville, MN: Liturgical Press 1992), p. 115.
30 Translation by James H. Charlesworth in Finn, *Early Christian Baptism and the Catechumenate*, p. 26.
31 *Nicene and Post-Nicene Fathers of the Christian Church*, vol. 5 (Oxford: James Parker & Co. 1893), p. 525.
32 *Life of Moses*, 2.22.4–5 and 118.

Although only a minor theme in his instruction to those preparing for baptism in fourth-century Jerusalem, Cyril of Jerusalem twice uses the trope of paradise in relation to baptism. The first is in his introductory address, where he expressed the hope that as the candidates, now purged of sin, approached baptism, the gates of paradise would be opened for them: 'Then may the gate of Paradise be opened to every man and every woman among you.'[33] And the second is in the first catechetical lecture where Cyril, looking forward to the moment of baptism, said: 'Henceforth thou art planted in the true/invisible Paradise' (1.4).

Such an imaginative thinking of baptism as a return to paradise, though less prevalent, is not lacking in early Western Christian writers. Cyprian (d. 258), Bishop of Carthage in North Africa, described by Tertullian as 'his master', is a distinctive Western voice who likens the Church to paradise. In a Letter to Jubaianus, Cyprian depicts baptism in these terms:

> The Church, setting forth the likeness of paradise, includes within her four walls fruit bearing trees . . . These trees she waters with four rivers, that is, with the four Gospels, wherewith, by a celestial inundation, she bestows the grace of saving baptism.[34]

This interpretation was certainly accepted by Augustine of Hippo (354–430), who in his *City of God* endorsed and reiterated the view that the image of paradise could be used in connection with the Church in so far as the visible Church is called to anticipate the ultimate destiny and God-given character of Christian people. In a chapter in which Augustine spells out both the function and the limitations of allegorical language in theological discourse, he summarizes what he regards as a proper reading of paradisal imagery in relation to *Ecclesia*, the visible Church as she prophetically witnesses to God's ultimate purpose:

> paradise stands for the Church itself, as described in the *Song of Songs*, the four rivers represent the four Gospels, the fruit trees, the

---

33 *The Procatechesis* 15, from *Nicene and Post-Nicene Fathers of the Christian Church*, Series II, vol. 7 (Grand Rapids, MI: Eerdmans 1893), p. 4.
34 Epistle 72.10, *The Ante-Nicene Fathers*, vol. 5 (New York: Charles Scribner's Sons 1925), p. 382.

saints; and the fruit, their achievements; the tree of life, the Holy of Holies, must be Christ himself.[35]

The reader could think that Augustine deploys here a precise semiotic schema, as in earlier typological exegesis, where 'x' represents 'y'; but given the range of metaphorical language linking baptism with the paradise, one could say by way of summary that as the Christian is grafted into Christ, the tree of life, so the baptismal waters enable that person to be fruitful, like the trees of paradise. To speak of paradise in this context is to use forward-looking language, a language qualified by a proper theological reserve, as throughout a Christian's earthly life the resurrection is and remains a future hope. Nevertheless, a theology of baptism that made no reference to resurrection would be deficient. So how can we account for this proleptic aspect of being joined to Christ in his death and in his resurrection, that promise first offered by Christ to the penitent thief: 'today you will be with me in Paradise'?

The resurrection aspect of baptism expressed by the term paradise does not mean that through baptism the candidate is literally placed in paradise but that in the sacramental action there is a reflexive movement from God's future back into the present. It is as though the present baptismal moment evokes the (mythical) past of Eden and anticipates the future (eschatological) paradisal scene of the heavenly Jerusalem and its temple. This is undoubtedly the sense evoked in the passage above of Cyprian of Carthage.

Cyprian's mention of the four rivers in this passage is a clear reference to paradise, but we may also detect in the figurative language faint allusions to the vision of Ezekiel of water flowing from the restored temple (Ezekiel 47) and to the apocalyptic vision of the flowing waters of life (Revelation 22) that flow 'from the throne of God and of the Lamb'; that is, from the sacrificed Christ himself. The source of this water is thus identified in Revelation as the wounded side of the crucified Christ, a familiar trope in the prayer of blessing over the water from the seventh-century Roman *Gelasian Sacramentary* onwards. The conflated image of living water flowing from the side of the Lamb who

---

35 *City of God*, Bk 13, ch. 22, trans. Henry Bettenson (Harmondsworth: Penguin Books 1972), p. 535.

was slain occurs in a developed form in a tenth-century poetic liturgical text in the so-called *Typicon*, which was originally sung in the atrium of the Holy Sepulchre in Jerusalem – significantly known as 'the garden' – on Good Friday.[36] This chant identifies the wounded side of Christ with the spring that 'would . . . water the whole face of the ground' (Genesis 2.6) and feed the four designated rivers of Eden (Genesis 2.10). To follow this imagery of flowing waters, one could say that the confluence of this biblical figurative language suggests that the grace conveyed to the baptized cascades back into the present time through the waters of baptism. The ultimate source of these waters is the eternal flowing fountain of life.

In his seminal paper, 'The Fountain of Life in Manuscripts of the Gospels', Paul Underwood comprehensively charts and illustrates the archaeological and iconographical antecedents of the fountain of life image that was used to decorate the Canon Table page of Carolingian Gospel Books of the Ada School.[37] In this comprehensive study, Underwood traces this exquisite manuscript illustration to the decoration of the free-standing baptistery of the cathedral church of St John Lateran, the alleged site of the Emperor Constantine's baptism. The baptistery stands on the site of a rectangular building that was originally a domestic thermal bath but was adapted in the time of Constantine to be a place of baptism. Archaeological evidence suggests that the baptistery has been rebuilt twice in its history. The first baptistery on the site, the first to be built in Rome in the mid 330s, may have been similar in structure to the Roman *mausoleum* and the *frigidaria* (cold baths) of the Stabian and Forum Baths in the neighbouring city of Pompeii.[38] However, the baptistery building was extensively remodelled during the pontificate of Sixtus III (432–40), and the octagonal walls that still

---

36 'And thy life-giving side, like a fountain bubbling forth from Eden, Waters thy Church, O Christ, like a reasonable Paradise, Thence dividing into sources, into Four Gospels, Watering the universe, purifying creation', cited by Paul A. Underwood, 'The Fountain of Life in Manuscripts of the Gospels', *Dumbarton Oaks Papers*, vol. 5, 1950, pp. 105–6.
37 Underwood, 'The Fountain of Life in Manuscripts of the Gospels', pp. 41–138,
38 See S. Anita Stauffer, *On Baptismal Fonts: Ancient and Modern*, Alcuin/GROW Liturgical Study 29–30 (Nottingham: Grove Books 1994), p. 19; Hugo Brandenburg, *Ancient Churches of Rome from the Fourth to the Seventh Century* (Turnhout: Brepols 2004), pp. 37–54.

stand today were constructed to enclose a large circular font sunk about one metre below the floor level.[39]

The font, placed in the centre of the baptistery, was over eight metres in diameter and surrounded by eight porphyry columns. This peristyle colonnade supports an octagonal architrave that bears the distichs, the often quoted inscriptions attributed to Sixtus' young deacon who would become Pope Leo I. It was these primary architectural elements – the capacious font, the pillars and the dome – that according to Underwood provided the pictorial elements for the composition of the fountain of life in the manuscript decoration. The baptistery, in other words, became the model for this key decorative motif. The way this image was rendered is particularly pertinent to the trajectory of our exploration, as in three of the four extant examples of Gospel Books[40] the fountain of life is placed in a paradisal setting. Familiar paradisal motifs, such as a profusion of plants, flowers, fruits, animals and birds, are to be found in the colourful rendering of the fountain of life decoration in the Godescalc and Soissons Gospel Books, and the iconographical link between these illustrative works of art and the Lateran baptistery at least implies an appreciation of a theological connection between baptism and the flourishing of creation.

This I believe is the third if somewhat understated strand woven into the other two more prominent theologies of baptism: the entering into the mystery of Christ's death on the cross and the Christian's rebirth through water and the Spirit. The deeply resonant symbols of death, rebirth and resurrection jostle for position in our theologies of baptism, but in the final analysis these three elements are indivisible.

The theology of baptism as rebirth was literally spelt out in the inscription around the octagonal architrave of the Lateran baptistery. What is inscribed here trades on the symbolic correspondence between the birth of Christ through the Holy Spirit and the watery womb of the Virgin Mary, and the birth of Christians through the womb of

---

39 See Olof Brandt, 'The Lateran Basilica and the Diffusion of Octagonal Baptisteries from Rome to Constantinople' in *Akten des XIV Internationalen Kongresses für Christliche Archäologie* (Vienna: Austrian Academy of Sciences Press 1999), and 'Understanding the Structures of Early Christian Baptisteries' in Hellholm et al. (eds), *Ablution, Initiation, and Baptism*, vol. 2, esp. pp. 1587–93.
40 That is, the Godescalc Gospel Lectionary, the Gospels of Saint-Medard of Soissons, the Gospels of St Emmeram.

mother Church, the *fons uitae*, 'font of life': '[Christians are] conceived by the breath of God, and born, fruit of a virgin, when birth-giving Church brings them from her waters.'[41] The inscription continues in the seventh distich to identify the wounded side of Christ on the cross as the origin of the baptismal waters of rebirth. So again the images of death and rebirth are juxtaposed. But what of the theme of resurrection, and where and how may this proleptic renewal of creation in relation to baptism be indicated? Robin Jensen finds an echo of Eden (Genesis 2) in the phrases that speak of those 'born from fruitful seed' and the 'waters [of] the whole world'.[42] A further clue may well be found in the interior decoration of the space for baptism. Although the original fifth-century mosaic decoration of the baptistery was largely lost in the massive redecoration of the interior during the seventeenth century, some decoration of the atrium or narthex remains to this day, and in this we may see a suggestion of paradise. Against a dark blue background there is luscious green foliage (possibly acanthus) heightened with gold and interspersed with orange trumpet flowers. Here indeed is a trace of a visual garden of delight, a paradise to meet the eyes of those who enter the waters of the font in the baptistery.

If Olof Brandt is correct in his assertion that the public meaning of an ancient building was expressed through its decoration as much as if not more than through its architecture,[43] then the decoration of the place of baptism is a clear index of the shared meaning of the ritual performed there. And it is in this light that we turn now to a consideration of two ancient fonts.

A reinstalled font in the Bardo Museum in Tunis was originally situated in a baptistery built on the south side of the basilica church of Felix at Kelibia in what is now Tunisia (see Plate 6). This is a sumptuously decorated late sixth-century cross shape font and the surrounding pavement is a luscious water garden just over two metres in diameter

---

41 Translation from Peter Cramer, *Baptism and Change in the Early Middle Ages, c.200– c.1150* (Cambridge: Cambridge University Press 1993), p. 276.

42 Robin Margaret Jensen, *Baptismal Imagery in Early Christianity: Ritual, Visual, and Theological Dimensions* (Grand Rapids, MI: Baker Academic 2012), p. 186.

43 Olof Brandt, 'Deer, Lambs and Water in the Lateran Baptistery', *Rivista di Archeologia Cristiana*, vol. 81, 2005, pp. 131–2; 'Understanding the Structure of Early Christian Baptisteries' in Hellholm et al. (eds), *Ablution, Initiation, and Baptism*, vol. 2, in which Brandt argues that the meaning of the rite is shown not so much by the shape and structure of the building as by the decoration, the 'make up', as he calls it (p. 1594).

and a good metre deep at its deepest point. The surrounding pavement includes an inscription saying that the font was dedicated to honour the memory of Cyprian, Bishop of Carthage, some three centuries earlier. As we shall see, the decorative programme of the font certainly recalls the words of Cyprian, cited above, in which he likened the Church to paradise. The font itself was probably set in a baptistery built on the south side of the apse of the church,[44] and its patterned mosaic decoration is remarkable. It makes visible some early North African and Roman themes of baptismal theology and practice. In the decoration of the round basin of the font are seen two Christograms, chi-rho (the first two letters of the Greek word for 'Christ') and the Greek letters alpha and omega (alluding to 'the beginning and the end', in Revelation 22.13), and these motifs are repeated in the inside of the four quarter-lobes of the cross. The symbol of a fish[45] (replaced by that of a dolphin in one section) is inlaid on the floor of each quarter-lobe, but in a symmetrical pattern on the walls of the font are four prominent trees, a date-palm, a fig, a fruit tree and an olive that are centrally placed and may well represent the four seasons of spring, summer, autumn and winter. The outer rim of the font is decorated with a scrolling grape-vine, growing out of four *canthari* or vases. The vines bear bunches of succulent grapes that twine around flowers (possibly roses) and provide shelter for birds, making the whole ensemble a composite image of an abundant and burgeoning and fruitful life. The whole decorative scheme, in other words, conspires to evoke not only the lost paradisal setting of Eden but also the fecund land of promise; a land described in all its lusciousness in Deuteronomy: 'a land with flowing streams, with springs and underground waters . . . of vines and fig trees and pomegranates, a land of olive trees and honey' (Deuteronomy 8.7–10).

Given the rich resonance of the decorative scheme of the font, it does seem that it was an intended index of the shared meaning of what happened and took place there. Indeed, it could be said that the art literally made visible the meaning of the ritual action performed at the font. In

---

44 Stauffer, *On Baptismal Fonts*, p. 38.
45 This may well illustrate the passage from the introduction of Tertullian's treatise on Baptism (*De Baptismo*, c.198–200) in which Tertullian describes Christians as being 'little fishes' who after the example of Christ are born in water. See Maxwell E. Johnson, *The Rites of Christian Initiation: Their Evolution and Interpretation* (Collegeville, MN: Liturgical Press 1999), pp. 61–6.

terms of ritual action, to approach the water of this font is visually to move towards the promised paradise of God, for the baptismal water is none other than the water of life itself.

In North Africa as in Rome at least until the sixth century,[46] the paradisal reference of baptism seems to have had an early ritual counterpart, namely in the giving of a cup of milk and honey in addition to the eucharistic wine during the Communion of the newly baptized. Milk and honey is a key biblical symbol of the land of promise,[47] and Tertullian makes reference to this practice in Carthage (*Adv. Marc.* i.14.3). Precisely how this happened, and whether the cup was given between the eucharistic gifts of bread and wine or after, is unknown,[48] but its significance is spelt out in *The Apostolic Tradition* ascribed to Hippolytus of Rome (*c.* 250). There we are told that the bishop gives thanks over 'milk and honey mixed together for the fulfilment of the promise that was to the fathers, in which he said, "a land flowing [with] milk and honey"' (ch. 28).

Whether the giving of a chalice of milk and honey to the newly baptized at their first Communion was practised by those baptized in the font at Kelibia is a matter of conjecture, but the combination of documentary and iconographic references to the promise of paradise certainly gives further weight to the resurrection aspect of baptism in the early centuries of the Church. In the mind and imagination of early Christian writers, the garden of paradise from which the four rivers of Eden flowed (Genesis 2) was a type of the Church (Ephrem, *Paradise* VI. 7–9). The appropriation of 'paradise' in Christian reflection is not simply a metaphorical garden but included a specific reference to the garden in which Christians are encountered by the risen Christ as Mary Magdalene was on the first Easter Day.

The paradisal imagery of fonts and baptisteries certainly conspired to heighten the resurrection aspect of baptism. This view is entirely consistent with Paul's view that those who through baptism were 'in Christ'

---

46 For documentary evidence, see the Letter of John the Deacon to Senarius describing the ceremonies of Baptism, written around 500, and the *Verona (Leonine) Sacramentary*, which contains a prayer for the blessing of the milk and honey for those baptized at Pentecost, in E. C. Whitaker, *Documents of the Baptismal Liturgy*, 3rd edn, rev. and exp. Maxwell E. Johnson (London: SPCK 2003), pp. 207, 211.
47 See texts in Leviticus 20.24; Deuteronomy 31.20.
48 Paul F. Bradshaw, Maxwell E. Johnson and L. Edward Phillips (ed. Harold W. Attridge), *The Apostolic Tradition: A Commentary* (Minneapolis, MN: Fortress Press 2002), p. 129.

already belong to the new creation (2 Corinthians 5.17). Part of what Paul is claiming here is that the baptized are able to share in that stupendous act of the creator God, decisively shown in the resurrected body of Christ, of making creation anew. This act of God in Christ is inseparable from creation, as the mature rendering of Paul's theology makes clear. God had indeed made all things through Christ, and it will be in and through him that creation itself will find its final perfection and purpose (see 1 Corinthians 8.6; Colossians 1.15–17; Ephesians 1.10). The baptized, in other words, are not only called to live as new creatures but to live as co-workers of the risen Christ as he renews his own creation as the final gift of the Son to the Father (1 Corinthians 15.24).

The question is how this rich rhapsodic nexus of the theology of baptism came to be visually and bodily expressed in the architectural settings of Christian baptism.

Traces of the resurrection motif are found in early Christian art painted around the third and fourth centuries by jobbing artists in the Catacombs of Rome, and are particularly seen in the recurring Old Testament figures of Jonah and the imaginary sea monster, and the visionary prophet Daniel.[49] Resurrection motifs may also be read in the surviving though heavily restored decoration of the baptistery in the excavated 'church-house' of Dura Europos, converted around the 240s, and located in the Syrian desert close to the River Euphrates. The appellation 'church-house' may suggest a comfortable domestic setting, but it could be argued on the basis of archaeology and pictorial decoration that this building was as much a ritual sacred space as the *Mithraeum* in the eastern border town of Dura. This was also an adapted domestic space, and was probably used exclusively for cultic purposes from the time the building was adapted for religious purposes as a sacred space.[50] The reconstructed baptistery in the Christian building, now at Yale University, has attracted and continues to attract extensive scholarly attention.

The fragmentary decoration is susceptible to different interpretations, but the facing arch directly above the baptismal font is decorated

---

49 Robin Margaret Jensen refers to these figures as 'pictorial typologies', Old Testament figures and events that were taken as prefiguring the resurrection of Christ. See especially her *Understanding Early Christian Art*, ch. 3 and *Baptismal Imagery in Early Christianity*, pp. 158–60.

50 See Carly Silver, 'Dura-Europos: Cross-Roads of Culture' in *Archaeology*, August 2010, <http://archive.archaeology.org/online/features/dura_europos/>.

with grapes and other fruits, which may have been intended to evoke the garden of paradise, as may the decoration above a niche in the south wall with its depiction of a prominent tree with small sketched figures of Adam and Eve set in Eden.[51] A more direct reference to the resurrection may be seen in the sketchily drawn and clumsily painted murals on the east and north walls. Those on the north wall depict a rather puzzling narrative scene.[52] The figures of three women, reconstructed from fragments of now faded decoration, and approaching a high-pitched roofed structure, can be read either as the wise virgins with torches in their right hands and bowls of oil or possibly incense in their left, waiting to escort the bridegroom to the bride's house (Matthew 25.1–13), or as the women who on the first Easter morning made their way with scented oils, while it was still dark, to the sepulchre in which Jesus had been laid (Mark 16.1). Scholarly opinion is divided, and although the most recent consensus favours the former interpretation,[53] the whole ensemble of the surviving series of narrative images does give some support to the latter reading of an Easter morning scene.

A richly decorative scheme of narrative mosaics and symbols is largely still to be seen in the late fourth- or early fifth-century shallow-domed baptistery of St Giovanni in Naples, now a part of the complex structure of the present cathedral church of St Restituta. It seems that the reference to water was the major factor in the choice of subjects for the narrative mosaics that decorated this particular compact, domed, octagonal space.[54] The exception is a mosaic of the empty tomb. And so the inclusion of this scene in the decorative scheme provides an illustration of what was apparently regarded as a vital aspect of the meaning

---

51 See Clark Hopkins (ed. Bernard Goldman), *The Discovery of Dura-Europos* (New Haven, CT: Yale University Press 1979), pp. 110, 116.

52 Ann Louise Perkins, *The Art of Dura-Europos* (Oxford: Clarendon Press 1973), p. 53.

53 The Easter reading of these figures was endorsed by Renate Pillinger in her article 'The Significance of Early Christian Monuments for the Study of Liturgy: The Example of Baptism', *Studia Liturgica*, vol. 25, no. 1, 1995, pp. 32–50. More recent opinion favours the interpretation of bridesmaids proposed by Thomas Mathews. See Dieter Korol, 'Neues zu den alt – und neutestamentlichen Darstellungen in Baptisterium von Dura-Europos', in Hellholm et al. (eds), *Ablution, Initiation, and Baptism*, vol. 2.

54 The severely damaged Gospel narrative mosaics of the encounter with the woman at the well, Peter walking on the water and the miraculous catch of fish: each have water, the element of baptism, as a common theme.

of baptism. This reference to the resurrection is reinforced by the decoration that divides the individual narrative scenes. Here we see the conventional Roman non-figural decorative images, which had been appropriated by Christians to function as symbols of the promised paradise, namely lambs, peacocks, the phoenix and pomegranates.[55] As Robin Jensen has pointedly observed, although early Christian baptisteries were often designed to resemble a mausoleum, their interior decoration actually reflected the life of Eden.[56] And so the baptistery annexed to the Christian basilica was the site where there was a dying to the old self, to sin, but also a rising with Christ through the paradisal and life-giving waters of baptism.

North African examples of paradisal imagery are to be found in the pavement decoration of the baptistery of Dermech 1 in Carthage,[57] at Timgad. A recently excavated example of a Tunisian baptistery with a seventh-century font decorated with birds and a profusion of vines, flowers and fruit is the baptistery of Bekalta that was discovered in 1993.[58] Other northern African examples are to be found, such as the quadrilobe baptistery at Tigzirt in present-day Algeria, where again we see pavement mosaics of flowers and verdant foliage.[59]

In the baptistery in Naples, the eight curving sections leading to the base of the dome, directly above the font, are decorated with a profusion of luxuriant foliage and fruit, against a blue- and gold-fringed background. On the side ribs of the structure, running down the vertical walls, foliage, flowers and brightly coloured birds cascade from fluted double-handled vases.[60] These decorative schemes effectively evoke an abundance of life, a luxuriant garden, which again we may read as an intentional pictorial representation of the site of resurrection encounter as it is described in

55 Paul Finney, in a discussion of the decorative scheme in the Catacombs of Callistus in Rome, cautions that the interpretation of these classical motifs is fluid and imprecise, but the context in which they are placed and seen does give them a particular symbolic frame of interpretation. See Paul Corby Finney, *The Invisible God: The Earliest Christians on Art* (New York and Oxford: Oxford University Press 1994), pp. 184–91. Augustine of Hippo alludes to the incorruptibility of peacock flesh in *City of God*, Bk 21, sec. 4.
56 Jensen, *Understanding Early Christian Art*, p. 212, n. 71.
57 Stauffer, 'Fonts: Baptism, Pascha and Paradise', p. 59.
58 Jensen, *Baptismal Imagery in Early Christianity*, p. 218.
59 See Robert Milburn, *Early Christian Art and Architecture* (Aldershot: Scolar Press 1988), p. 211.
60 The baptistery is described by Milburn, *Early Christian Art and Architecture*, p. 208.

the Gospel of John (John 20.11–16). In this narrative, when the grieving Mary Magdalene is met by the risen Christ, she mistakes him for the gardener. And as the garden was for Mary, so the font is for the baptizand, a place of restoration and a meeting with that abundance of life into which we are brought to share with the living Christ, the new Adam. Indeed, we could say that in entering the waters of baptism, the *competentes*, those candidates for baptism, have a foot in Eden.[61]

This message of restoration was visually transmitted by the decoration of those Norman twelfth-century fonts that were decorated with sculpted reliefs of the creation and the so-called fall. English examples are to be seen in the font at All Saints' Church at East Meon in Hampshire and the font at Kirkby near Liverpool. The square font at East Meon, which was sculpted from the grey/black marble from Tournai in Belgium, has four carved panels, about one metre in length and 40 centimetres in depth. Sculpted on the north- and east-facing panels are the creation of Adam, the making of Eve from the rib of Adam, the temptation and the expulsion of Adam and Eve from the garden of Eden. This iconographical schema follows the logic of 'type' and 'anti-type' first seen in the narrative mural paintings on the walls of the baptistery room at Dura Europos, and reveals an understanding of the mystical water-washing of baptism as being the repristination of creation and the restoration of that which was lost at the fall.

A modern working of this classic theme is to be seen in the font in the baptistery of the abbey church of St Maurice in Switzerland. This baptistery is located in a Romanesque tower and was designed and executed between 1987 and 1994. At its centre is a trefoil font, designed and made by the Swiss artist Madeline Diener (d. 2005). Carved into the surface are bas-reliefs of Adam and Eve, representing humankind called to become children of God, various animals, including a stag and a hind, representing the baptizand 'athirst for the living God' and finally the tree of life as a fruiting vine. The font is deliberately set in an octagonal base representing the eighth day, the day of resurrection, and running down from the surface of the font to its base are seven grooves representing the seven days of creation. So what we see here is a coherent decorative scheme that visually presents the complex meaning

---

61 See Edwin Muir's poem 'One Foot in Eden' in *Edwin Muir: Collected Poems* (London: Faber & Faber 1979), p. 227.

of baptism as the renewal of creation, and the grafting of the newly baptized into Christ, the fruitful vine.

Having considered the decoration of fonts, we turn now to adduce possible evidence of the semiotics of resurrection and paradise in the architectural design and shape of fonts and baptisteries. As scholars of the liturgy of the early Church have cautioned against assuming a conformity in the structure and content of baptismal rites, both chronologically, as if there were a single line of development, and across different geographical regions,[62] so archaeologists and art historians have also warned equally stringently against seeing a conformity in both the shape and possible meaning(s) of fonts and spaces for baptism even within the space between three centuries and in different cultural and social locations.[63] In an earlier and highly influential work, J. G. Davies was more confident in charting a chronological development to the design and shape of fonts and baptisteries and in assigning meanings to these different designs.[64] But given the sheer variety of extant and excavated font design, and the different architectural shaping of spaces for baptism and of how these spaces related to the larger church building, it is difficult to postulate a single evolutionary line of development either geographically or chronologically. Furthermore, attributing symbolic significance to each different shape of font and space for baptism is also uncertain because of the inconsistency and paucity of explicit contemporary explanations.[65] Different shapes of fonts are found in a number of different regions, and baptisteries where the sacramental action took place were often built as adjuncts to the main church building. Some included an ancillary room, presumably for the rites of renunciation and adhesion

---

62 Paul F. Bradshaw, *The Search for the Origins of Christian Worship: Sources and Methods for the Study of Early Liturgy* (London: SPCK 2002, 2nd edn); Johnson, *The Rites of Christian Initiation*.

63 See Brandt, 'Understanding the Structure of Early Christian Baptisteries'; Robin Margaret Jensen, 'Womb, Tomb, and Garden: The Symbolism of the North African Baptismal Fonts', paper delivered at the Annual Meeting of the American Academy of Religion, November 1997.

64 J. G. Davies, *The Architectural Setting of Baptism* (London: Barrie & Rockliff 1962), pp. 18–25.

65 See Everett Ferguson, *Baptism in the Early Church: History, Theology, and Liturgy in the First Five Centuries* (Grand Rapids, MI: Eerdmans 2009), p. 820, n. 4.

and for the stripping of candidates, as in Jerusalem and elsewhere in Palestine.[66] Although architectural arrangements varied from one geographical location to another, the placing of a baptistery was evidently significant in the understanding of the meaning of the baptismal rite.[67] In fourth-century Jerusalem the baptistery was integral to the Anastasis rotunda complex, although its exact location and design remain something of an unsolvable puzzle. Looking at Charles Couasnon's ground plan of the whole fourth-century church complex, it appears that the baptistery could have formed a triangulation point with two sacred sites – the site of the cross (Golgotha) and the tomb (Anastasis). This physical alignment reinforced the meanings that were ritually enacted in the rite of Initiation. From the evidence of the *Mystagogical Catecheses* and the pilgrim Egeria's *Journal*, we know baptism was celebrated there at the Easter Vigil night service. It would be entirely probable that the candidates for baptism stood in the dark vestibule of the baptistery for the renunciations and the adhesion (the turning to Christ). On the basis of the scant and conflicting early archaeological evidence, it is impossible to plot exactly where the baptistery was located.[68] What we do know, however, is that candidates faced west for the renunciations and then turned to the east for the act of adhesion. In facing east, they would probably have seen either the sepulchre or even the open door into the baptistery.[69] In either case the meaning coincides, and in his commentary on the pre-immersion rites, Cyril alludes to this moment in these terms: 'the gates of God's Paradise are open to you, that garden that God planted in the East.'[70] So in general terms it can be said that the topography of the location of the baptistery in Jerusalem highlighted the death and resurrection motif of baptism, and in addition it may well be that the architectural arrangement and the orientation of the pre-baptismal ritual made an explicit reference to the resurrection in terms of paradise.

66 See Juliette Day, *Baptism in Early Byzantine Palestine 325–451*, Joint Liturgical Studies 43 (Cambridge: Grove Books 1999), pp. 18–27.

67 Robin Margaret Jensen, 'Ancient Baptismal Spaces: Form and Function' *Studia Liturgica*, vol. 42 2013, pp. 108–29.

68 For a succinct discussion of the literature, see Day, *Baptism in Early Byzantine Palestine 325–451*, pp. 18–24.

69 John F. Baldovin sj, *Liturgy in Ancient Jerusalem*, Alcuin/GROW Liturgical Study 9 (Nottingham: Grove Books 1989).

70 *Mystagogical Catechesis* 1.9, from Yarnold, *The Awe-Inspiring Rites of Initiation*, p. 74.

Italy is of course famous for its separate baptisteries, such as those in Ravenna, but in other regions the baptistery was more integral to the structure of the basilica. And yet once again there was a variety of architectural plans and arrangements. Some churches had a baptistery at the west end of the building, some on the north side and in others it protruded from the apse. This variety of placement either within or adjacent to the main church building makes the question of how the baptismal rite was actually celebrated in any given location rather conjectural. Similarly, it complicates the question of how the baptistery and its font were originally read and understood by those celebrating the rite, both ministers and candidates for baptism. We do of course have early liturgical texts and extant catechetical instructions and baptismal homilies, and this documentary evidence can shed some light on the theological significance of the baptistery and its font. The temptation is to argue from silence or over-generalize from a particular source, whether a written document or a particular artefact.

Nevertheless, it is possible to construct a broad taxonomy of different early font designs in such a way as to recognize the diversity of design, say from the third to the seventh centuries, within a variety of geographical locations. Certain font designs seem to be prevalent in particular geographical regions (cruciform shapes in Syria and Greece, octagonal and hexagonal in Italy, for instance), but detailed analysis presents a more nuanced picture of the distribution of different font designs around the early Christian world. Pioneering work was carried out by Anita Stauffer and others, such as Robin Jensen, have undertaken extensive field research and analysis of font design.[71] From the results of their work it is possible to suggest a number of basic categories:

1 circular
2 rectangular/tomb shape
3 square
4 cruciform
5 hexagonal
6 octagonal.

71 See, for example, Stauffer, *On Baptismal Fonts*; the comprehensive study of Sebastian Ristow, 'Frühchristliche Baptisterien' in *Jahrbuch für Antike und Christentum: Ergänzungsband 27* (Münster: Ashendorff 1998); Robin Margaret Jensen, *Living Water: Images, Symbols and Settings of Early Christian Baptism* (Leiden and Boston: Brill 2011); and the ongoing Baptisteria Sacra Project at the University of Toronto in Canada.

The map, however, shows a varied picture – some font designs are found in a spread of geographical locations, and some of these combine two or even more elements from the geometric shape of the six basic design categories, such as a circle within a square.

As we saw in the case of the Lateran baptistery, some design elements are combined in the architectural plan of the baptistery and the actual geometric shape of the font, such as a circle within an octagonal arrangement of surrounding pillars and structural walls. The greatest number of surviving and excavated early fonts are round, and although it is tempting to attribute a symbolic value to the circular font and say that a circle represents eternity and is therefore apt to represent the 'heavenly rebirth' of baptism, we must also allow for the fact that its manufacture may rest more fully on quite pragmatic reasons. Although it is wise not to overstate the symbolic significance of the shape of a font, there is archaeological evidence in some early baptismal sites that the shape was changed – a change that may reasonably be attributed to a more symbolic rather than functional preference. At the excavated baptistery of the old basilica in Aosta in northern Italy, for instance, an early, possibly fourth-century, cross within a circle shape and a later, possibly seventh-century, octagonal shape font are to be seen. More could be said about all this, but for our purposes the point to be drawn is that a number of design features seem to indicate a reference to the resurrection and to God's purpose to creation made new. The hexagon speaks of the sixth day; that is, the day humankind was made (Genesis 1.26–31) and the day of crucifixion, through which humankind is made new. The octagonal pattern points to the eighth day; that is, the cycle of creation beginning again and the eschatological day dawning when God creates 'a new heaven and a new earth'.[72]

This is likely to have been the case of the octagonal font in the Ambrosian baptistery of St Giovanni in Milan, which is sunk into the floor and measures some five metres in diameter.[73] In his instructions to baptismal candidates and neophytes, however, Ambrose does not explicitly make this link between the octagonal shape and the theme of new creation. The eight-sided walled font, excavated under the piazza in front of the present cathedral (Santa Maria Maggiore) in Milan, is reputedly the site where Ambrose baptized Augustine of Hippo in 387

72 See Robin Margaret Jensen, *Baptismal Imagery in Early Christianity*, pp. 160–4.
73 Stauffer, *On Baptismal Fonts*, p. 24.

and, like the Lateran baptistery, it had a series of distichs inscribed around the font. Underwood reckons that these inscriptions were made during a rebuilding of the baptistery during the time of Laurence, a fifth-century Bishop of Milan. Although the dominant theme of the inscriptions is the cleansing waters of baptism, the first distich remarks on the appropriateness of the octagonal design for a font while the third in the series spells out how salvation was brought by the light of Christ rising again, the Christ 'who opens the gates of death and raises the dead from their tombs'.[74] Here is a direct reference to the resurrection as the raising-up work of God in Christ, the firstborn of the dead. It is the work of resurrection, the second cycle of God's work of creation. In this connection Underwood cites the Epistle of Barnabas. In a densely polemical passage addressing the question of the Sabbath,[75] the writer speaks of the eighth day when God begins to make 'another world'.[76] It is likely that during the reconstruction of this font in the fifth century, four pipes were installed to feed water into it, deliberately recalling the four rivers of paradise. If this is the case, the whole arrangement suggests a strong sense of the resurrection as the renewal of creation, and of baptism as the Christian's way of re-entering paradise.

A fairly general feature of ancient fonts that may well bear a reference to the resurrection aspect of the baptismal rite is the arrangement of steps leading down into the deepest part of the pool, and then steps up to the level of the floor. Again there is considerable variety in the positioning and orientation of the steps, and among the extant fonts some have three steps but others have two and some four. Although not all ancient fonts are arranged so that the candidate enters the deepest part of the water on the west side of the font and then emerges on the east, a greater number do have this arrangement. One prime example of this west–east orientation with three steps is the excavated cruciform font in Augustine's city of Hippo in North Africa.[77] Another notable example

---

74 Underwood, 'The Fountain of Life in Manuscripts of the Gospels', p. 81.

75 Paul F. Bradshaw and Maxwell E. Johnson, *The Origins of Feasts, Fasts and Seasons in Early Christianity* (London: SPCK 2011), pp. 12–13. The Epistle is attributed to Barnabas by Clement of Rome.

76 The translation cited here is J. B. Lightfoot, *The Apostolic Fathers* (London and New York: Macmillan & Co. 1891), p. 284.

77 See G. Radan, 'The Basilica Pacis of Hippo' in Joseph C. Schnaubelt and Frederick Van Fleteren (eds), *Augustine in Iconography* (New York: Peter Lang 1999), for a review of archaeological evidence, and Augustine of Hippo, *Serm.* 125.6 for an allusion to the symbolic significance of the steps into and out of the font.

is the fourth-century cruciform shape font in the Church of a Thousand Gates at Paros in Greece. In terms of its design this font is a basic Byzantine cross shape with four equal arms of just under three metres wide and a metre deep. There are three steps descending into the font on the western armature and three steps at the east end,[78] so that as the candidates stepped down into the baptismal water they literally entered into the cross and then ascended from the water into the life of the risen Christ. For this west–east orientation also speaks of the eschatological hope of the appearing of Christ. Whatever the exact arrangement of steps, it would seem that the celebration of baptism had assumed the character of a mimetic ritual involving a physical descent and ascent. The stepping down into the water was a descending with Christ into the depths of death, the stepping out a being raised with Christ into newness of life. This movement ritually enacted the paschal *transitus* of Christ, the passage from death to life that was a central theme of the baptismal teaching of Cyril of Jerusalem. Addressing candidates for baptism in the church complex in Jerusalem, which encompassed the reputed site of Golgotha and the sepulchre, the place of death and resurrection, Cyril exploited the topography and spoke vividly of baptism as both a tomb and a womb, the occasion when the candidate was drawn into the paschal mystery and was made new through being joined with Christ in both his death and his resurrection.[79]

This teaching gives us a picture, if not a total description, of the different rituals around the celebration of baptism, and one may reasonably assume that the points that were drawn, particularly in post-baptismal mystagogy, were considered to be the salient ones, or what we may describe as the official and public meanings of the rites. But there is the question of how the participants experienced the ritual actions around baptism and the setting in which it was celebrated. In this respect, the mystagogies of both Cyril and Ambrose of Milan have an added value, as they both expressly seek to draw out the meaning of what was actually experienced by the neophytes and give due weight to the primacy of the candidates' experience of these 'awe-inspiring rites of initiation'.

---

78 See plate 15 in Ferguson, *Baptism in the Early Church*.
79 See Yarnold, *The Awe-Inspiring Rites of Initiation*, p. 78, and Juliette Day, *The Baptismal Liturgy of Jerusalem: Fourth- and Fifth-Century Evidence from Palestine, Syria and Egypt* (Aldershot: Ashgate 2007), p. 81.

In Milan, Ambrose suggested that the journey to the water of baptism began with the cross. The catechumens, those under instruction for baptism, are virtually defined as those who 'believed in the cross and were signed in it'.[80] Baptism itself, signifying the identification of the candidate with the Crucified, was a sacrament of the cross of Christ, a *sacramentum cruces*.[81] But in Ambrose's teaching, as indeed in the writings of the Apostle St Paul, the cross, representing the death of Christ, is inexplicably bound up with resurrection, and there are sufficient hints and intimations that the resurrection was understood at least in part as the renewal of creation. In the mystagogical catechesis *De Sacramentis*, for instance, Ambrose spoke of the immersion in the baptismal pool in terms of the candidate's being plunged into the paschal mystery of Christ's death and resurrection. Perhaps the surprising element in this teaching is the emphasis Ambrose placed on the resurrection reference of the ritual action. Addressing the neophytes who had been baptized at Easter, Ambrose refers specifically to the octagonal font of St Giovanni in which they were to be baptized, and spells out the meaning of the rite they had recently experienced: '[The one] who passes through the waters of this font . . . [through] these waters does not die: he rises again.'[82]

Contemporary Syrian sources appear to witness to the same understanding of the candidate entering the water and rising from it as a ritualized entering into Christ's death and resurrection. The composite Church Order known as the *Apostolic Constitutions* is quite explicit on how the baptizand's participation in Christ's death and resurrection is ritually enacted in the entering and leaving the water of the baptismal pool: 'The descent [into the water] the dying together [with Christ], the ascent [from the water] the rising together [with him].'[83]

---

80 Cesare Alzati, *Ambrosianum Mysterium: The Church of Milan and its Liturgical Tradition*, vol. 1, trans. George Guiver CR, Joint Liturgical Studies 44 (Cambridge: Grove Books 1999).
81 See *De Sacramentis*, II.23. Yarnold suggested that this line may refer to the action of signing with the cross – *The Awe-Inspiring Rites of Initiation*, p. 119, n. 39.
82 See *De Sacramentis*, I.12 for the full passage. See Yarnold, *The Awe-Inspiring Rites of Initiation*, pp. 104–5; also *De Sacramentis*, II.20, 23; III.2 and *De Mysteriis*, III.II.14–21. Note that these passages of Ambrose are omitted by Johnson in his enlarged edition of Whitaker's collection of baptismal documents in Whitaker, *Documents of the Baptismal Liturgy*.
83 *Apostolic Constitutions* III,17,3, from Whitaker, *Documents of the Baptismal Liturgy*, p. 36.

A similar interpretation was articulated by John Chrysostom, probably in the late 380s when he was still a priest in Antioch.[84] In one of his baptismal homilies, the 'golden mouthed' Chrysostom describes the descent of the candidate into the waters of baptism in language that is compressed from Pauline sources and susceptible to being read in terms of the Christian's participation in Christ's resurrection.[85] The one baptizing, he explains, 'takes you down into the sacred waters, at the same time burying the old nature and raising the new creature, which is being renewed after the image of its creator'.[86] As Chrysostom repeatedly insists, baptism is burial and resurrection together.[87]

But what artistic evidence of the resurrection aspect of baptism are we able to muster in support of the argument? Apart from the paradisal iconography we have already reviewed, what might count as direct resurrection motifs are quite rare in font and baptismal decoration. Although not by any means common, there are some extant medieval fonts that include in their sculpted decoration a direct resurrection scene, such as the raising of Lazarus[88] or Christ stepping out of the sepulchre.[89] One resurrection sculpted motif, exceptional in terms of both its design and its crafting, is to be seen around the font in the church of St Mary Magdalene at Eardisley in Herefordshire. The font dates back to the time when the Normans ruled the Welsh Marches, and it belongs to the so-called Hereford School of sculpture. This has striking similarities to Romanesque sculpture and is famously known in the church at Kilpeck, also in Herefordshire, and at Hereford Cathedral. It is thought that the patron of the work on the font at Eardisley was familiar with established Continental models and with contemporary currents of intellectual thought, and that he (Ralph de Baskerville) advised the sculptor in the choice and execution of the images for the chalice shape font at Eardisley.[90]

---

84 Juliette Day, *The Baptismal Liturgy of Jerusalem*, p. 86.

85 See Colossians 2.12; 3.10.

86 *Baptismal Homily*, II.25, Yarnold, *The Awe-Inspiring Rites of Initiation*, p. 161.

87 For a summary of pertinent texts, see Raymond Burnish, *The Meaning of Baptism: A Comparison of the Teaching and Practice of the Fourth Century with the Present Day* (London: Alcuin Club/SPCK 1985), pp. 29–30.

88 An example is to be seen in the Norman rectangular finely carved stone font with its quatrefoil bowl at Lenton in Nottingham.

89 Examples can be seen on the early thirteenth-century lead font at Brookland and the fifteenth-century font at Northfleet, both in Kent.

90 For a more detailed discussion of the Eardisley font, see Malcolm Thurlby, *The Herefordshire School of Romanesque Sculpture* (Almeley: Logaston Press 1999), esp. pp. 123–7.

The particular section of the elaborate programme of decoration that bears on our consideration of the resurrection reference to baptism is the carving of a Christ figure, shown in motion, holding a Greek shape processional cross with his right hand as he pulls a smaller-scale figure, probably Adam, out of a thicket of interlaced carving with his left hand. The image is part of a wider representation of the Trinity, and a dove representing the Holy Spirit perches on the arm with which Christ holds Adam by the wrist. This dynamic iconography presents the salvation of the triune God in action, for depicted here is God in Christ, through the Spirit, drawing humanity into the unshackled freedom and life of the resurrection. The composition recalls the literary tradition of the Harrowing of Hell,[91] and although in a very different medium and style, the iconography of the *anastasis*, the traditional Orthodox icon of the resurrection showing Christ drawing Adam and Eve out of the dark cavern of death into the light and life of the resurrection. As well as this explicit reference to the raising up power of God in baptism, we may also infer that the chalice shape of the Eardisley font, and also the font at nearby Castle Frome, and in more common Scandinavian examples,[92] signals an understanding that the newness of life into which the baptized are brought is offered and repeatedly given in the Eucharist.

The theme of resurrection in relation to baptism is fraught with theological difficulties. If resurrection is a future eschatological hope, then how and in what sense can it be a present reality for the baptized Christian? The problem has long been recognized. Theodore of Mopsuestia (393–428), a fourth-century contemporary of Ambrose of Milan and John Chrysostom, wrestled with the question in the sermons he preached to those being prepared for baptism. For Theodore, the resurrection was a future reality that could only be known once a person had been through the physical processes of dying and death, and so the question in its sharpest form was the sense in which the resurrection as a future event could be known in the conditions of this present life. In the answers he gave to this question, Theodore maintained what we

---

91 The story of the Harrowing of Hell is grounded in the allusion to Christ descending into hell to preach to the souls of the departed in 1 Peter 4.6a, is recounted in the apocryphal *Gospel of Nicodemus*, expanded by the seventh-century English poet Cynewulf in his *Ascension*, and embellished in later medieval writing such as the Exeter *Harrowing of Hell*.

92 See Davies, *The Architectural Setting of Baptism*, p. 66.

would call the eschatological tension of 'even now' and 'not yet', and was able to do so for two reasons. The first was his Platonic view of reality, the second his thoroughgoing typological reading of Scripture. A Platonic world view allowed for a greater shading of reality and a typological reading of Scripture yielded the vocabulary of 'figure', 'first-fruits', 'promise' and 'gift'. And it was precisely through these terms that Theodore set out his account of how the baptized Christian was enabled to do this through the sacramental grace of baptism – first by participating in the reality of the future hope of resurrection, second by being disposed to receive the gift of life being renewed.[93]

The resurrection life, we could and probably should say, belongs to God's future. It lies beyond this life, and yet for the Christian baptized into the death and resurrection of Christ, this hope impinges even now on the present, making and remaking the baptized person a 'new creation'. Incorporated into Christ in baptism, the Christian has to live as a 'new creature' within the conditions of the old creation.[94] In practical terms this means that the actual day-to-day living out of the Christian life has to be for each individual Christian a rehearsal, a continuous *practice* of living the resurrection life so that the 'new creation' may be implanted in the old. To speak in these terms brings us to the modern discourse of virtue ethics, with its emphasis upon *habitus*, those dispositions that set our ways of seeing, thinking and feeling, our commitments and shared values.[95] The theoretical concept of *habitus* has its roots in the writing of the French philosopher and social anthropologist Pierre Bourdieu. Bourdieu uses the term in a range of quite different ways, making a single definition rather difficult. Suffice it here to say that *habitus* is primarily a disposition, a way of seeing and doing things that are part of and express a community's collective memory, ongoing practice and future hope. These are set down, as in a process of gradual sedimentation, as the meaning of what is unselfconsciously performed by members of a given community. In this sense *habitus* is a

---

93 For a full discussion, see Enrico Mazza, *Mystagogy: A Theology of Liturgy in the Patristic Age*, trans. Matthew J. O'Connell (New York: Pueblo 1989), pp. 93–105.

94 Von Balthasar sees this as being parallel to the Johannine paradox of the Christian being *in* the world, but not *of* the world. See Hans Urs von Balthasar, *Theo-Drama: Theological Dramatic Theory*, vol. 4, *The Action* (San Francisco: Ignatius Press 1994), p. 477.

95 For a classic working out of what is known as virtue ethics, see Alasdair MacIntyre, *After Virtue: A Study in Moral Theory* (London: Duckworth 1981).

socially acquired knowledge or a capacity, inculcated over time through the individual's participation in the defining and constitutive activities and repeated behaviour of a community.[96] Although the *habitus* of a particular community or society is bound up with how individuals see and respond to stimuli, Bourdieu insists that it transcends subjectivity and is structured through the objective conditions of the environment in which the community lives its daily life.[97] He also spoke of *habitus* as the basis of perception and the appreciation of present and future experience,[98] and as such it comes close to the notion of particular ways of seeing that was sketched in the opening chapter, and the capacity of the worshipping community to *see* liturgically.

Further, we can also add that as embodied creatures our thoughts and feelings, our outlooks and attitudes, are gained and inculcated in us through repeated practice; that is, by the actual living out of life in intentional and habitual ways. In addition, the observation could be made that etymologically the term *habitus* relates also to habitat; literally, to where we are placed. Thinking of the hints and intimations in the baptismal imagery in liturgical texts and the decoration of fonts and baptisteries, we could speak of the baptized Christian being placed in paradise. This is not to say that the Church is or even should be a kind of social utopia – it certainly is not. Indeed, like the individual Christian, the Church has a history that is flawed and constantly in need of the refashioning hand of God's grace and mercy.

Nevertheless, there is a sense in which baptism does bring us to the very verge of paradise, to that place where the power of Christ's resurrection is present and at work in human lives. And so on this basis, and by way of some concluding remarks, we can say that knowing the resurrection is living *as if* one could be in paradise even now. Such a way of living may become a visible reality in the lives of Christians when in practical ways they promote God's purpose for the whole life of creation to be free to grow and flourish, bloom and be fruitful. In this sense we move from a liturgical seeing to a way of living that arises from a rich liturgical life in the worshipping environment where art

---

96 See Pierre Bourdieu, *Outline of a Theory of Practice*, trans. Richard Nice (Cambridge: Cambridge University Press 1977); *Distinction: A Social Critique of the Judgement of Taste*, trans. Richard Nice (London: Routledge & Kegan Paul 1986), p. 170.
97 Bourdieu, *Outline of a Theory of Practice*, p. 77.
98 Bourdieu, *Outline of a Theory of Practice*, p. 78.

and rite coincide. The lifeblood of this liturgical life is the sacrificial self-giving and donation of Christ, seen on Calvary and played out day by day, Sunday by Sunday, as Christians gather before the living cross to celebrate the Eucharist, and there to receive the first fruits of creation made new. It is in the environment of such focused worship that the Christian can receive what the prophet and the visionary have seen; that is, a new heaven and a new earth (see Isaiah 65.17; Revelation 21.1). This vision, which eludes and refuses to be confined to any single human strategic plan or programme, is something given, and given as both a future vision and a present task as we work out the salvation that has been seen.

Select index of works of art

Index

Note: artworks are listed under the artist's name, where known; churches are listed under place name.